The New Nativism

The New Nativism

Proposition 187 and the Debate over Immigration

Robin Dale Jacobson

University of Minnesota Press
Minneapolis
London

Published by the University of Minnesota Press
111 Third Avenue South, Suite 290
Minneapolis, MN 55401-2520
http://www.upress.umn.edu

Library of Congress Cataloging-in-Publication Data

Jacobson, Robin Dale.
   The new nativism : Proposition 187 and the debate over immigration / Robin Dale Jacobson.
        p.   cm.
   Includes bibliographical references and index.
   ISBN 978-0-8166-5027-9 (hc : alk. paper) — ISBN 978-0-8166-5028-6 (pb : alk. paper)
   1. Illegal aliens—Government policy—California—Public opinion. 2. California—Emigration and immigration—Government policy—Public opinion.   3. United States—Emigration and immigration—Government policy—History—20th century.   4. Immigration opponents—California. 5. Public opinion—California.   I. Title.
   JV6920.J33   2008
   325.794—dc22   2008001828

Printed in the United States of America on acid-free paper

The University of Minnesota is an equal-opportunity educator and employer.

15 14 13 12 11 10 09 08   10 9 8 7 6 5 4 3 2 1

Contents

Preface

I began this project out of a deep dissatisfaction with polarized debates around the politics of race. Public dialogue on race, when it finally took place in the open, did not seem to move us any closer to a satisfying resolution. Look, for example, at the famous cases involving Rodney King, O. J. Simpson, or Clarence Thomas. Accusations of racism flew in all directions and caused people to become further entrenched in their original positions. One side accused the other of racism; the other side answered with accusations of reverse racism. We seemed stuck, like children in the school yard yelling with all our passion, "No, you!" As if that would somehow, miraculously, prove us right.

Throughout these moments of national debate on the issue of race, I kept returning in my mind to the directive I give my students in the classroom: "Attack the idea, not the person." Demonizing your opponent, I always tell them, is not intellectually fulfilling, democratic, or, in the end, pragmatic.

The label "race card" has become common coinage because many times race has been used uncritically (not necessarily wrongly, but not analytically) in public and political dialogues. Accusations of racism have been thrown out in the same spirit one would discard before calling gin, as if that were the winning move. Unfortunately, asserting racism where we see it hasn't helped progressives win the game. It is time for a new tack, if for no other reason than we haven't managed to stop the serious backsliding of racial progress that began in the 1980s.

Leaving Baltimore and arriving on the West Coast for graduate study in 1997, I was shocked to find a radically different racial terrain and a radically similar racial dynamic. Despite differences in the demographics of the area, its racial history, and the main political issues at hand, the same demonization and polarization repeated itself; the same dueling accusations of racism characterized public discourse. Now, on the West Coast, the process recurred, most vividly, around issues of immigration.

A 1994 California voter initiative, Proposition 187, designed to deny social services to undocumented immigrants was a defining moment in racial politics, not only in California but in the country as a whole. Opponents accused the measure's supporters of being motivated by racism. According to the opposition, the measure was a result of white racism and specifically targeted Latinos. Its supporters, on the other hand, suggested that they were concerned only with immigration status, a race-neutral phenomenon, and that it was opponents, in fact, who were racist in their narrow assessment of the measure. These mutual accusations of racism led to an extremely polarizing debate, which drastically altered the political terrain of California. The battle over how to understand Proposition 187 continued long after the citizens of California finally voted on the initiative.

The struggle around Proposition 187, then, suggested itself to me as an ideal case in which to examine the role of racism and the "race card" in contemporary political struggles. To this end, I visited and interviewed supporters of Proposition 187. The thirty-three people I talked with circulated petitions, wrote letters to the editor, engaged in debates with their communities, and donated money to help ensure passage of Proposition 187. I spent hours with each supporter talking about the measure, the campaign, immigration, and their lives outside of this issue. The activists were not all of the same mold. I talked to a Japanese American, a former "lefty" who had moved "right of Attila the Hun," a Libertarian school counselor, an environmentally minded engineer, an unemployed truck driver who listened to a lot of talk radio, a well-traveled college professor, and many more individuals, each with a unique story. In this book, you will hear the voices of these people; you will read about their childhood experiences, family histories, jobs, political experiences, and the views that led them to support Proposition 187. While no two stories are alike, through an exploration of similarities and differences in their journeys, we learn about mobilization and the politics of immigration restriction. By studying the varied pathways that led to support of the measure, we can uncover the role that race played in the battle over immigration.

These men and women have been labeled racists by many social historians. I did not undertake my study to "let them off the hook." The policy changes this initiative proposed are not ones with which I agree, and I would struggle against similar measures wherever they are brought forward. I am, however, convinced, after recording at length the impressions and recollections of those who endorsed the initiative, that most of them did not understand their activity as being grounded in racism. I do not believe, moreover, that their denial of racism was a public expression used to hide their racist motivations.

Was Proposition 187 about race? Absolutely. But *how* did race play a role in the minds of its supporters? What was the connection between race and immigration that led individuals to believe that cutting off social services to some of the most vulnerable in society was a good idea? These are the questions this book explores. In so doing, I am attempting to transcend the divisiveness without pardoning racist policies, a fine line to walk, indeed.

Faye Ginsburg's work on the abortion debate in Fargo, North Dakota, in the 1980s is an inspiration for my approach, since it points to a way out of unproductive, polarized debates. Ginsburg enters the lives of women activists on both sides of the abortion issue. In doing so, she discovers how and why each woman eventually came to political activism. It is here she discovers common ground. Her breakthrough book demonstrates that once we begin to deconstruct assumptions about who our opponents are or what motivates their political activity, we discover human beings, albeit with a different set of experiences and ways of looking at the world. We might disagree with their perspectives, but we are likely to be able to identify with some parts of their stories, share some of their theoretical goals, and even engage them in legitimate dialogue.

To find this common ground does not require that we agree with opponents or that we find the implications of their political positions any less repulsive. It does compel us, however, to try to understand their motivations and the fundamental differences between their perceptions and ours. We may, after doing this, still believe their policies are ill advised or even immoral. If so, our study of their viewpoint will have provided the basis for a tactical approach much more effective than name-calling or crying foul. To address the concerns of our opponents in a way that is more democratic is not only a noble aim but sound strategy as well. Such a strategy, which entails restraining our impulse to demonize our opponents and instead seeing them as people with whom we can engage in fruitful political dialogue, is the ultimate goal of this book.

I hope it is with that in mind that the participants of the study read this book, for my first debt of gratitude is to them; they shared their ideas and gave of their time to help me understand what was and is happening in the realm of immigration politics.

I am also grateful to a number of funding sources that enabled me to complete the initial research of this project, including the Center for Diversity and Community, the Risa Palm Scholarship, and the Stephen L. Wasby Dissertation Fund at the University of Oregon. Also crucial to getting through the first stages were a large number of people at the University of Oregon. In particular, the intellectual and emotional contributions of the following individuals were invaluable: Deborah Baumgold, Max Brown, Rich Crook, Jeff Klein, Joseph Lowndes, Beatrice McKenzie, Ron Mitchell, and Kelly Shelton. Jeff in particular helped me on my long research trips up and down California.

I was lucky to find myself at Bucknell University while turning my research into a book. My colleagues in the political science department have been role models for me: people who care about the academy as I envision it, a cooperative venture in learning, teaching, and generating new knowledge. Everyone here seems to do each with a grace that I hope comes with time. I especially want to acknowledge my brutally supportive, good-humored writing group, who read most of this book, sometimes more than once: Michael Drexler, John Enyeart, and Scott Meinke. Others who have read drafts of portions of the book and made it a much better product include Kim Geron, Beatrice McKenzie, and Melissa Pashigian.

I owe my passion and my approach to issues of race to Howard Winant and Peggy Pascoe. I feel incredibly lucky to have had Howard Winant read the manuscript; he is a scholar who would have appeared in these acknowledgments in any case for the incredible intellectual debt I owe him. It was my introduction to his work as an undergraduate that inspired me to pursue studying the politics of race. Given that, I am still in disbelief at my good fortune that he agreed to read the manuscript, and I am grateful for his thoughtful comments on the book. Peggy Pascoe clarified the centrality of race in American life for me. Working with Peggy early on in my graduate career set me on my path; it was some of the most challenging work and therefore, as always, the most rewarding. She served as an incredible critical reader and teacher.

Julie Novkov and Gerald Berk served as cochairs for my dissertation and provided invaluable advice in turning this project into a book. I am so thankful my "parents" didn't make me choose. They worked together wonderfully, and I couldn't imagine being raised by just one of them. I was reassured why I wanted to continue with this project and in political science in general every time I left Gerry's office. After a discussion of my research, a book, or just the state of the field, I would walk away with my head spinning and with the drive to go immediately to my computer. In addition to intellectual commitment and excitement, he provided me with invaluable tools and guidance and pushed me at just the right moments and just the right places in this project.

Julie Novkov provided me with the support both intellectually and emotionally that I had been told would be essential, but I didn't quite understand how much until it was all over. She was the perfect role model with her work, both in her substance and diligence and with her mothering. She read drafts of the book, even after kicking me out of the nest. Her encouragement saw this project to its end and me through my graduate career and my first years in a job. She has always been there for me—always, as she proved when she returned my phone call while in labor.

Finally, the people who are closest to me on a daily basis deserve the biggest congratulations for putting up with me and helping me through this. I'd like to thank my father, who always gets more excited about my accomplishments than I do (and yes, Dad, my "paper" is now finally done). I'd like to thank my mother, who serves as my first wall to bounce ideas off of and my last line of defense for my writing. Milo Mowery put up with the additional craziness this book brought into our lives and helped to keep something resembling order when I couldn't. He juggles contradictions with grace. He talked through ideas when I wanted to, and he knew when I needed to work through things on my own. He was able to express his reservations about the content of the project while at the same time providing unwavering support for my endeavor. All of this made it a much smoother process than I know it would otherwise have been. And finally, my best teachers: Lily's and Stephen's arrival during this project kept me sane and grounded. They taught me about listening to others and trying to understand the world from their perspective. They taught me about possibilities.

INTRODUCTION

The Legacy of Proposition 187

In November 1993, ten people in California, including former agents of the U.S. Immigration and Naturalization Service, a mayor, and a state representative, wrote the Save Our State initiative. This document, which would become Proposition 187, comprised a number of different components that dealt with illegal immigration in California. The voter initiative proposed stricter penalties for false residency documents and reversed existing laws by mandating cooperation between the police and the INS. The sections that produced bitter, protracted public debate and made Proposition 187 a landmark in immigration politics and race relations were those that denied illegal immigrants social services, including nonemergency health care and public education, and required officials who delivered public social services to report any suspected undocumented person to the INS.

From the time of Proposition 187's introduction until the November election a year later, the debate over curtailing social services to undocumented immigrants became central to California politics and intensely mobilized individuals on both sides of the issue. After the introduction of the measure, Proposition 187 dominated conversations about the election and politics more generally in California. The public and the press repeatedly forced politicians running for election in November 1994 to take a stand on the initiative. The passionate debates spilled onto the pages of newspapers. In September, 313 letters to the editor in the *Los Angeles Times* were about Proposition 187, while only 191 were about all November election candidates combined. By the middle of October, the number of people who said they intended to vote because of the proposition equaled the number who were motivated by the contentious gubernatorial election. (Both outnumbered those who were interested in that year's senatorial race two to one.) By the end of October, officials were expecting voter turn-out to set records; political analysts attributed this to Proposition 187. In November 1994, the California electorate overwhelmingly supported the measure. More than 59 percent of voters favored this initiative to deny so-cial services to the undocumented.

The day after the proposition passed, lawsuits were filed, and the court placed an injunction on the measure. U.S. District Court Judge Pfaezler ruled it unconstitutional, calling it an attempt by the state to regulate im-migration, a federal responsibility. Instead of appealing, the state requested that the case be mediated. The central provisions of the measures, those denying the undocumented access to government services, were never implemented.[1]

The immediate court injunction against the measure, and the subsequent court ruling finding Proposition 187 unconstitutional, did not come as a surprise to those on the ground in California. Few believed the measure would ever be implemented. Proponents of Proposition 187 acknowledged that it was highly unlikely any tangible change in policy would result from passage of the initiative. This acknowledgment was made publicly just as forces on both sides were intensifying mobilization, about three months before the election. How, then, do we explain that more Californians went to the polls because of this issue than any other? Although the newspapers, organizations, and activists involved agreed, and acknowledged, that the measure would not be implemented, why did so many individuals work so fiercely to pass an initiative they knew would not make it past the courts?

The court injunction raises another intriguing question about Proposi-tion 187: the question of its legacy. Despite the failure of its stated policy goals, Proposition 187 is regarded as a watershed in contemporary race re-lations. Nearly a decade after the court's ruling, politicians are still asked about their stand on the initiative.[2] The measure is credited with copycat initiatives in other states and with creating the political space for other racialized measures in California. These initiatives include campaigns that ended affirmative action and bilingual education, most recently Measure 54, which, had it passed, would have prevented recording race on a variety of different government forms. Proposition 187 has also been credited with major shifts in the national political scene: changes in the Republican Party's platform on immigration between 1996 and 2000, provisions in the 1996 federal welfare reform that denied services to legal immigrants, politicization of Latinos, increases in the rates of naturalization, and even rising illegal immigration. How can Proposition 187, a measure that was never implemented, have had such long-term and wide-ranging impacts?

The legacy of the measure and mobilization in its support are intertwined and help explain the role of race in contemporary immigration politics. Mobilization in support of the initiative was part of a highly contentious, racialized battle over citizenship. By passing the measure, supporters of Proposition 187 hoped to render illegal immigrants (read "Hispanic illegal immigrants") politically voiceless, with no economic claim on society, outsiders even within the community. While the measure did not directly address the entrance into the state of illegal immigrants or undocumented workers, it distinguished among people already living inside the state. Even without implementation, the initiative separated and redefined: the "people" of California—that is, the electorate—decided that undocumented aliens living in the state did not have a right to education or health care, that they could make no social claims on society. The stakes were far from symbolic, as the redefinition of community had far-reaching impacts on people's lives.

How? If such redefinition wasn't backed up with legislation, how were people's lives changed? Through the very act of debating and supporting Proposition 187, proponents developed new racial understandings of citizenship. Changed conceptions of terms such as *race, immigrant,* and *citizen,* ratified through their vote, became lenses through which they understood subsequent events. Proposition 187, although never officially ending access to social services for the undocumented, redefined the community and redefined racial characterizations of the immigrant population, and in doing so redistributed resources—political, social, and economic.

By exploring support for Proposition 187, we gain insight into these new definitions of race and citizenship and the legacy of the measure. We can understand contemporary immigration politics in the United States and race politics more broadly. We gain insight into activity to restrict immigration in the post–civil rights era, when race is, at least publicly, disavowed by most political actors as a factor in creating immigration policy. By looking at how racial depictions of immigrants and citizens were reconstructed by supporters of Proposition 187, we can also construct a model for understanding the rise of the Right, one that explains how various factions of the Right are brought together, and the critical role of race in that ascent. Finally, exploration of the mobilization in support of Proposition 187, and of the legacy that endured even after its legal nullification, shows how racial depictions of citizenship and immigrants evolve and how these social constructs have real impacts on politics and on people's lives.

The Passage of Proposition 187

Popular and scholarly explanations of the appearance and passage of the measure have focused on elites, economics, and threat. Pete Wilson, when faced with the possibility of losing reelection for governor, embraced Proposition 187 as a key to his campaign. California was in the midst of a recession in 1994. Additionally, significant demographic changes were taking place, and there were projections that whites would soon no longer be a majority in California. Such analysis goes some distance toward explaining the political struggle over the measure and is important in considering the context of the racialized struggle.

However, neither elite manipulation nor the economy nor fear of threat explains the form of the measure itself—the specific policy pursued—nor are these forces sufficient to tell the story of mobilization. Unless we assume that all economic downturns will lead to nativist movements or all attempts to mobilize by elites are successful, we must include, but go beyond, economic recession and demographic changes to understand this moment of nativism.[3] We must dig into the specific narratives of individual supporters to understand the specific policies that emerge at times of nativist movements. In other words, we need to explore how elite activity and economic and demographic changes were interpreted by individuals at the time.

The Save Our State initiative entered the spotlight in 1994, but illegal immigration was already on the stage. The creators of Proposition 187 and the electorate that voted for the initiative were involved in a heated national and state conversation about illegal immigration that came to a boil in 1993.[4] By that time, California had been facing four years of recession and continual closings of military bases and reductions of contracts in the once-large aerospace industry. Pete Wilson, then governor, was a facing a tough reelection campaign. He championed and helped bring the anti-immigrant measure to the forefront of the political agenda.

Governor Wilson's budgetary move in 1993 contributed to the centrality of illegal immigration in California politics. The state had endured a recession and had a huge deficit. In the fall of 1993, Wilson's proposed budget for 1995 relied on a reimbursement from the federal government of $2.3 billion. He asked for the money to cover the state's expenses in paying for illegal immigration. By the spring of 1994, that sum was cut to $760 million dollars, but Wilson had also filed three lawsuits against the federal government in an attempt to retrieve money for incarcerating, educating, and providing emergency medical care for illegal immigrants. Not only did the request for the money and the lawsuits highlight the cost of illegal immigration during a difficult fiscal era, but the reliance on such a sum for a balanced budget indicated that the state could achieve fiscal health if it was not paying for illegal immigrants.

Wilson was not the only state politician pushing the federal government to deal with illegal immigration. Localities in California followed Wilson's lead and began requesting money to cover services that they were providing for undocumented immigrants. Members of the state legislature also focused on immigration, requesting action from the federal government and proposing legislation to deal with the issue of illegal immigration.[5]

While politicians like Wilson certainly publicized and probably altered the way people talked about immigration and undocumented people living in California, they clearly did not control the state's voters. If anything, the trends in the polls and the changes in his stances show that the balance of power swung the other way—the California voter controlled Wilson's views.[6]

Even if the lines of influence had been reversed and Proposition 187 had been instigated from the top, we would still need to understand why it was taken up from below. An initiative begun by ten people required many volunteers and over 385,000 signatures to make it to the ballot. People came to the voting booths in November 1994 *because* of Proposition 187. Certainly, then, it owed at least part of its support to a movement from below.

Citizens took up the call for dealing with illegal immigration through the initiative process. They did not focus on border control or employer sanctions or identification cards. The path they chose, social services, was more questionable. Many of the proponents of Proposition 187, both politicians and the public, acknowledged before the election that, given the content of the initiative, passage would not lessen the influx of illegal immigrants or save the state money. But this did not slow the mass mobilization of forces on behalf of the initiative.

National and local preexisting organizations mobilized support for Proposition 187 through networks, leadership, and money. Alan Nelson, a coauthor of the measure and a former immigration official, worked part-time for the national Federation for American Immigration Reform (FAIR), earning $70,000 a year at the time the measure was crafted (Stefancic 1997, 129). Although there was no consensus on the proposition, the top backer was the California Republican Party.[7] The third-largest donor was a California senator (Stefancic 1997, 128). FAIR, though remaining at a distance from the campaign, reserved time to air radio ads during the last week of the campaign (Feldman 1994c). The California Coalition for Immigration Reform, Stop the Out-of-Control Problems of Immigration Today (STOPIT), and other local groups designed explicitly to deal with immigration issues proved essential to generating volunteers and providing an organizational backbone (Stefancic 1997, 128).

Other networks also served to mobilize citizens, including homeowners' associations, which played a large role in the pro–Proposition 187 struggle (Lennon 1998, 91–93). Area branches of Ross Perot's American Reform Party proved useful to the proposition's proponents, providing a popular conduit for gathering volunteers. Citizen volunteers proved essential, in terms of both time and money. Letters poured into local newspapers arguing for the passage of Proposition 187, and its supporters raised $860,432 (Gibbs and Bankhead 2001, 81).

At times, however, these resources did not seem up to the task. While pro–Proposition 187 forces originally planned to use only volunteers to gather signatures, in the end they needed a paid signature-gathering service to meet the deadline. Other problems with their resources emerged. They ended the campaign with over $250,000 of debt.

The opposition also mobilized with great force, raising $3,214,255, over three and a half times more than the proponents did (Gibbs and Bankhead 2001, 81). A variety of preexisting institutions, such as churches, medical associations, schools, police associations, and immigrant rights groups, also stood against the measure. The *Los Angeles Times* came out in opposition to Proposition 187. Many politicians made a strong and vocal stand against it during the election campaign. Kathleen Brown, the Democratic candidate for governor, who was leading Wilson, a champion of Proposition 187, in the polls until a few months before the election, took an antiproposition stand and eventually lost. Additionally, opponents to the proposition were also able to garner large numbers of activists and volunteers. One of the biggest demonstrations in decades in California gathered between 70,000 and 100,000 people to rally against the measure (McDonnell and Lopez 1994). Given the resources and number of opponents, how do we understand the decisive passage of Proposition 187?

Scholars attempting to understand the passage of Proposition 187 have looked at the demographics of individuals who supported the measure and at opinion poll data (Tolbert and Hero 1996; Alvarez and Butterfield 2000). Whites supported the measure two to one, while over 70 percent of Latinos voted against it. Blacks and Asians marginally opposed the measure, with around 52 percent voting against it. Alvarez and Butterfield (2000) found that individuals with a negative perception of the state's economy tended to vote in favor of Proposition 187 (although one's personal economic assessment did not seem to affect the tendency to vote for or against the measure). They also established that educational attainment had a negative relationship with voting in favor of Proposition 187, and southern Californians were more likely to vote in favor of the measure than northern Californians. Alvarez and Butterfield concluded that Proposition 187 is an example of cyclical nativism brought on by economic downturns.

In an attempt to include contextual factors, Tolbert and Hero (1996) looked at county levels of support for the measure. They found racial context influenced individual support for the measure. Counties with a large white population and a large Latino population produced higher levels of yes votes. Similarly, counties with a relatively homogeneous white population also supported Proposition 187 in higher percentages. Racially or ethnically heterogeneous counties produced lower levels of support. That is, counties that also had significant populations of African Americans or Asian and Asian Americans in addition to the white and Latino populations produced more no votes.

Discovering who favored passage of the measure is an important place to begin to understand Proposition 187. Uncovering who supported the measure in large numbers—for example, whites or Republicans—provides insight into how the measure was understood by the electorate. These contextualized demographic variables give us hints about the racialized characterization of citizens and others or about the connection between this issue and fiscal conservatism. However, while these snapshots of individuals after they voted provide a window onto who was mobilized to act, they fail to tell us how or why.

To fill this gap, people have explained the passage of Proposition 187 as the result of immigration influx or economic deterioration. White native interests, so the story goes, were threatened by demographic changes (e.g., Frey 1996; Tolbert and Hero 1996) and economic decline (e.g., Nesbet and Sellgren 1995; Citrin et al. 1997; Alvarez and Butterfield 2000), and therefore white voters passed Proposition 187. Immigration did indeed account for 50 percent of the growth in population and labor force in the 1990s (Gibbs and Bankhead 2001, 78). And these immigrants were predominantly of color.[8] As mentioned previously, the early 1990s saw discussions of the near-approaching time when white Californians would no longer be a majority. Additionally, California was facing the worst recession since the Great Depression. Closing military bases and losses of aerospace contracts central to the southern California economy, combined with a general recession in the early 1990s, made for difficult economic times. These economic and demographic changes played a key role in creating an environment in which Proposition 187 could emerge and pass.

While these demographic and economic transformations established a fertile ground for *something* to happen, they are not sufficient to explain why *this* particular measure appeared. Unless we are willing to accept that the interests expressed in the measure were a "true" expression of the interests of the white native population in California, analysis that relies on changing demographics or economic conditions is not sufficient. Such analysis is grounded in the assumption that the categories of white, native, and the attendant interests are objective and knowable and not a product of political struggle—that they can be used as variables.

Such assumptions do not allow us to explore Proposition 187 as a battle over the meaning and content of these terms. Instead they take for granted the categories of people and the notions of self-interest as expressed by the native population, without questioning how narratives of interest, competition, and belonging are constructed and used. When we ignore such questions, we reify definitions of *citizen, foreigner,* and *interest* without exploring the ways that political battles, in fact, construct identities and interests.

Nativist Narratives before Proposition 187

By looking at Proposition 187 after the mobilization phase is over, most studies have ignored the political contestation surrounding this racial project and therefore cannot look at how mobilization results in "new interpretations of racial meanings" (Omi and Winant 1986/1991, 69). To truly understand nativist reactions, we must question how people are mobilized by nativist narratives and from where those narratives emerge.

Historians and others working with historical methods have demonstrated the ways race is constructed (e.g., Roediger 1991; Hale 1998; Lopez 1996; Lipsitz 1998). Scholars still struggle with how to understand contemporary problems through this lens. While (almost) all scholars can agree that race is a socially constructed phenomenon, when dealing with the contemporary moment, they tend to regard variables like *white, white interests,* and *ethnic groups* as explanatory or at least knowable quantities, not in need of explanation. The multiple ways in which the definitions of citizenship and race are fought over get lost.[9]

To understand Proposition 187 as a powerful racial project, we must look at the construction of racial meanings through action. We must look at Proposition 187 as a moment of contestation, not a predestined reaction to change. And we must study Proposition 187 in historical context. That context includes the histories of American nativism and of California's race relations. As we will see, proponents of Proposition 187 drew on a wide range of historically available racial tropes, in the context of the contemporary political era, as they re-created their state's racial terrain.

Nativism, opposition to a minority on the basis of their "foreignness," is a consistent, and evolving, strain in American history.[10] While its various manifestations may look the same on the surface, the specific nature of the racial tropes behind each has significant implications for the policies it engenders. Past periods of nativism provide images and conceptions of dangerous others that are used and re-created to match a current need and context. To understand any moment of nativism requires an understanding of the images and concepts inherited from the past and how they are reconstructed in light of the current political terrain.

American nativism, while a consistent impulse, has targeted different groups, contained myriad goals—from exclusion, to detention, to persecution—and reached varying political outcomes. At particular moments, generally of social, political, and economic upheaval, nativism has come to the fore of American politics.[11] During the 1840s and 1850s, anti-Catholic nativism culminated in the million-member Know-Nothing Party and successful electoral campaigns. Following the Civil War, anxiety over Asian immigration, beginning on the West Coast and spreading east, led to the Chinese Exclusion Act of 1882 and subsequent violence and agitation against Asian immigrants. Another period of anti-immigrant sentiment and political action, beginning in the late nineteenth century, focused on a new wave of immigrants from southern and western Europe, culminating in the 1924 National Origins Quota Act, which set the first quantitative limits on immigration. In the midst of the Great Depression, fear of migrants arose and was accompanied by repatriation campaigns targeting Mexicans. During

World War II, the mistreatment and internment of Japanese Americans received widespread social and legal support. Following World War II, "Operation Wetback" forcibly repatriated over 3.8 million people to Mexico, some of whom were American citizens. Each of these nativist moments contained common elements, but also unique features, political imperatives, and results.

Similarities first: Complaints about unassimilability, dirtiness, backwardness, hostility to American values and institutions, sexual immorality, and criminality have been leveled against Irish, German, Italian, Chinese, Japanese, and Latinos, as well as Jews and Catholics. Women immigrants have come in for a healthy share of such negative stereotyping, with Chinese women suspected of being prostitutes and Irish women accused of being fecund. Most immigrant groups have been associated with criminal conduct and anti-American sentiments or behavior; Japanese, Chinese, and Germans have all at some point been accused of having a distinctive culture that threatened "American" culture.

Although they share similar concerns about foreignness, each moment of nativism uses these racial tropes in distinct ways. While Chinese women, depicted as prostitutes at the end of the nineteenth century, were suspected of criminal conduct and denied entry into the United States, the concern over Irish fertility coincided with the early-twentieth-century rise of eugenics in the United States. Thus Irish women's perceived sexual immorality was connected with concerns of an inferior stock engulfing the American population through reproduction. Concerns about multiplying paupers and racial takeover contributed to the idea of national-origins quotas. Numerical limits were a tool to battle against race suicide; exclusion was not necessary. Similarly we see nativist concerns about culture having very different political goals and outcomes depending on the time and the group of consternation: while concerns over the threat of Chinese culture led to exclusion, concerns over German culture led to Americanization campaigns.

Racial tropes, expressed by the state, science, and popular culture, are reinterpreted in light of the current political moment. While similar racial tropes are used by different groups at various times in history, the specific forms of these accusations, and the connections between the broad claim and the specific group, differ from their predecessors. They are transformed as they are applied to new peoples at new times in a different context. And it is in such transformations that racial politics are redefined.

Accusations issued by proponents of Proposition 187 of Mexicans being hyperreproductive, backward, criminal, and dependent have been leveled at other groups and at Latinos at other times. A key to understanding the contemporary racial or nativist moment in American politics, though, is to understand how these racial tropes are applied to the immigrant group of consternation, Latinos, and how they are used in the California political and racial terrain in the post–civil rights era.

The restrictionist movement of the early 1990s emerged from a racial terrain shaped fundamentally in the 1960s. Changes wrought during the civil rights movement in race relations in general and in immigration policy and patterns in particular created three key reactions on the right: the Far Right, which fights for "white rights" and sees open racial conflict; the New Right, which sees racial mobilization "as a threat to 'traditional values'" and "engages in race coding" (Winant 1994, 31); and color-blind conservatism, which denies the importance of race and argues against recognition of race by the state (Winant 1994, 31). The appearance of a powerful restrictionist movement in the early 1990s stemmed from the ability to create a coalition of these three forces around the issue of immigration.

California's conservative movement beginning after World War II led the way for the revival of the Right, including the color-blind conservatism central to racial politics after the 1960s. Orange County, which was to be the heart of Proposition 187, became a hotbed of conservative activism during the McCarthy era. This political climate, together with the economic and demographic boom after the war and the centrality of the military-industrial complex to the area's prosperity (McGirr 2001, 51), fostered a strong sense of anticollectivism and antisecularism in Orange County. This conservatism was both connected to a national movement and unique to the locale.

Race did not occupy the same central, explicitly segregationist role in the California conservative movement that it did in the South of the 1960s (McGirr 2001, 130). White supremacy, while having a long history in California, took a different form than in other regions of the country. From its origins as a U.S. state, the uniqueness of race in California is clear. Manifest destiny and free-labor ideology defined the first debates over race in the new California. The California constitution, adopted in 1849 amid the growing national debate over slavery, evidenced free-labor ideology. This belief system was "grounded in the precept . . . that free labor was economically and socially superior to slave labor" (Foner 1970/1995, ix). From this

constitutional debate over admitting blacks to concerns over Chinese own-
ing land, mining, and immigrating, European American Californians "repeatedly associated nonwhite people with various unfree labor systems"
(Almaguer 1994, 13). When whites encountered, for example, the Mexican
elite ranchers following the annexation of California, they connected the
ranchero with southern plantation slaveholders (51). Free-labor ideology
combined with white supremacy and led to a series of policies that were
used to exclude or make invisible racial minorities, creating the illusion of
a homogeneous white state. From sundown laws to policies allowing land
to be taken from Mexicans and Asians, California consciously constructed
itself as a white society. Unlike the hierarchically bifurcated South, California
attempted to create a "free" society that denied the presence of the "unfree"
others. The illusion of a raceless state contributed to the unique evolution
of conservatism in California following World War II and helps explain
why color-blind conservatism found a ready home there after the civil rights
movement.

One origin of contemporary California color-blind conservatives can
be seen in the battle for Proposition 14 in 1964. This voter initiative was designed to abolish the state law prohibiting racial discrimination in housing. The measure passed overwhelmingly.[12] Proposition 14 "contained the
seeds of the controversies that would fragment the California electorate
over affirmative action, immigration, bilingual education, and urban crime"
(Gibbs and Bankhead 2001, 177). The debate around this proposition included the ideas of freedom, individuality, government-as-enemy, and
racialized notions of the other. These values and worldviews, as we will
see, recombined in new ways with new realities in the early 1990s around
the issue of illegal immigration.

The new realities in which these conservative ideas were used and reformed leading up to Proposition 187 include the closing of military bases
and vast reductions in military contracts, an extended recession, and increasing immigration and racial conflict. In 1992 the Los Angeles riots served
as a touchstone that would inform conservative action in the subsequent
years. Not only Proposition 187 but a string of other citizen initiatives were
influenced by the television images of daily racial uprisings (Gibbs and
Bankhead 2001). Proponents of Proposition 187, as we will see, cite the Los
Angeles riots as a turning point in, or a confirmation of, their perceptions
of the problems in California.

Proposition 187, having some similarities to nativist movements that preceded it, is unique in the ways racial tropes were recombined with colorblind conservatism in light of the contemporary social and political terrain. Through their activism, proponents redefined racial categories and the meanings of citizenship in California in the 1990s—the legacy of Proposition 187.

This book uses the personal journeys of proponents of Proposition 187 to explore this legacy. These narratives show how mobilization around Proposition 187 emerged from, and changed, the cultural and political landscape. Chapter 1 explores how various theories on race and social movements can explain the mobilization, passage, and legacy of Proposition 187. Here I contrast new racism, based on a static notion of race, with racial formation theory, which proposes focusing on the changes in race over time. By looking at such changes, we can see the struggle around Proposition 187 as a dynamic contest over the meaning of race and racial categories. Racial formation theory also suggests a turn to current social movement theory; however, current social movement theory fails to help us explain mobilization behind a judicially doomed measure. Finally, by placing a theory of agency center stage, I hope to solve some of the problems found in social movement theory and encourage readers to understand mobilization in favor of the initiative as part of the creative reconstruction of notions of race.

Chapter 2 explores the ways in which claims to color blindness and racialized understandings of immigration shaped the mobilization of support for Proposition 187. This study suggests that the two metaschemas in the campaign may be identified as color-blind conservatism, which holds that race should be treated as irrelevant and that the use of racial categories inherently interferes with fairness, individualism, and equality, and racial realism, which maintains that race is a fundamental dividing category in society and that each race has singular interests that compete with the interests of others. The rest of the chapter explores the central bridging strategies that connect these two seemingly contradictory sets of commitments.

Each subsequent chapter explores a theme or notion of citizenship that is central to the debate over Proposition 187: legal, economic, cultural, and political citizenship. For each theme, respondents have commitments to both a color-blind notion of citizenship and a racial realist version. Chapter 3 discusses legal citizenship and supporters' construction of Mexicans as criminals. Bridges are drawn between proponents' concerns about the rule of law governing migration and a Latino tendency toward criminality. This mobilizes individuals to support Proposition 187. After passage of the measure, the court ruling declaring Proposition 187 unconstitutional is read as a sign of increased lawlessness emanating from the traditional protector of the rule of law. As a result, these bridges are maintained and become a central lens for viewing subsequent events. Criminalization of Mexican migration is one of the principal legacies of the measure.

Chapter 4 looks at the role of economic arguments in the struggle over the measure. Much of this debate takes the form of a cost-benefit analysis to determine the "worth" of the undocumented to the state of California. The color-blind concern about fairness to taxpayers was not about the "bottom line" but about taking care of "economic" citizens before those deemed noncitizens. To determine who is an economic citizen, supporters connect this color-blind schema with notions of Latino dependency. Bridges are constructed between this racial realist concern about dependency and work ethic and the color-blind concern about fairness to taxpayers. These bridges maintain immediate power and result in serious policy shifts at the federal level; however, they lose saliency in the long run, as they provide little leverage for understanding subsequent state action and political events.

Chapter 5 examines the debate over culture. Proponents suggest that they are concerned with the process of assimilation because a homogeneous culture is essential for a functioning society. They argue that they are not concerned with maintaining any particular culture, but that for pragmatic reasons, there should be only one. This idea, however, is accompanied by expressions of disdain for Mexican culture. Mexican culture is described as dirty, communal, and ultimately uncivilized. Proponents use a notion of loyalty to connect advocacy of assimilation and a functioning society with concerns over cultural invasion by an uncivilized group. Cultural assimilation is understood as an indication of loyalty, a connection that gains power as issues of national security take on increasing prominence.

Chapter 6 considers the role of population concerns in the campaign around Proposition 187. Proponents used race-neutral concerns about the environment and quality of life in California to explain their support for the measure. However, we cannot understand this support without looking at the bridges between color-blind concerns about growth and racial realist concerns about Mexican hyperfertility. Concerns about population become equated with concerns about Mexican invasion at the ballot box through reproduction. After the court injunction against the measure, worries about political power struggles and political invasion come to the fore as discussions about the environment fall into the background. The collapse of this bridge leads to a distancing between the environmental movement and the restrictionist movement.

The final chapter revisits the notion that social action theory and a framework of transposing schemas help us understand the mobilization and legacy of Proposition 187. The transformations that resulted from the battle for Proposition 187 highlight the failure of "new racism": new racism has a static notion of race that fails to explain why Proposition 187 had such an impact on the racial and political terrain. The legacy of Proposition 187 is the creation of racial meanings through bridges between racial realism and color-blind conservatism. I conclude by exploring how this is evidenced in a number of key political events after Proposition 187, including the 1996 welfare reform, the debate over the granting of driver's licenses to the undocumented, the reaction to 9/11, and copycat initiatives in other states. These crucial political and legal milestones were all influenced by the new racialized conceptions of economic, cultural, and political citizenship created by Proposition 187. Only by looking back to the roots of these events in 1990s California can we claim to fully understand our nation's current racial constructs.

CHAPTER ONE

Bridging Race

Opponents of Proposition 187 repeatedly leveled charges of racism at the measure's proponents, arguing that it represented a thinly veiled attempt to penalize the state's Latino population. The proposed measure called on providers of social services to report those they "suspected" of being undocumented. To opponents, such an enforcement mechanism required discrimination against those who looked and sounded different. Proponents rejected the claim, arguing that their stance was race neutral; it was the opponents who were themselves playing the "race card." Because the measure's provisions were grounded in documentation status, not race, proponents insisted, they were the victims of race-conscious political opponents.

These dueling accusations of racism are an example of the central dilemma of racial politics in the contemporary moment. In an age when race is understood as a social construction, in an age when race is consciously up for grabs yet politically off the table, how do we begin to wade through competing charges of racism? We can begin by exploring the debate as an active redefinition of race.

Defining race today means grappling with an acknowledgment of race as a social construction, an artifact of human invention, while at the same time recognizing its formidable power. These goals may appear to be at cross-purposes with each other. To recognize race as a social construction may lead us to want to ignore it or wish it away. However, the continuing impacts of race, the very real ways it channels relations and resource distribution and creates our intersubjective reality, demonstrate the substance of this deeply embedded concept.[1] The challenge of addressing race as at once being socially constructed and having material impacts is a dilemma that faces everyone from scholars to activists to people on the left and the right. This is the stuff that racial politics are made of: competing interpretations of the meaning of race and racial categories.

Racial formation theory provides the best guide to understanding contemporary racial politics. Racial formation theory posits race as the dynamic product of political struggles. Through this lens, we can explain the unfolding and the legacy of political battles more clearly. It also helps us understand immigration politics, where activists of all stripes are struggling with how to interpret the role and meaning of race. Proposition 187, then, is both an important case study in its own right and a way to explore the role of race in the broader contemporary political order. With a carefully theorized notion of agency, racial formation theory leads us to understand proponents of Proposition 187 as individuals who are creatively recombining historically available racial tropes and other worldviews to reinterpret the world around them and the political and racial terrain.

The Colors of Conservatism

Proposition 187 was spurred by the color-blind conservative movement, which contends that if race is a social construction, then it is not real. Therefore race should not be mentioned in government policy, law, or business dealings. Color-blind conservatism "denies the salience of racial 'difference' or argues that it is a vestige of the past, when invidious distinctions and practices had not yet been reformed"; as a result, "any collective articulation of racial 'difference' amounts to 'racism in reverse'" (Winant 1994, 31). Color-blind conservatism is a central reaction to the changes in the racial terrain following the civil rights movements and subsequent racial projects like the 1965 immigration reform act and affirmative action. Color-blind conservatism uses certain schemas from the civil rights movements and from American liberal individualism to challenge advances made toward equality.

Color-blind conservatism is a product of the struggle with the notion of race as a social construction. The ideology has its roots in the questioning of race as a biological or cultural category, a response to the anthropologist Franz Boas's pioneering studies and the decline of scientific racism (Pascoe 1999). One important response to the shifting racial terrain of the time was to separate the powerful cultural forces from the biological forces. Race became "merely biological" and therefore unimportant. Race as a powerful marker had been part of a racist culture that could now be altered by ignoring race. Because of this legacy, we find ourselves in "an Alice-in-Wonderland interpretation of racism in which even those who argue for racially oppressive policies can adamantly deny being racists" (Pascoe 1999, 482).

Recent nativist movements, exemplified by the movement to pass Proposition 187, are an extension of color-blind conservatism and illustrate the contradictions within the ideology. Nativism that arose in the late 1980s focuses on questions of fairness by highlighting the problem of the illegal immigrant and the impacts of an increasing population. Race is no longer a central platform on which immigration restrictionists stand publicly (Reimers 1998). This is true of the many variants within the ranks of immigration restrictionists, from those concerned with culture to those concerned about the economic impact of immigration and fairness to citizens in the labor market. Recently, some environmentalists, who argue that overpopulation resulting from immigration causes environmental degradation, have joined the restrictionist movement. Organizations and individuals concerned with population and immigration argue that they are in fact "color-blind" regarding their activism.

When we begin to interpret, however, what individuals mean by fairness regarding the labor market or how they perceive threats to the environment or culture, we frequently stumble on race-based understandings of these problems. Conceptions of who the immigrants are, and what they are doing to violate fairness and hurt the quality of life, are grounded in racial categories. So-called race-neutral language about immigration, newcomers, and foreigners is, in fact, loaded with racial images. This is because words are understood and interpreted by individuals who have a particular set of racial characterizations about who, for example, constitutes a newcomer or who is a "native."[2]

New Racism

One explanation of the role of race in color-blind conservatism, and projects like Proposition 187, is that activists have simply taken racism underground in an attempt to conform to what is socially acceptable. Activists, it is proposed, are using the idea of race as a social construct to veil racist motivation and policies. According to such theories, Proposition 187 and other contemporary racial projects are examples of "new" or "symbolic" racism.

Unfortunately, by highlighting the dynamic nature of racism, new racism creates a static conception of race and fails to confront what is really at stake in racial political struggles: the meaning of race.

The idea of new racism emerged from attempts to understand the role that race continued to play in the minds and actions of white Americans in the wake of the civil rights movement. Struggling with how to account for the continuing relevance of race in politics despite a common belief in race as a social construction and a commonly expressed commitment to equality, scholars have introduced a slew of different names: "symbolic racism" (Sears and Kinder 1971), "modern racism" (McConahay 1986), "subtle racism" (Pettigrew and Meertens 1995), and "race resentment."[3] According to these theories, racism remains a potent force but has adopted a less-explicit expression. Race plays the same role but is talked about through code words rather than explicitly. In other words, latent racism is the foundation on which the veneer of equality is laid. Beneath the surface, politicians and elites can still tap into subconscious racism.

While the various depictions of new racism differ, they also share certain themes, as well as certain fundamental problems. Proposition 187 highlights the dangers of drawing a distinction between new and old racism.

New racism is distinctive, according to scholars, for three reasons: it acknowledges race as a social construction; it uses American values at its core; and it is more subtle or less explicit than pre–civil rights discrimination. First, scholars historically demarcate new racism by focusing on a perceived shift from biologically grounded notions of race to cultural categories (Jacobson 1998; Pascoe 1999, 465–67). If race is socially constructed, it resides within a purely cultural category. Scholars focusing on new racism note that we live in an "era that has generally renounced ... biological theories of superiority" (Sears et al. 1997, 20). New racism, "instead of invoking genetic inferiority ... attributes outgroup disadvantage to cultural differences" (Meertens and Pettigrew 1997, 58). Kinder and Sanders (1996), for example, caution against equating the decline of biological racism with the demise of racism in general and trace the historical evolution of modern racism in terms of culture (97–98).

Second, most conceptualizations of new racism suggest that American values constitute a key cultural category. The new racism is "expressed less in the language of inherent and permanent difference and more in the language of American individualism" (Kinder 1998, 422). There is an emphasis on values and a subtle prejudice expressed through the "defence of traditional values" (Pettigrew and Meertens 1995, 58). A group's failure or difference is explained by its members' failure to act in accordance with the social and cultural values of the larger society or simply by their failure to respect such values. A common tenet, then, that characterizes the various formulations of new racism is the belief that racism today is "the *conjunction* of prejudice and values" (Kinder and Sanders 1996, 292).

Third, the use of values and culture as key concepts in racial attitudes allows this new form of prejudice to be less explicit or more subtle. Pettigrew and Meertens (1995) suggest that the "common theme across all these new forms [of conceptualizing racism] is that they are *covert* means of expressing prejudice that differ from the old-fashioned forms" (58). Code words and talk of American values can frequently allow racial political messages to be conveyed without using language that explicitly refers to race. The tactic of "covert" racial politics allows those who use racialized images to hide the racial content of their message from others, and even from themselves, in an era when egalitarian principles are largely accepted (Kinder and Sanders 1996, chap. 5; Meertens and Pettigrew 1997, 56). New racism's reliance on cultural exaggerations allows people to distance themselves from accusations of prejudice because they are merely "report[ing] on actual and obvious intergroup differences" (Pettigrew and Meertens 1995, 60).

In sum, new racism suggests that many individuals have responded to the deconstruction of race by replacing biology with culture in their rationales and taking the notion of race underground. Race continues to be relevant because individuals have thought of new ways to talk about the same categories less explicitly. Codes are used to get at the same ideas. Racism, theorists maintain, continues to make race relevant by morphing into more socially acceptable forms while at the same time upholding earlier divisive notions of race.

The passage of Proposition 187 has been understood in just these terms. Hasian and Delgado (1998) illuminate the multiple styles of propaganda supporting the measure, presenting color-blind language as a "tactic designed to deflect frontal assaults and [claims that Proposition 187] was motivated by racism, nativism and ethnocentrism" (256). Racist ideas, they contend, are "couched" in other terms, and cues are used to generate support for this racist measure. Lennon (1998) talks about the dangers of the initiative system in relation to Proposition 187. She argues that anonymity at the voting booth may actually encourage the passage of racist measures:

"While public proclamations of racist attitudes have lost their respectability, prejudice continues to receive an airing of privacy in the voting booth" (Julian Eule, quoted in Lennon 1998, 94). She concludes that racial and nationalist discourses in Proposition 187 were masked by liberal and democratic language (96). Both these accounts of Proposition 187, then, suggest that the measure tapped into a deep-seated racism while providing a cover with false commitments to equality.

However, looking more closely at the campaign around the measure and investigating its supporters (instead of asserting their intentions) show that this explanation is lacking. In fact, my exploration of Proposition 187 proves that drawing a distinction between new and old racism is a faulty, even dangerous, endeavor. New racism provides little room for considering the context and the dynamism of race because it ignores the process through which racial meanings are constructed and reifies racial meanings as they emerge. In other words, new racism takes a snapshot of a racial project and freezes it in the moment, preventing us from learning how and when race is transformed historically.

Dangerous Distinctions

The central distinction based on subtlety or explicitness is inaccurate and misleading.[4] The battle for Proposition 187, its passage, and aftermath show this distinction to be mistaken. The measure's wording, if taken out of context, may appear subtle or to have little to do with race. But words have meaning only through the context of people's lived experiences, and those experiences are racialized.

This is evident in the infamous television commercial used during California's heated 1994 gubernatorial campaign. The ad shows twelve Hispanics swarming over a fence, crossing into America. The image is in black and white and is accompanied by pounding rhythms and a voice-over that warns, "They keep coming." This ad, part of Pete Wilson's successful campaign, predicted what would happen if someone weak on illegal immigration occupied the governor's office. Putting the issue into pictorial form makes the intersubjective understandings of the initiative starkly clear. There is nothing subtle or "less explicit" about hordes of brown-skinned people climbing fences. The racial context of this political message is not an undertone but its directly accessible and explicit meaning. The television commercial was created and received within a specific racial terrain. Racial projects are embedded within history, within the racial terrain from which they emerge.

Recognizing this requires that we use race as a dynamic category, an approach for which new racism is ill suited. New racism takes race as a static category, meaning the same thing over time, or at least within a single campaign. According to its scholars, the devices that people use may change, but they are designed to get at the same underlying set of ideas; the fundamental nature of race does not vary. For example, Tali Mendelberg (2001) writes about the use of race cues in elections. She talks about tapping into people's prejudices in new ways. Politicians, she suggests, are capitalizing on a contradiction between a norm of equality and personally held racial stereotypes. According to Mendelberg, campaigns that use racial messages mobilize but do not challenge or create notions of race. Her concept of race, then, is static; she views it as simply a tool and fails to account for the reconstruction of racial categories that occurs *during* mobilization.

Additionally, new racism does not provide room for individual change and growth. Scholars of new racism suggest that others can tap into the deep-seated racism buried within people. This view makes racism fundamental to the nature of individuals who respond to the racial codes. Such theories offer no way to understand why some respond to new racism and others don't, why for some, commitments to equality are real, and for others they are something to merely parrot. New racism offers us instead the troubling conclusion that some people simply *are* racists, almost a biologi cal fact. Once we buy into this "predestination," we have no leverage to explain shifts in support of similar policies or ideas, which in turn leaves us at a loss to explain the rise and fall of coalitions or individual mobilization.

A Way Out

Michael Omi and Howard Winant's racial formation theory suggests a corrective by pointing to the shifting notions of race. Racial formation theory begins with the premise that race, a fundamental organizing principle of society, is constantly contested through racial projects at all levels. Therefore understanding race means understanding the process through which it is defined. Changes in the definition of race shift the racial terrain, guiding political interpretations of the world and shaping political possibilities.

This theory stresses both the consistency of racism—racism "creates or reproduces hierarchical social structures based on essentialized racial categories" (Winant 2000, 19)—and the changeability of race—race is "an unstable and 'decentered' complex of social meanings constantly being transformed by political struggles" (Omi and Winant 1986/1989, 68). If Winant is right, scholars need to be studying the *process* of racial formation. We need to examine the structural and historical contexts, contexts in which racial attitudes are enmeshed, the macrosocial processes that shape approaches to race (Winant 2000, 18–22). Shifting the meaning of race to center stage and increasing work on understanding the ways in which such meaning is formulated highlight the ways in which racism is perpetuated (Pascoe 1999). Such a shift in focus, away from studying, labeling, and identifying the changes in racism to a focus on changes in the meaning of race, provides an avenue for understanding how and why individuals' racialized perceptions can alter over time, as well as the reasons behind the rise and fall of political coalitions. Looking closely at the meaning of race across time, place, and project is, in fact, the best basis for reconciling the dynamic nature of race and the consistency of racism.

As we will see, the campaigns for and against Proposition 187 involved the creation of new racial categories. "Native" and "foreigner," "white" and "Mexican," are not static concepts. The struggle over Proposition 187, specifically the mobilization for the measure, was a struggle over the racialization of citizenship. Individuals were mobilized to support the measure as they connected color-blind American values about individualism, fairness, and equality with raced notions about group competition. Both were sets of genuine commitments. The legacy of the measure, its impact on subsequent politics, is a result of the new versions of economic, political, and social citizenship that emerged from the creative connections drawn between color-blind commitments and racial worldviews.

The following chapters show the campaign around Proposition 187 as a struggle over racial categories. Actors involved in the political battle (re)constructed racial categories. In turn, the political fallout from the measure resulted in strengthening, disposing of, or re-creating those racial categories. Previous studies, based on new racism's static notion of race, fail to explain the continuing legacy of Proposition 187. This failed initiative's lasting impact cannot be accounted for if it merely tapped into existent and static conceptions of race. If neither people nor policy was transformed, why is Proposition 187 still so politically salient? While new racism suggests that mobilization uses existent racial categories, the theory of racial formation highlights how mobilization can *reconfigure* racial categories. In doing so, racial formation theory provides a framework for understanding how racial terrains are shifted and how the battle around Proposition 187 created distinct and enduring raced conceptions of citizenship.

Social Movement Theory

Racial formation theory points us toward social movement theory to understand the mobilization around a racial project. During mobilization, transformations occur in the racial project and its meaning. To understand these transformations, racial formation theory relies on tools for understanding collective action. I therefore consider the state of social movement theory and how it can help understand racial transformation and the mobilization and legacy of Proposition 187. Social movement theory is plagued by a strict divide between material and cultural accounts of mobilization, which proves problematic for understanding Proposition 187, as well as racial formation and social movements more generally. Material explanations do not allow for transformations in the racial terrain that occur during mobilization. Resources are mobilized, but people and conceptions of race and community are untouched. This is similar to the problem identified in theories of new racism: race and racists become static conceptions that elites and organizers tap into for mobilization. On the other hand, cultural accounts of collective action provide no guideposts for understanding the extent or limits of change during mobilization. Individuals appear as free agents unbounded by history and structures. Conceptions of race and possibilities for change are not clearly linked to the current racial terrain.

Scholars have recognized problems with the material-culture divide in social movement theory and attempted to offer some integration approaches.[5] These approaches, while suggesting ways to understand the interactions between culture and structure, replicate some of the problems found in previous versions of social movement theory. They fail to answer the mobilization mystery behind Proposition 187 because they subsume issues of culture within a material framework. I argue that an account that places agency at the center of movement activity can overcome the material-culture divide. To understand racial formation and mobilization in favor of Proposition 187, we need to focus on the role of creative political action by individuals firmly grounded in a specific historic context and racial terrain. This is essential for grasping the dynamism of race and the transformative power of mobilization.

Resource mobilization (e.g., McCarthy and Zald 1977; Tilly 1978; McAdam 1982) is a structural explanation that focuses on observable variables such as organizational and political structure and resources and downplays the importance of emotion, identity, and culture. According to this theory, tactics can be understood by looking at the resource and political constraints a group faces, and the success or failure of a movement can be explained by a group's ability to mobilize resources, including money, labor, and membership. At the base of resource mobilization is a purposive or rational notion of agency (Crossley 2002), where social movement leaders or potential participants engage in cost-benefit calculations to set goals and determine tactics. Rational-actor models are grounded in a methodological individualism, which denies sociability, subjectivity, and variability in humans.

This version of agency is problematic for understanding racial formation in general and Proposition 187 in particular. Proposition 187 is especially puzzling for resource mobilization theorists because they focus on the attempt of a group to attain instrumental change. Because of its rational-choice foundations, the theory is best at explaining instrumental goals such as legislative, structural, and other sorts of tangible change. The inevitability of the judicial intervention forced proponents of the measure to say that the proposition had symbolic value. The rational actor at the base of resource mobilization is not easily congruent with such goals. Additionally, the rational-actor model of agency takes preferences as a given. It ignores questions about the construction of preferences. It ignores how society and social interpretations of goods create the value of any goal. In a similar fashion to new racism, real changes in racial politics over time are occluded, and outcomes seem predetermined. With culture located outside the traditional notion of structure, structures "tend to appear . . . as impervious to human agency, to exist apart from, but nevertheless to determine the shape of, the strivings and motivated transactions that constitute the experienced surface of social life" (Sewell 1992, 2). The traditional notion of structure has therefore resulted in deterministic or near-deterministic understandings that focus on stability and do not adequately account for change. Culture and identity do not play a critical role in resource mobilization theory, and as such, it has trouble accounting for the mobilization around Proposition 187 and the measure's influential legacy.

Theories of collective action grounded in cultural explanations or identity-oriented approaches provide room, but not grounding, for understanding mobilization around Proposition 187. Identity-oriented approaches developed from insights about culture and identity found in new social movement (NSM) theory and in earlier theories of collective behavior. These approaches point to the need to look at intersubjectivity, expressive goals, and the construction of interests and identity. Identity-oriented theories place cultural interpretations at the center for understanding both strategies and goals. In so doing, they can explain a range of protest activity that resource mobilization has difficulty accounting for, such as consciousness-raising, street theater, and witnessing, as well as fighting for measures that will most likely never be implemented, even if passed.

However, the focus on identity, collective values, and cultural interpretations is not connected with material and structural concerns and therefore also leaves many questions unanswered about Proposition 187. Culture is a changeable product of human action; therefore human action governs movement activity. Agency, while given a central place, is not theorized. Because of a strict material-culture divide, we are not given tools to understand agents' actions. We are left with little leverage for understanding why some goals arise, why some tactics are chosen, or how movements develop. Why did Proposition 187 appear when it did in the form it did? And how did Proposition 187 impact people's daily lives? Agents appear free from the constraints of structures and history. Culture appears infinitely mutable, and the ways that culture impacts structures are lost. To understand Proposition 187 as a transformative moment, we need to understand the activists involved in the campaign firmly embedded in the Californian and national racial terrain in 1994.

Scholars have attempted to integrate cultural and material approaches to social movements. Framing and the political process model (PPM) are two central examples of attempts to incorporate culture into material explanations. These examples of integration highlight where social movement theory still needs to advance.

Framing focuses on the ways that social movements set issues or construct frames for constituents to view and understand events around them. "Social movements frame—that is, assign meaning to and interpret—relevant events and conditions in ways that are intended to mobilize potential adherents and constituents, garner bystander support, and demobilize antagonists" (Klandermans 1992, 80). Culture becomes one of a number of resources that leaders of social movements can use to reach new constituents or sustain members. Framing theory, similar to resource mobilization, posits rational social-movement elites struggling for tangible goals. Frames are designed to attract constituents, and leaders can be understood as attempting to read the cultural mood of some section of people. Therefore it is not so clear who is really doing the framing—the people through the leaders reading their desires or moods, or the leaders in shaping the way people understand the events. Framing fails to provide a clear account of agency and thus fails to truly incorporate culture and structure.

The political process model, forwarded as a synthetic approach (Ayres 1997), also makes connections between institutions and culture, but with a clearer theory of agency to avoid relegating culture to a micromobilization role. PPM places the political environment at the center of its understanding of social movements and as such is an advance in social movement theory. Changes in the political system or the elite structure provide opportunities for social movements to emerge. Preexisting structures, social networks, and established institutions, such as those stemming from schools, churches, and fraternal organizations, are necessary to take advantage of the opportunities provided by the changes in the political structure. By contextualizing the movement, PPM connects actors to history and to each other. Cultural understandings, identity, and consciousness shifts become important in a third level required to generate collective action, the micromobilization process. This process enables participants to perceive the potential for change, generates solidarity, and therefore "help[s] to overcome the perennial 'free-rider' problem" (Ayres 1997, 55). Culture becomes important to understand how organizations attempt to gather popular support.

While this integration begins to question the connections between structure (e.g., political systems) and cultural understandings, culture is still seen primarily as a resource that enables mobilization. The ways that culture, identity, and mobilized people interact with, and possibly contribute to, shifts in the political system are not really considered. PPM considers resource mobilization issues and addresses questions of identity, but the connections *between* them have not been fully explored.

Integration attempts fail to solve the puzzle of Proposition 187 because they do not integrate; they consolidate. Combining culture and structure has resulted either in making one dominant over the other or in depicting each as working in its own separate stream. Proposition 187, a "symbolic" struggle that takes place in a traditional political venue, is a clear example that structure and culture cannot be so easily divided into separate arenas or separate analytical categories. Culture, in both examples of consolidation approaches, becomes a tool for rational action, and therefore many of the same problems that resource mobilization had in addressing Proposition 187 still arise. Framing or PPM still cannot understand the battle as a whole. A struggle over a nonimplementable measure eludes a theory that posits rational social-movement elites struggling for a tangible goal. To fully understand the events surrounding Proposition 187, we require tools that supplement social movement theory and allow us to collapse the material-culture divide.

Social Action Theory

Social action theory, stemming mostly from sociology, explores collective action without cornering off material and cultural explanations from each other. Developments in social action theory suggest a useful version of structure that truly incorporates culture at its core and provides us with new terminology that helps overcome the problems of the previous integration approaches. Such a model permits us to understand precisely what was problematic in the social movement theories explored in previous sections by providing a theoretical underpinning to the notion of agency. This allows us to understand multiple responses to change, the unpredictability of resources, and action that originates from various places of power. Such a model allows us to understand the transformative moment of mobilization in Proposition 187.

A reformulated notion of structure that incorporates culture at its core can provide room for human creativity and change necessary to account for the mobilization and changes in the racial terrain wrought by the passage of Proposition 187.[6] Structure is made up not simply of material resources but also of the interpretative devices that give meaning to those resources. Structure is made up of resources and schemas, which re-create and transform one another and the structure.

According to the sociologist Pierre Bourdieu, resources or capital are "all goods, material and symbolic, without distinction, that present themselves as *rare* and worthy of being sought after in a particular social formation" (Bourdieu, quoted in Mahar et al. 1990, 13).[7] Resources can be money, a diploma, or an accepted legitimacy—social capital. For capital or resources to have meaning, they must exist within a field of struggle and within a structure. Resources are actual, in that they exist in time and space, but they are also the effects of schemas—they rely on interpretive tools to have meaning.[8]

Schemas, or what Bourdieu calls strategies, are "society's fundamental tools of thought, but also the various conventions, recipes, scenarios, principles of action, and habits of speech and gesture built up with these fundamental tools" (Sewell 1992, 8). Schemas are part of structures, which reproduce social life, power relations, themselves, and resources. Shifts in racial meanings therefore change the distribution and meaning of a whole range of resources and should not be separated from other, more "real" changes. This becomes clear in a reformulated notion of structure that truly incorporates material resources and culture. If we recognize the power of social constructions for interpreting and giving meaning to resources, then the question of how to deal with race as both a social construction and a powerful force in our daily experience emerges as nonsensical.

While resources are not virtual, they do depend on the schemas for their meaning, and here the door opens for change in structures: "An array of resources is capable of being interpreted in varying ways and, therefore, of empowering different actors and teaching different schemas" (Sewell 1992, 19). While resources require schemas for meaning, schemas also require resources for them to have any power. Schemas need to be reproduced and reinforced, and without resources to do so, schemas would be discarded. While schemas reproduce resources, and resources reproduce schemas, structures are not forever regenerative. Change occurs in structures because of the relationship between resources and schemas and because of people's ability to apply schemas in new settings.

Schemas are constantly in flux regarding their breadth and their relationship to resources. Schemas are "intersubjectively available procedures" that can be used in a variety of situations, which are never fully known. Schemas can be used in multiple ways if there is a certain similarity between the domain in which the schema originated and the target domain. There is no "fixed limit to the possible transpositions" because one cannot say a priori if a given problem is similar enough to use a given schema (Sewell 1992, 17). It is in the reciprocally reinforcing relationship between schemas and resources, and in the ability to transpose schemas to new situations, that we get change. Through the act of transposing schemas from one context to another, structures change.

As structures are always changing, an actor can never be sure of the effect her behavior will have and the type or quantity of resource she will accumulate. There is a perpetual instability to the structures. Structures intersect and overlap across schemas and resources, allowing for schemas to be transposed, resources to be unpredictable, and change to spread.

This change relies on creative human agency. Schemas can be used in new contexts because structures are multiple and overlapping and the meaning of resources is never fixed. This axiom illustrates human agency and creativity in all people: "If this is so, then *agency,* which I would define as entailing the capacity to transpose and extend schemas to new contexts, is inherent in the knowledge of cultural schemas that characterizes all minimally competent members of society" (Sewell 1992, 18).

Using schemas in new contexts is about collective action. Agency, as defined, can really be understood only in light of collective action. Schemas are understood, and gain their power, intersubjectively, because others recognize and share the same interpretation of the meaning of resources. To enact a schema is therefore a collective action from the beginning. Additionally, individual acts of agency gain their power only through affecting others: "Agency entails an ability to coordinate one's actions with others and against others, to form collective projects" (21). Collective action means instantiating new schemas in new contexts, changing the meaning and distribution of resources.

Social action theory therefore suggests exploring mobilization around Proposition 187 by looking for transposition of schemas, contexts that allow for or necessitate the creative act of transposing and the effects of transposing schemas on resources and behavior. Without a strict material-culture divide, human agency becomes theoretically grounded, and we can explore the ways that people interpreted events and resources creatively, why they chose certain actions, and how the struggle unfolded. These tools allow for a dynamic notion of race, movement goals, and intersubjective understandings. There is room for understanding whether and how the mobilization phase of a movement can transform structures and resource distribution. Additionally, such a theoretical background contextualizes and historicizes the racial formation process. We can explore how the struggle over Proposition 187 was redefined through the mobilization process and how racial meanings were affected, and in doing so, we can provide insight into the future possibilities for immigrant reception and racial politics.

Introducing schemas to new domains necessitates reconciling the various schemas within a domain. For example, if racialized conceptions of new immigrants are brought to bear on the immigration debate, one needs to reconcile them with the schema that depicts immigrants as the backbone of our nation. Through attempts to fit multiple schemas into the same domain, one creates pathways or *bridges* between the schemas. Bridges are tools of thought used to connect schemas during the act of transposition. If the bridge proves useful—is able to reproduce and be reproduced by the resources in the domain—then the bridge itself may become a new schema used in that domain and available for transposition elsewhere.

Bridges are the ways in which people deal with their contradictory world-views. Bridging does not make contradictory worldviews mesh seamlessly. Bridging is a way of managing these opposing outlooks, not reconciling them completely. And the fact that reconciling is difficult to accomplish is what allows for change in the meaning and import of race. The racial terrain is unstable and will inevitably change, because bridges do not make a coherent whole out of contradictory beliefs.

Constructing bridges is a creative act. To say it is creative, however, does not mean individuals are creating these schemas and bridges from scratch. Creativity in this context is not inventing something from nothing but recombining old forms in new ways. Individuals find new contexts for schemas and in so doing transform their scope and their meaning. Racial characterizations of immigrants are not new, but proponents of Proposition 187 recombined notions of race and American values in new ways with new bridges to address the political issue in front of them. In doing so, they re-created economic, political, and social citizenship in California in 1994.

Method

To explore the transformations of the racial terrain resulting from mobilization around Proposition 187, and to explore the central schemas and how they were transposed, I turn to supporters of the measure. Work done thus far on Proposition 187 has left out the voices of proponents, those who worked and voted for the measure. And it is just those people who might provide insight into what schemas mobilized individuals to act. I used semistructured interviews to explore the mobilizing schemas and the transformation that occurs during mobilization. Surveys, polls, and structured interviews can get us some distance toward hearing their voices, but on complex topics such as fairness, justice, equality, the economy, and race, the people need to be allowed to speak for themselves (Hochschild 1981, 21). I then contextualized this information and supplemented it with newspaper accounts, speeches by elites, and organizational propaganda distributed by supporting groups during the campaign.

Open-ended conversational interviews with mid- to low-level activists form the centerpiece of this study. The interview process was open-ended and generally followed a conversational format, allowing supporters to reconstruct stories of how and why they were mobilized to act in favor of this measure. Each interview lasted between ninety minutes and three hours.

The individuals interviewed did more than vote for the measure; they donated money, circulated a petition to qualify the measure for the ballot, and wrote letters to the editor, but they were not heavily involved in organizational work during the campaign, nor were they in leadership positions. If we are to take agency seriously, speaking with mid- to low-level activists is critical to understanding the mobilization phase. Such individuals can reveal information not evident in organizational propaganda or surveys. They can provide insight into how they perceived their activity, how they responded to elite and organizational arguments, what mobilized them to action, and how they came to those understandings.

I conducted interviews with thirty-one individuals. Ten respondents were women. Twenty-nine respondents were white. Three interviewees were immigrants: one was a naturalized Japanese American male, one was a male immigrant from Poland, and one was a naturalized woman from Guatemala. The respondents ranged from lower middle class to upper middle class. We met at a place of the individual respondent's choosing, which varied from a modest home in Hawthorne, California, in a transitional neighborhood to an elegant house in a well-manicured development in suburban Los Angeles, from fast food restaurants to country clubs. The respondents' occupations varied, including, for example, an unemployed trucker, an engineer, teachers, farmers, an accountant, an owner of a successful advertising firm, stay-at-home moms, and two interviewees who were retired and struggling to make ends meet. Sixteen of the interviewees identified as Republican, one as a Democrat, and one as a Libertarian; the rest did not identify with a party. Interviewees were between the ages of thirty-six and seventy-seven at the time of the interviews, or twenty-nine and seventy at the time of the campaign, as interviews were conducted seven to eight years after the passage of the measure.[9]

The intervening time between the campaign and the interviews and contextualizing the narratives that emerge from the interviews with documentary evidence produced at the time of the campaign (e.g., newspaper accounts, organizational propaganda, and political speeches) help us address questions about the legacy of the measure. We can see how the campaign for Proposition 187 affects individuals' interpretations of current events and political projects and how those political projects use Proposition 187.

While scholars acknowledge the ways in which memories affect people's interpretations of their world,[10] the reverse also needs to be considered. What an individual emphasizes or interprets in the retelling of an oral history may be a result of current consciousness as much as past consciousness. Proposition 187 was passed and deemed unconstitutional and has since been renounced by many who originally supported it, including the Republican Party in California. Such events alter how interviewees explain their support of the initiative. Comparing the narratives that emerge from the interviews with the documentary evidence produced at the time provides insight into the ways people are reconstructing their stories. I used letters to the editors of major newspapers, propaganda put out by elites and groups supporting the measure, and newspaper accounts of events in the early 1990s to contextualize the interview data. Additionally, since the passage of the measure, California's economy has improved, immigration impacts are understood differently, a new president has been elected, and the United States finds itself in a radically different international context. There have been continued efforts for immigration reform and some changes in national policy. An individual's involvement in, and understanding of, these events and current political goals change the ways he or she recounts previous political activity. Memory is a political act. And this act is central to understanding the legacy of Proposition 187.

The interview and analysis process therefore takes advantage of the time that has passed since the campaign over the proposition in an attempt to show not only what motivated individuals to support the measure but also how the measure impacted subsequent events. For example, when individuals talk about their reaction to the court process after the measure, we are able to discern which bridges were reinforced by subsequent political action and which were not. That is, we see change in response to subsequent political action, which provides insight into the point of origination as well as the point of arrival. We gain insight into how the passage continues to have an impact, despite never being implemented. We gain insight into the role of Proposition 187 in constructing the current racial terrain.

Bridging Race: A Preview

Proponents, opponents, and scholars all agree this was a racialized campaign; however, they disagree on why that was the case. Race was central to respondents' memories of the measure. I never introduced the topic of race in an interview. I allowed each respondent to bring up the issue of race and how it relates to Proposition 187. Respondents generally did so extremely quickly, within the first couple of minutes of talking about the measure.[11] They struggled with how to understand the role that race played in their mobilization. The campaign over Proposition 187 was both a raced struggle and a struggle over how to understand race.

Proponents held two seemingly competing schemas about race. The first is the schema of color-blind conservatism. This involves a commitment to individuality and equality and a denial that racial differences matter. The best way to handle race, according to this schema, is to ignore the category in policies and politics and focus on fairness to unraced individuals. The second central schema is racial realism. Here race is a fundamental dividing category in the world. Races have distinct and competing interests. I use the term "racial realism" as an analogy to the international relations theory of realism. Realism in international relations views states as unitary actors pursuing their own interests. As they do this, states are locked in a perpetual power struggle.[12] In an analogous fashion, racial realism is the belief in a perpetual power struggle between races pursuing their own interests. Similar to the unitary actor of the state, races are understood as having a single interest. Racial realism is used to define the worldview of proponents of Proposition 187 from their perspective. Commitments to racial realism and color-blind conservatism may appear to be contradictory, but it is in fact just at the moment when a bridge is created between these concerns that supporters are moved to act on the measure.

During mobilization, supporters were able to hold these two schemas simultaneously. The construction of bridges, or tools of thought needed to connect schemas around a single event or issue, mobilized respondents to act on the measure. These bridges were a creative act that caused, and was caused by, political activity around the campaign. Supporters, however, did not simply apply color-blind conservatism and racial realism to the measure but created connections between the two schemas. This connection generated political activity. Their political activity altered the context or the structure reinforcing or modifying the bridges. Activity on the measure served to reinforce the bridge between the two, allowing them to be complementary, not competitive. Bridges are an element of creativity essential to simultaneous transposition of these two schemas and essential to mobilization.

Respondents reveal three basic bridges. I call them the racialization bridge, the association bridge, and the defense bridge. I name these after the central dynamic in each and explain each in detail in chapter 2. These bridges become the new schemas through which subsequent political action can be understood. The construction of these bridges took place during the mobilization phase, and they generated new tools of thought for viewing the world. Again, supporters use these bridges to evaluate events in a creative fashion, altering what is not reinforced and maintaining what appears to work. Here we can see change occurring and the racial terrain being altered. The racial terrain, the unique landscape on which the politics of race play out, is time and place specific. Its defining features, though shifting with locale and moment in history, are the languages about race and the main fault lines in racial politics. These include the meaning and import of race and racism, the content of racial categories, the set of policy issues associated with race, relevant political coalitions, and the distribution of resources along racial lines.

Figure 1 illustrates how the racial terrain is changed during the mobilization phase. Racial realism and color-blind conservatism are connected with a number of bridges by proponents. This leads to a mutually reinforcing relationship with their political activity on Proposition 187 and the

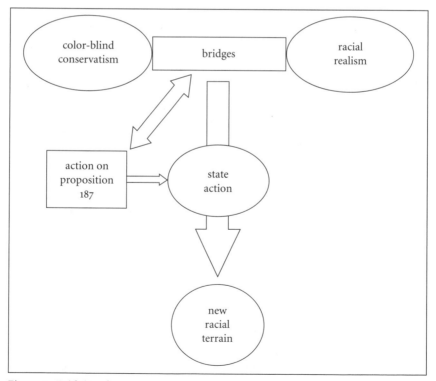

Figure 1. Bridging change

	Color-blind conservatism	Racial realism
	is concerned about fairness and creating a raceless society	is concerned about race invasion and racial power struggles
The law (chapter 3)	focuses on documentation status; wants to achieve rule of law and equality	sees Latinos as criminal; concerned about physical danger to the individual and community
Economics (chapter 4)	wants to achieve fairness to taxpayers	sees Latinos as dependent and lacking an American work ethic
Culture (chapter 5)	wants to achieve assimilation to any single culture; concerned about functioning as democratic society	sees Latinos as uncivilized; concerned about losing a culture war
Population (chapter 6)	wants to achieve a reduction in population; concerned about environment and quality of life	sees Latinos as hyperfertile; concerned about physical and political displacement

Figure 2. Schemas and metaschemas

bridges. The bridges become a new set of schemas, which supporters draw on to interpret or read state action. It is the application of these bridges-turned-schemas to state action that generates shifts in the racial terrain. The legacy of Proposition 187 can be found in the bridging strategies.

Racial realism and color-blind conservatism and the bridging strategies employed are a framework for understanding how supporters responded to the various issues in the campaign. Debate on Proposition 187 included discussions on immigration law and race but also on the economy, health, crime, education, culture, and more. Respondents use the schemas of racial realism and color-blind conservatism to create stances on each issue. Seemingly competing concerns arise around issues of the law, the economy, culture, and population. Figure 2 illustrates how twin concerns about fairness or color blindness and invasion or racial realism appear as proponents of Proposition 187 consider each of these themes.

The bridges used to connect the metaschemas of color-blind conservatism and racial realism serve as pathways along which these other twin schemas are connected. A racialization bridge, an association bridge, and a defense bridge appear between each set of mirror schemas. The specific logics of the bridges vary according to the particular issue, but the basic pattern remains the same. However, the specific logics are important to understand change. As each is used to read state action, some bridges are reinforced, others prove less salient, and others break apart as their logics do not fit the unfolding of the political events. Both the construction of these bridges and their continuing utility after Proposition 187 explain the mobilization around the measure and its legacy.

CHAPTER TWO

Color-Blind Conservatism and Racial Realism:
Two Sides of the Same Coin

It's when you form the ghettos is your problem. When they become the "other people." When it becomes a problem they've created and there's the "us" and the "them." There is always "us" and "them" but it's where you consider "us." Where the borderline between "us" and "them" is. And if it's very sharply divided, you've got problems. I just think that 187 was meant to solve more problems than it was going to create.
—Bob, respondent

KATHY: If anybody listens to this tape, they'll say, oh, you're listening to a bunch of racists.

CHORUS: Exactly.

BERNIE: But they're not living where we're living; we're living it.

FRAN: You can tell them we're a bunch of gray-haired old racists.

BERNIE: Gray-haired old ladies.

KATHY: If I'm a racist, fine. I don't really care. I want to defend this country.

To understand mobilization in support of Proposition 187, we must investigate how two seemingly competitive conceptualizations about race and politics work together: color-blind conservatism and racial realism. Color-blind conservatism argues that race is no longer a relevant category and people should not behave otherwise. References to race in government programs and policies serve to perpetuate the false category. Individualism and equality are highlighted as keys to achieving fairness, the paramount value in this schema. Racial realism, on the other hand, suggests that race is a fundamental dividing category in society and that races have singular interests that compete with the interests of other races.[1] During the struggle over Proposition 187, experiences were interpreted through these two racial schemas at the same time. They worked together to observe and create resource distribution that led supporters to focus simultaneously on the problems of fairness and invasion. These twin concerns underlie contemporary nativism and the passage of Proposition 187.

When supporters constructed bridges between these two worldviews, they were mobilized to act on the measure. Constructing these bridges also altered the racial project as initially articulated. Through this creative collective action, they were altering the racial terrain. By exploring the bridging strategies that produced supporters' actions on the measure, we understand what was at stake in the struggle over Proposition 187, how those at the bottom were (re-)creating the racialized categories and resource distribution norms.

While theories of new racism suggest that mobilization uses existent racial categories, racial formation theory highlights how mobilization can *reconfigure* racial categories. The transformative role of mobilization with a theorized account of agency is key to understanding Proposition 187 and racial politics. A notion of agency that is creative yet grounded in historically available schemas allows us to answer the difficult question presented by theorists of new racism: how to understand expressed commitments to equality and fairness and a continuing central role of race. A notion of creative action based in a particular social, cultural, and economic context—a context including both resources and schemas—allows us to view the dynamic relationship between ideological commitments, racial understandings, and action. Doing so illuminates that neither racism nor equality is the fundamental base; people draw on both, and other schemas as well, simultaneously in creative ways to engage the world and the issues they encounter—this *is* action.

By maintaining a dynamic notion of race and exploring the interactions between commitments to equality and racialized views in the campaign around Proposition 187, we see what the fight was over and how the racial terrain was altered. Understanding the relationships between these two outwardly contradictory worldviews gets to the heart of understanding Proposition 187. Barbara Fields (1982) suggests that the key to understanding what is happening when looking at seemingly oppositional southern racialist ideologies is to ask, "What kind of social reality is reflected—or re-fracted—in an ideology built on a unity of these particular opposites?" (155). We must do the same to understand Proposition 187 and the contemporary politics of immigration. To that end, we turn to proponents' expression of color-blind conservatism and racial realism in light of Proposition 187.

Color Blindness and Fairness in Proposition 187

Responses to accusations of racism expose the importance of a notion of color blindness to the campaign over Proposition 187. A "Fact and Fiction" sheet put out by Citizens for Legal Immigration Reform and the Save Our State Committee suggests that the measure has nothing to do with race but is about control of the border. The fiction is that the measure is about race; the fact is that the measure asks, "Will we have an immigration policy enforced by law, or will our borders be open to anyone?" When supporters addressed the question of the role of race in the measure, all but one re-spondent contended that their support stemmed more from color-blind concerns than from racialized ones.

Proponents generally introduced the issue of race by expressing outrage at the accusations of racism.[2] A variety of different tactics were used to challenge the accusation of racism; many times these different tactics were used in concert with one another. One method was to suggest that support from minorities is evidence that Proposition 187 could not possibly be a racist measure. A respondent who was involved in organizational work in favor of the measure offered, "I respond with a very simple answer: Oh, is that right? Why don't you ask some of our Hispanic, Asian, Latino, and a zillion other members who are not Caucasian. Why don't you go ask them?" The use of minority supporters to demonstrate the measure was not grounded in race ranged from the anecdotal to statements on the magni-tude of support. Jason, a Japanese American, answered by pointing to the success at the polls that Proposition 187 had among Hispanics: "And I think that the Hispanic population, Latinos felt that's what it was [anti-Hispanic]. . . . But without the Hispanic vote it wouldn't have passed either." Donald, a white education administrator, reported, "I actually knew some-one very close to me that went through the legal process who was a Mexi-can and was supposedly being discriminated against who was for the meas-ure. 'Cause he still had a lot of brothers in Mexico who wanted to come over, but they were going to do it the way he did it, which was legally."

Additionally, the supporters very quickly and frequently brought up their own credentials as color-blind members of what should be a color-blind society. Cliché responses emerged unselfconsciously. Mentioning of friends and contact with other races was designed to show that support could not have stemmed from a concern over race for them:

> I want to say this, I was raised [around] and loved the Mexican people very much. I used to play marbles with Alberto, he used to win all my marbles. I went to school with these kids . . . went to school with some blacks also. Across the board. You name it, we had it in our high school. I loved everybody. . . . I have many, many friends who are dear of many, many races.

Another lamented his inability to convince others that his support didn't stem from racism: "You know, it is extremely difficult for me to convince people that I have no hostility toward Mexicans. Individually or collectively. In fact, I kind of like Mexicans! Um, that's not what it is."

Supporters suggested that they were not racist, but also not color conscious. To prove this lack of color consciousness, they turned to their past experiences. As children they had not been aware of differences, or if they had been, color really didn't matter to them. Kyle, a television producer for a public station in southern California, remembered, "My high school—first-, second-generation kids with Japanese names, whatever, everyone was American, it didn't even cross my mind."

Bob, a white self-employed worker in his late fifties, acknowledged that others might have been reacting to a fear in changing racial demographics. However, his support for the measure didn't stem from that concern. Evidence of this is found in his color-blind experiences. He described the smooth racial mixing in the neighborhood in which he purchased his first house: "You know, my next-door neighbor was Hispanic on one side and not on the other. But I didn't really—you know, as I think back, I remember that was the way it was, but there was not 'Oh, they're Hispanics, and they are whites.' No, you didn't think that." The denial of race prejudice is a function of having lived with a variety of races. The experience of being around people of other races precludes the possibility of prejudice for Bob and others. An engineer in southern California reported: "I've grown up with all kinds of people at all times, and so that's just normal. For me, racial prejudice just doesn't make sense." The contact thesis extends to the whole state: "I think most of California is much more tolerant out of necessity."[3]

While supporters acknowledged the existence of individual racism and that there may have been a small portion of supporters who voted for Proposition 187 for racial reasons, most did not. On the whole, society treats minorities fairly, according to supporters: "Anyone who is different can be attacked just because they are different, but that's not a national thing, it's an individual thing. We're not nationally ethnocentric or racist." A question regarding America's contemporary reception of immigrants elicited positive responses. America may have had some ugly moments, but today immigrants are welcomed and treated fairly: "They move right in. The ones that are legally accepted in, I think fit in very quickly." Another respondent echoed a similar sentiment: "Well, I think in general the country is pretty open to, I don't know how especially in the Bay area, this area here is very cosmopolitan. I'd say it's very open. I think that, ah, I think that there are very few stereotypes. That most people, for the most part, that people take on people."

Supporters want to promote a color-blind society. Every supporter of the measure also supported Proposition 209, the measure that ended affirmative action in California, although some respondents' support was not unqualified. One respondent suggested that affirmative action according to income would be a beneficial policy. Another suggested that though historical discrimination might have some impact on people's life chances, affirmative action in California had gone too far. Opportunity should be provided regardless of race:

> What you really want is a color-blind society. I think my company is pretty good at that, because you need that skill so bad, you don't care what color they are. Again your best rebuttal is to provide opportunities for education, and empower people; strength comes from within, and if they are as good as you are, then they can prove it, and they are given the opportunity to prove it. That's what the country is about. No one is guaranteed anything, you just get a good crack at it.

While it is good to be inclusive, "When it gets to the point where it's hurting the institution because you're bringing in people who are totally unqualified and things like that, then obviously it's not a good thing. But if it's such a small number and it's giving people opportunity, then I don't have a problem with that, you know then it's a good thing." Yet another respondent found value in having minorities in schools as role models but thought that affirmative action was actually about supporting unqualified applicants over qualified ones:

Teachers in California are by and large white. There are way more white teachers. It would be good to have role models that kids could identify with. . . . I'm not against, ah, I'm not against minorities having every single opportunity that whites have, but I'm against whites losing out on jobs just because of affirmative action. I'm against hiring a minority who is less qualified than a white, and that is what was happening. That's what the intent of the proposition [209] was, to stop that from happening.

Proposition 187, according to supporters, was another initiative to create color blindness and a fair society.

In 75 percent of the interviews, fairness was identified as being central to respondents' support for the measure. Richard, a retired teacher, explained his mobilization around the question of fairness: "I just didn't like what was happening. The unfairness of it. So I got involved." Philip, who had lived in many different parts of California, described why Californians in general supported the measure. While there may have been some racism, most of the support was about fairness: "People felt that the basic rules of fair play were being violated. That people shouldn't be able to break the law and then come in and take advantage of the system, that that really violated people's sense of right and wrong." He also described his own support in those terms: "But the main reason I was in favor was not that it was costing us a lot of money, 'cause I don't think that it was, but that it was violating the sense of fair play and what it means to be an American, which is that everybody should try to work unless you really can't."

The current immigration situation in California, and that of 1994, is understood as being unfair to immigrants to whom supporters are sympathetic, other minorities, and all "native" Americans. The system around undocumented immigration punishes some and not others or requires some to follow a set of rules but not others. This is reported as being unfair to other immigrants: "For people to come into the country illegally, it's not fair on the people that do it legally; they go for years and years [and] do the whole green card thing. And to have someone coming in here getting the benefits right away, it's just not right." Respondents used stories of personal friends or acquaintances who went through the legal system: "He did it all legal, so he had to wait, comes over and pays taxes, and it just wasn't fair to me. That the ones breaking the law could just slide by and the ones being punished were the ones actually following the process! And I think 187, ah, took, tried to rectify that." Jason went through the official naturalization process when he was a teenager. Jason is a man in his thirties with a good sense of humor. He described himself as having turned from a "west-side, left-wing, semi-pinko" to "right of Attila the Hun" as a result of the 1992 Los Angeles riots. He joked throughout most of the interview. At one moment, however, his humor left him, and he became visibly agitated. He was answering the charge that Proposition 187 would increase infectious diseases by limiting access to health care. He contrasted his own experience emigrating from Japan:

> Yeah, but the fact that illegal aliens are coming here brings their own infectious diseases. I had to have, to come to the United States, we had to have complete physical exam, you know, to make sure we didn't have tuberculosis, we didn't have any diseases. We gone through all of that and plus immunizations to come here, so we didn't bring disease to the United States. Okay? So that argument about having infectious disease . . . they're [illegal immigrants] the one who's . . . bringing infectious disease to United States!

The situation is unfair because it treats differently those who should be treated equally, those who want to enter America legally.

The situation is also understood as being unfair to all Americans, as well. The situation is unfair because it treats those who are not equals as equals. American citizenship entitles you to first consideration. Those who are not citizens should not have the same access to resources: "Too many people and unfairly the system had given so many dollars in there for these services, and these people come in, more and more of them are coming in and taking the resources that are supposed to be for everybody." The impact of immigration on resources such as natural resources, education, health care, and infrastructure is unfair to Americans. Kyle noted impacts on the classroom as an example: "Is it fair that kids who are used to thirty to a class or whatever, now there are forty-two in a class? Or where there are kids speaking a foreign language?" Kyle understood the changing demographics as unfair to whoever was there first, to the kids who are experiencing the change by an influx of additional students or an increase in foreign languages. The battle over Proposition 187 for some is described as being about reinstitutionalizing the supremacy of native interests, not about the race of either the natives or the newcomers. When discussing moves to restrict the granting of citizenship based on birth within the United States, John, a member of the organization Zero Population Growth, stated: "I would support that. We have naturalization procedures that work, and it seems to give us some control over our borders and our numbers, and you have to be able to plan for things. The top obligation being for the people who are already here. So I think out of fairness to them."

Racial Realism and Invasion

While fairness was central to supporters' responses, so were concerns over invasion. Discussions of race realism, the reality of race and the inherent competition between races, emerged from the very respondents who wanted to promote color blindness. Bob, who touted his experience in his first house as being a color-consciousless experience within a racially diverse neighborhood, contrasts that with his experience in childhood. In his school, he had a segregated social experience:

> We were still two groups, okay. "We" were the newcomers and "they" were the people who had lived here at the time. ["We" were] the white kids who came from the suburbs and had the money and everything else, and "they" were the Mexican kids who had come from the farm families, and, um, we didn't get along. We don't know why. Yeah, two different—the languages, uh, I don't know why. But as a kid you don't ask. You know where you walk and where you don't walk. That's it.

Some respondents suggest that it is human nature to divide into groups and that race is a by-product of that inclination. Race is a clear marker. Bob could not explain why the white students and the Mexican students did not get along. It was not necessarily reducible to language or class. While Bob acknowledged that those factors played a role, in the end he said there was something ineffable that was just felt, a racial realism. Milton, a Jew who had lived through the Nazi occupation in Europe, suggested that many of the problems since the end of World War II had resulted from people wanting to ignore human nature's drive toward separation based on ethnicities or race:

> The proletariat of the world didn't unite themselves because people want to preserve ethnicity. That is what the war is about in Kosovo, that is what the war is about in Chechnya, that is what the war is about in Indonesia, and so on and so on, okay? Number one. And secondly, you know, so who else? Hitler tried to unite Europe under an Aryan empire, and it didn't work either. People are not going to be globalized, it's as simple as that. You know we're not that far away from the animal kingdom. Whenever I look at the animals, you know the lions eat, the lions and tigers will never mate. And

certain, in the same way, the only people who really believe in this globalization are people who love each other forever and don't make any claims to
ethnicity, that is in the eyes of some starry-eyes liberals, as I pointed out.
In Palo Alto there is a group who believes this is really true. But I wish it
was true, but it is not going to happen.

Milton talks about a variety of other international situations that he feels
are a result of this fundamental misreading of human beings. He relates
domestic problems and the battle over Proposition 187 to the same phenomenon. He thinks white Americans are in particular trouble because of the
current political correctness, which blinds white Americans to the inevitable
continuance of race struggles.

Bob understands his segregated school experience in part through universal laws of human behavior. Interaction between two sets of people will
breed trouble: "You don't have a problem if in [the] middle of nowhere in
a big population you take two, three percent of somebody else. That's not
going to be a problem, generally. Well, they'll absorb, and everybody looks
after the people next door. You don't have a problem. It's where a large,
two large segments come together, where those borders happen is where
you get [problems]."

According to this perspective, the meeting of two peoples inevitably
causes problems because races are inherently in competition with one
another. Here supporters are demonstrating a racial realist understanding
of the world, where races have unified interests that put them in a perpetual state of war with other races. Active fighting, or "problems," occurs
only when there is a perceived threat, that is, when there is not a clearly
superior power. Respondents perceived the threat of Mexican presence to
be about invasion. As the numbers and power of Mexicans grow, the danger
is heightened. Milton reported:

> They've never merged into the culture. And when you look at this country,
> you can see it's kind of an island of English-speaking people surrounded
> by Latinos. Lots of Mexicans. You've got Guatemala, you've got Puerto
> Rico, you know you're an island here and eventually that island's gonna be
> swamped. Fifty years from now, things are gonna be completely different.
> Thank god I'm not going to be around, but this is going to be a problem.
> I'll tell you one thing, I know things are going to be rough.

The fear of losing the country is evident in other interviews. Charles is a
retired man in his seventies who is in a precarious economic situation because of early retirement, plummeted stock values, and very low interest

rates. Before I met Charles, he sent me a packet in the mail that included photocopies of the U.S. military records for his grandfather and great-uncle. Charles understands his right to this country as stemming from his predecessors' willingness to fight for it. He reports that the changes are causing him to lose his country:

> I have no ties to any other country. I'm monolingual. I feel like I'm lost in my own country. And I know it's my country because my great-grandfather went through a lot . . . and his father before him. It turns out when I look back at the 1840 or 1830 census, I see there was a Joseph Sullivan before him. His father was named Joseph. And I don't know where my family came from. And I think there might have been three of them in the Revolutionary War. But, uh, I feel like I'm a person without a country, although I shouldn't be. I don't know where to go.

Charles talks about wanting to go to New Zealand but is certain they wouldn't want him at his age. He suggests that immigrants threw their country away. He hasn't, yet he feels that owing to demographic changes, he is still losing his country. "I feel like I've lost my country and I have nowhere to go. I'm worse than an immigrant. I'm a nothing in my own country. My government left me; I didn't leave my government."

The idea of fighting an invasion emerges from other respondents as well. I talked with five highly active members together with an elite leader involved in the campaign for Proposition 187. This group interview allowed for respondents to play off each other, frequently hitting crescendos of agreement where they echoed each other's sentiments and kept raising the ante. Denise, a woman in her forties, was relatively quiet through most of the interview. However, she became vehemently animated when I asked about their decisions to stay in southern California. Her excitement spurred Kathy and the others:

> DENISE: I'm fighting. It's my house, my country, my state, my city, my block, yes.
>
> KATHY: Where are we going to run to? It's getting all over the country.
>
> CHORUS: We have no place to run to, we have no place to run to.
>
> KATHY: They come into our country and they want things run their way, and they get it and we don't have a chance. Where do we go? . . .
>
> DENISE: If I'm a racist, fine. I don't really care. I want to defend this country.
>
> [Chorus agrees.]

DENISE: Call me anything you want to call me; just get out.

KATHY: I was in the air force for seven years. I'm not about to give up this country, I'll fight till the last . . .

FRANNY: Till the last dog is home.

The use of military language was not simply metaphorical. Many see race riots or race wars as a real possibility. Milton, the immigrant from Poland, sees armed racial conflict on the horizon: "In time probably twenty years down the pike. We'll have a hell of a problem. We may have a little guerrilla war here, you know. People [in] Texas, California, 'This is ours, what are you doing here. This is our country.' You know they say that right now." Americans are naive to think that such things couldn't happen here, Milton said, and he warned more than once about the impending situation: "Thank god I'm not going to be around, but this is going to be a problem. I'll tell you one thing, I know things are going to be rough here. What you saw in Europe in 1945, the one with Hitler incident, is going to be kid's play. We're talking about bigger numbers here. You're going to have racial conflict here."

Over breakfast at his country club, Dean, an advertising and marketing executive, told me about potential armed racial conflict. As we sat in the fine dining room looking out over the manicured golf course and club grounds, he reported what would happen if "Mexicans who live in America" as opposed to "Mexican Americans" were elected to office in large numbers:

If they start electing Mexicans who live in America, and they want to turn this into another Mexico, are in fact leading efforts to succeed and become back part of Mexico, which of course will be resisted. Not just at the ballot box, that would be the turning point, that would be the second civil war. Uh, unfortunately, Robin, it could happen. That's how emotional this thing is. It's a tinderbox.

Given the potential in an issue like this, Dean repeatedly commented on the restraint of those running the Proposition 187 campaign. He mentioned that there was compelling information included in internal meetings that was not used publicly: "Yeah, it was thought, you can take issues like 187 and turn it into the next civil war if you're not very careful. And we may get that anyhow, but because of that, they decided to just back off." There is the implication that the truth would reveal the extent of the invasion. When whites realize the extent of what was going on, they will rise up with arms. Eight other interviewees talked about Reconquista or Aztlan, two names given to a supposedly widespread Latino plot to take back the southwestern United States for Mexico. In the minds of these respondents, what prevented a defensive war was the ignorance of most Americans about the plot.

Supporters' narratives highlight the importance of looking at invasion via the ballot box, as well. Supporters perceive Latinos to hold critical political power. Politicians are depicted as cowering from taking a stand on issues because they fear the power of the Latino vote. Electoral politics are a central stage on which racial realism gets played out, according to supporters. Minority political activity expresses the unified interests of a racial group. Races support their own: "Hispanics could take over. Now, they don't have the power to do it militarily; they are going to do it legislatively. And there are already radical forces within the Latino community that promote that, and the Latinos' lawyers and lawgivers will always promote Latino."

Jim is a white unemployed truck driver in southern California. Through his past jobs, he has had long-term contact with a number of Latino drivers. He reports frequently having heard Hispanics talk poorly about other Hispanics, based either on economics or on time of arrival in this country. Despite these negative feelings Hispanics have expressed toward other Hispanics, Jim perceived the racial connection to override their "real" political beliefs: "There are some of them who have been here third, fourth, fifth generation or whatever the reason . . . they don't like 'em, either. The funny thing is when they don't like them, to go to the polls to do something about it is something else."

Latinos, according to respondents, tend to vote together or have a similar set of interests that they express through the political system. Because of this color-conscious voting, others are forced to respond in kind. Dean explains how there has come to be a "white" interest that politicians are ignoring. He reports that ethnic groups in general and immigrants in particular have formed powerful voting blocs. The result of these ethnic and racial groups with electoral power is a growing reactionary white voting bloc. The white vote will coalesce as a result of the threat posed by others who are voting based on race. Dean, while wanting a color-blind world and feeling that folks generally accept others, is a racial realist when it comes to political power:

> The voting patterns are segmented, and they tend to vote as blocs. Literally voting blocs. Now it's not 100 percent but just as blacks vote 90 to 95 percent Democratic liberal. Jewish vote 80 to 85 percent liberal. Well, what you're

getting is all these little blocs, so what you still have or what you are starting to have, what you had in the state of California which created 187, you had another bloc vote, and the bloc vote was white male.... So what you're now getting in California is all these little bloc votes. You have the Korean vote, the Cambodian vote, I don't know if the Hmong count as a bloc or not, but you know if there is such a group, we've got them in California. Black vote, Jewish vote, what's happening is 187 brought out this incredible white vote—white males vote, not white females, white males vote one way... eventually the white female vote will follow it. What we're going to have is a split in this country along party lines which will eventually be the minority vote on one side and the Caucasian vote on the other, and although it will be read liberal [versus] conservative, I suspect it will not necessarily be that way. That's what's going to happen in national politics.

The combination of racial realism, shifting demographics, and "corrupt" political parties means that Latinos will be able to "take over" the area. This takeover is a conscious plan by Hispanic forces, according to some respondents: "They think that, and just rightly so, that they can take over southern California. And they will. And they don't care how." Color-conscious minorities are waging a political war and have the upper hand, according to respondents: "So it's just a trend that's going to happen.... Eventually this will all be, entire southern California, will be Mexican politically controlled."

Supporters were driven by concerns about racial power struggles. Because race was understood as a unifying force, little distinction was drawn between Mexican immigrants, regardless of status, and Mexican Americans. Latinos as a race threatened to gain control over Americans physically, culturally, and politically. Supporters constructed Latinos' interests as being in direct competition with white interests and American interests. Whites therefore needed to be aware and act against the invading force.

Racializing Fairness

How is it that respondents would say on the one hand that Proposition 187 was not an "Anglo/Hispanic issue" and later in the interview talk about racial polarization, balkanization, and power struggles? Individual supporters engaged in the creative process of connecting a racialized assessment of the problem with race-neutral concerns about fairness by drawing on propaganda, personal experiences, newspaper and other media accounts, conversations, and schemas from other political campaigns and areas of their lives. The three central bridging strategies that supporters used to connect

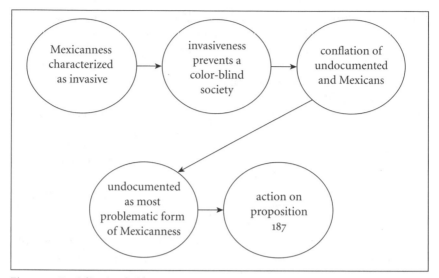

Figure 3. Racialization bridge

schemas about fairness and invasion led to, and were reinforced by, their actions in favor of Proposition 187. These strategies drew on and created the political and racial terrain of the time, including demographic shifts, economic conditions, and political power distribution.

The first strategy is the racialization bridge, which connects fairness and invasion around an initial racialization of Mexicans as threatening (Figure 3). Because of the racialization of Mexicanness, supporters cannot act as if they were in a color-blind world as they would like. The presence of Mexicans within the community threatens invasion and simultaneously subverts fairness because of their particular racialization; Mexicanness consists of a set of invasive properties. Because the undocumented are understood as being Mexican, a measure that focuses on the undocumented will deal with the problematic racial group. Once this racial group is marked as being outside the community, supporters can then live in the color-blind world they desire. Deviations by Mexicans (read: the undocumented) from what is understood as a color-blind norm prevent the full flourishing of a color-blind society.

The second strategy, the association bridge, inverts the process by positing the undocumented as a particularly problematic population with undesirable characteristics that threatens invasion (Figure 4). The conflation of the undocumented and Mexicans creates an association between Mexicans and the undesirable characteristics. Mexicanness, regardless of citizen-

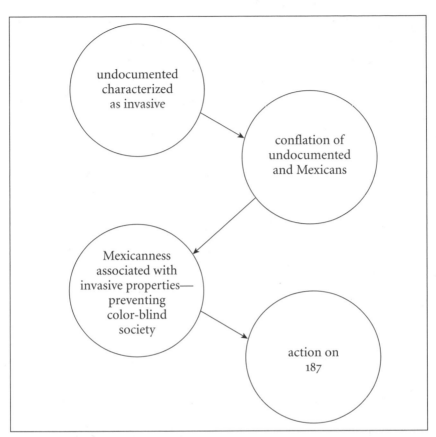

Figure 4. Association bridge

ship or status, becomes part of the problem initially understood as being a function of undocumented migration. Mexicanness is related to the invasive properties, although Mexicanness, in this strategy, does not create the problem. Again, removing the problematic population, removing the ability of the problematic population to construct the community, or at least mitigating the most troubling aspects of this racial group, would allow fairness to return and proponents once again to act in a color-blind manner.

Both the racialization bridge and the association bridge rely on a conflation of "the undocumented" and "Mexicans." The racialization of the immigrant is part of the intersubjective reality of Californians in the mid-1990s. Unless otherwise qualified, immigrants are understood as being Mexicans. This racialization was a reaction to both the state racial terrain and the local racial terrain. While all respondents understood the undocumented as being primarily from south of the border, other racial groups took on some role depending on the local racial terrain. This role was always secondary or supplementary, however, to the role of the Mexican illegal immigrant.[4] When I asked respondents whether they had any familial or other intimate connections with immigrants, almost everyone who had talked about connections with Latino immigrants. It required further prodding on my part about possible family connections to get respondents to discuss their immigrant heritages or European immigrant relations. If one is asking a Californian about immigration in the early years of the twenty-first century, especially in the context of discussing Proposition 187, one, I discovered, is asking about Latino immigration.

The labels "Hispanic," "Latino," and "Mexican" are used interchangeably. "When I say 'Mexico,' that's a metaphor for anything south of the border. Not really all Latin America, either; it's mainly Mexico, El Salvador, Guatemala, Honduras, that sort of thing." And Mexicans/Latinos are conflated with immigrants. Throughout interviews there were seamless transitions between discussion of immigration and discussion of Latino populations and Mexicans. Individuals sometimes checked themselves, only to fall back into the use of "Hispanic," "Mexican," and "immigrant" as synonyms. One interviewee caught himself: "Hispanics, let's say illegals—don't necessarily have to be Hispanic—can receive free medical care at this clinic up the road." He then proceeded to use the two terms interchangeably for the remainder of the interview.

Maria, an immigrant from Guatemala, married Bob a few years after arriving in the United States. Bob had worked with United We Stand to support the measure, and Maria had also voted in favor of it. Maria suggested that Proposition 187 probably started in Orange County, where she was based at the time, "because of all the immigration. We have a lot of Hispanic and Mexican, well, mainly Mexican, I would say, and Central American." Bob and Maria talked about the impact of immigrants on the labor market:

> BOB: If you go to any light manufacturing in the area, you'll find almost all Mexicans working, or Hispanic. There are a lot of South, um, Central Americans.
>
> MARIA: Yeah, you have to stop saying "Mexicans" because they aren't the population.
>
> BOB: That's my old United We Stand days. Anyway, um, the restaurants, the busboys, all the cleanup jobs, all the gardeners. They used to be, what, Japanese or Chinese, and you won't find them anymore.
>
> MARIA: That's right . . . the Mexicans knock down the price.

The groups working for Proposition 187 were described as having furthered the conflation, and supporters clearly had a hard time not viewing the world through that lens. Maria, who criticized Bob for not noting the differences between Hispanic and Mexican, fell into the same pattern with her very next comment.

This conflation of "Mexican" and "immigrant" intensified when the qualifier on immigrants was "illegal." Illegal immigrants, according to the intersubjective understanding in California, are Mexicans: "Chinese same thing. And the Vietnamese and Chinese came here, all came on whether or not they liked the laws or not, all came under the law. . . . They did it by the law. And even they, when I talk to some of them, they resent the fact that how come they can't get their relatives here, but if you're from Mexico you can."[5]

Proposition 187 targeted the racialized Mexican immigrant. As one respondent put it, Proposition 187 was a response to the "Mexican impact on the state of California." The problematic immigrant was understood as coming from Mexico. An interviewee who suggested he was merely responding to the large numbers clarified unselfconsciously at one point that the large numbers of immigrants are Mexican: "So I just wanted something to be done about too many Mexican people all of a sudden." One supporter, who said that his support of the measure stemmed purely from an environmental concern, that there were too many people, unabashedly stated that he hoped the measure would address the population problem by sending a message to those in Mexico: "Well, I was hopeful, I thought it was reasonable to assume that quite a lot of people who were in Mexico would say, 'You know, it's not quite such a good deal to go to California, I think I won't go there right now.'" These statements seem consonant in supporters' minds because population growth and immigration are defined as Mexican.

The construction of the undocumented Mexican leads to a conflation of the undocumented and Latinos in general, regardless of status or country of origin. Because it is impossible to determine documented status simply by looking at a person, all Latinos become undocumented. As images are used to depict the struggle over this measure and the issues surrounding it, race becomes a proxy for citizenship or belonging. As Ono and Sloop (2002) write:

> In public arguments concerning Proposition 187, the "we" consists of citizens and documented immigrants (insiders), while the "other" consists of undocumented immigrants (outsiders). Furthermore, because one cannot

see the difference between a "legal" Chicana or Chicano and an "illegal" Mexicana or Mexicano, the media environment helps create a situation in which all Mexican-descent peoples are under suspicion as "other."... News media representations of "apparent" Mexicans conflate nonresidents and nonpermanent residents of the United States with permanent residents and citizens. (37)

These racialized categories of outsider or undocumented were reconstructed in the battle over Proposition 187. The passage of the measure and the reaction to this racial project by the state and others enforced these racial meanings. Proposition 187 was a racial project that instituted a racializing of the immigrant or a foreignizing of a race. The struggle was over the role and meaning of race in defining outsider and citizen.

The central place of race in the struggle can be seen in the language and images that proponents used throughout the debate. The Wilson campaign television ad that used the scene of a group of Hispanics swarming over a fence (see chapter 1) shows the primacy of race in this campaign. So did statements by Ronald Prince, one of the originators of the Proposition 187 initiative, who wrote that any "attempt to inflame racial hatred can only hurt us" (Hasian and Delgado 1998, 256). Prince said to a crowd of supporters, "You are the posse, and SOS [Save Our State] is the rope" (McDonnell 1994; Ramos 1994). Despite disagreements on how to interpret this statement, scholars, opponents, and proponents all note that the campaign was racialized.

The third strategy that respondents used to connect concerns over fairness and race neutrality with concerns over a racialized invasion, the defense bridge, revolves around the race consciousness of others (Figure 5). Respondents suggest they would like to see the world without racial divisions or that *they* are in fact color-blind. It is others, immigrants or the broader category of powerful minorities and their allies, who perpetuate the system of racial categories. Respondents must live in that world created by others. Other people, of other races, are racial realists, and consequently respondents must act to defend themselves in this racial power struggle. Proposition 187 is therefore either part of a self-defense battle whites have been cornered into or part of a battle to reinstitute a color-blind world; both are accomplished by taking power away from the color-conscious forces.

Respondents who use this strategy understand race as a social construction and therefore as being fictitious; the use of such a social construction is a violation of fairness. Race is perpetuated for respondents by minorities

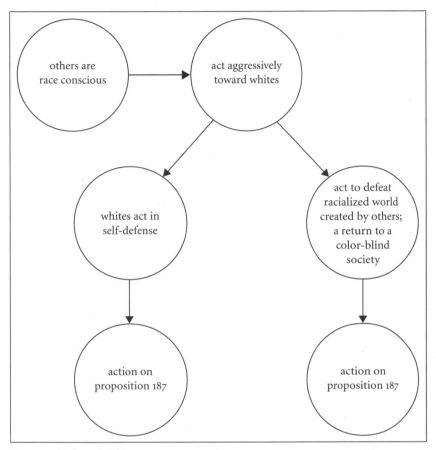

Figure 5. Defense bridge

and the immigrants themselves. Proposition 187 was in fact understood as countering racialization. Bob expressed anger at the opponents of Proposition 187 because he felt that they were creating a racialized distinction that is detrimental to the community:

> That's why I hate the other side's rhetoric . . . because they wish to make an us and a them for their own benefit. They don't wish to be us. They want to be them. And they want to be identified by us as them and vice versa for their own political reasons.

This sentiment is echoed in one of the more widely circulated pieces of propaganda, a question-and-answer pamphlet put out by the Save Our State Committee in 1994: "Our opponents are trying to confuse the issue by claiming that we're racists. In truth, we represent all the people of California, of every race, creed, and color." Not only political leaders opposing the measure but those on the ground who opposed it are understood as being responsible for adding the component of color to the battle. Respondents attribute race consciousness alternately to elites, immigrants, and human nature. Respondents talk about the ways media and elites played the "race card." While never using that term, respondents suggest that media and opponents injected the issue of race to discredit a political movement striving for fairness.

Philip, an environmental scientist concerned about fair play and environmental resources, explains, "I think the hardest thing about 187 and things like it is that it appears to be an insult to Mexicans, and they perceived it that way. And I just think that's wrong, but you know, you can't change the way people perceive things." Minorities in general are seen as culprits for the continued importance of race. Respondents suggest that minorities are responsible for removing themselves from a potentially inclusive society: "Many of the minorities even do not feel like they're Americans. But when they go somewhere else, they find out they are." Immigrants, specifically the undocumented/Latino immigrants, also perpetuate the notion of race by creating demands based on race. Maria believes that race becomes powerful by other immigrants' focusing on it. She noted that her husband does not call himself a German American, but some immigrants still insist on the dual label, which creates the distinction: "If your child is born in that country, they belong to that country. Even if it's the first generation. But they don't learn that. They sit around, 'I'm not white.' Even children, it's incredible." Race therefore continues to be a powerful marker because immigrants, liberals, and opponents of Proposition 187 make it so. Bob noted that it is not a discriminatory society that perpetuates racial distinctions:

> But they're [illegal immigrants] arguing for the wrong things. They should be working for more citizenship, more "I wanna be a part," rather than "I want to be treated separately. I want to be treated differently. I'm being discriminated against." Or all of these things. Those are things you take and you go with and you work with—you work around them. People don't discriminate against you if you don't let them. In a way. You just work around them. If they can't tell you apart, okay, and they're not so blind as to tell you apart just on skin color or the slant of your eyes or the accent in your voice.

Fairness, however, is violated not only by the perpetuation of the categories of race socially but more importantly by political activity and policy based on race. Our immigration laws are not being enforced, according to one respondent:

> I don't know, some people, I think, just have got this view that if you're a certain minority, not just any minority, certain minorities, that we shouldn't do anything to interfere in whatever your doing. . . . I just looked at it as unfair. And it was unfair because it was so biased against many of the people I knew and liked. Who happen to be from China, Russia, Vietnam. And how come they were different. . . . I've often wondered how we would have reacted if China were on our border instead of Mexico. If a billion people tried to get in. . . . Yes, I think it would be much different. We'd have tanks and everything at our border.

Latinos are an advantaged minority in California, not only over other immigrants but also over native whites, according to respondents: "There is also a blind eye, you know; when you are a minority or a Latino, you can do things that if you were a white person, you can't do, okay?" Others are being hurt by this favored treatment, according to one respondent: "People are leaving us, California. . . . They say, 'Hey, what's happening? We're not being treated equally, fairly as some of the other so-called minorities,' okay?" He continued to explain that this disproportionate treatment is a result of political concerns: "Over here our legal system protects them and protects them because of the electoral system, which says we must, we have more Latino voters and therefore, uh, we can't be too tough on these guys."

Proposition 187 was a mechanism for rectifying the unfair situation that favored some people. Ed, a college professor in southern California, explained that his support of the measure was grounded in a notion of fairness. Other immigrants, he asserted, resent the favored status given to Mexicans, and Proposition 187 was a way to rectify that:

> It's really discriminatory. That says, "We've got a special class of people. And that is: people who come from south of the border get special privileges. And if you come from somewhere else, you don't." And the way I saw 187, it just leveled the playing field for all of them [immigrants]. And it even leveled it with respect to people from Arizona or Minnesota. You want to go to Cal Berkeley from Minnesota, you got to pay an out-of-state tuition. You come from Mexico, you don't. But under 187 you would.

Proponents of Proposition 187 are caught in a bind here. Their understanding of the problem of immigration is racialized, yet they want to assume a color-blind world. To deal with this conflict, the theoretical view of a color-blind world within a heavily racialized world, they suggest it is others who are in fact perpetuating racial categories. Race continues to exist, not because it is real but because others insist on using it. Race is used by others as a dividing line along which to strive toward self-interest. Others are constructing and then attacking along racial lines. Respondents, who would like to act in a race-neutral way, are placed in a group, "white," and then are being threatened as a member of that group. Respondents would prefer a more individualistic world, but because of others' antagonistic use of race, respondents must be race conscious as well. Proponents of Proposition 187 are caught in a power struggle, and responding is a matter of self-defense.

Defense is one of the three central bridges that allow racial realism and color-blind conservatism to work together and mobilize individuals to act. The three bridges become new schemas through which to view state action. Through the reading of state action, the racial terrain is altered as respondents redefine citizenship and race. The post–Proposition 187 world consists of a different racial and political terrain because of the new understandings of fairness, immigration, and race created through mobilization. These new understandings were used to read state reaction to Proposition 187. The state response to the passage of Proposition 187 generated an altered coalition of restrictionists. After a district court declaration of unconstitutionality and a subsequent mediation that gutted the major provisions of the initiative, the emphasis of the California restrictionist organizations, while not abandoning the notion of fairness, changed to invasion.

Invasion, or the so-called Reconquista, is a central concern of immigration restriction organizations in the post–Proposition 187 era. The California Coalition for Immigration Reform (CCIR) was a cosponsor of Proposition 187 and served as a major organizing arm for the campaign both in southern California, where the organization is based, and in the state as a whole. The group pulled together Republican groups, immigration activists, and population groups. It worked with Ron Prince and other central political figures in 1994. At the time of the campaign, the information put out by CCIR focused on the monetary and cultural effects of mass illegal immigration. CCIR currently is most closely aligned with Glen Spencer's Voices of Citizens Together and Terry Anderson's radio talk show, both parts of a more radical arm of the restrictionist movement. During the campaign, notions of fairness and color blindness were highlighted in the materials distributed by CCIR. The question-and-answer and fact sheets discussed ideas of illegality and use of tax services. In the group's recent publications, the perceived secret plot to take back the American Southwest has held a central place. Uncovering politicians who support the "seditious" groups involved in that plot is also a main focus of CCIR. Invasion is central, as evidenced by the political cartoons selected for the front pages and the products for sale produced after 1994, which include an audiotape set, *Takeover of America,* and a video titled *Attack on America.*[6]

The restrictionist movement currently encompasses a more narrow range of individuals and politicians. The coalition of the color-blind Right, the New Right, and the Far Right around stances on immigration restriction has begun to fray. The Republican Party, which supported the move to pass Proposition 187, has distanced itself from such causes in the aftermath of the measure. This is also evident in the party's retreat on welfare restrictions to immigrants. While passage of Proposition 187 is credited with the institution of the 1996 laws limiting immigrants' access to social services, most of those restrictions have been overturned or mitigated. The result has been a polarization of active immigrant restrictionists. Themes of invasion, appealing to the New Right and the Far Right, have taken center stage in the restrictionist movement. The centrality of invasion has been heightened by an increasing concern over globalization and the role of the nation-state and the "War on Terror."

Conclusion

To understand the impact of Proposition 187 on racial politics, we need to understand the competing claims of race neutrality and race consciousness that surround the measure and contemporary politics more generally. The theory of new racism provides one option for understanding those claims. New racism suggests that arguments about fairness in Proposition 187 are used as a cover to mobilize individuals on a measure that draws on people's latent racism. However, talking to supporters of the measure reveals that color-blind conservatism and racial realism were both schemas held by people who worked on behalf of the measure. Neither schema trumped the other in consistent or predictable ways; neither was the base or fundamental truth of a supporter's character. Individuals were committed to both worldviews and drew on them in complex ways. The bridges between these competing schemas and political action on Proposition 187 were mutually reinforcing. Through an illumination of the different bridging strategies, we gain insight into how supporters read state action after the measure and therefore into the lasting legacy of Proposition 187.

Racial realism and color-blind conservatism are metaschemas that are played out around a number of different themes. The bridging strategies between the metaschemas serve as models for bridging between race-specific and color-blind notions of citizenship. Proponents use each bridging strategy as they struggle to define various forms of citizenship: formal, economic, cultural, and political. We can understand how membership in the community and the nation-state was redefined in the campaign over Proposition 187 by highlighting the bridging strategies. As we shall see in subsequent chapters, Proposition 187 was about defining illegality, immigration status, and citizenship as much as it was about responding to those issues.

CHAPTER THREE

Criminalizing Mexican Migration

The real issue here is do we or do we not live according to law? This is
an all or nothing question. If you choose to ignore the laws you don't
like, then you have no position to complain when you are a "victim
of crime." Has your car been stolen? Yourself robbed? Raped? Too bad.
If we don't enforce the laws, then might makes right. Illegal immigrants
are not needed. They are exploited. They should all be deported. They
are not here legally.

— Letter to the editor, *Los Angeles Times,* October 11, 1994

The struggle over Proposition 187 was a critical modern moment criminal-
izing Mexican migration. During the campaign, proponents connected
notions of danger and criminality with the act of undocumented migration through race. What had been a discrete act of violating immigration
law became, in the eyes of the measure's supporters, a criminal tendency in
Mexicans. Through their criminal behavior or their propensity toward
criminal behavior, the undocumented were seen as forfeiting their rights
and benefits of membership and therefore should be denied social services.
Mobilization for Proposition 187 combined and transposed schemas about
criminality and illegality around a raced notion of Mexicanness. In doing
so, supporters reconstructed racial meanings and redistributed resources
of economic and cultural citizenship along racial lines.

A central mobilizing narrative revolved around the importance of upholding the law. This schema of illegality was embedded in the metaschema
of color blindness with an emphasis on race neutrality and fairness. This
schema, however, worked in conjunction with, and relied on, racialized

notions of criminality. Mexicanness in the campaign is associated not just with undocumented status but with criminal behavior in other areas as well. The schema of criminality was embedded in the metaschema of racial realism and depicted racialized characteristics that threaten the safety and power of others. Notions of Mexican criminality have a long history in the United States in general and the Southwest in particular. However, it was as supporters created bridges between race-neutral notions of law enforcement and raced concerns about criminality that they were mobilized to act on the campaign.

Supporters use the three bridging strategies of racialization, association, and defense. The racialization bridge, or the culture of crime, conflates Mexicans and the undocumented through an initial racialization of Mexicans as criminals. Because Mexicans have criminal tendencies, they are also more likely to be the ones to violate immigration laws. The association bridge, or the border, conflates the undocumented and Mexicans around the prominence of the Mexico–U.S. border. The central place of the border in the minds and lives of Californians in particular leads to a naturalization of the connection between the undocumented and Mexicans. The role of the border, however, is ignored as respondents suggest that the connection between Mexicans and the undocumented is evidence of a propensity toward crime, not a result of geographic and historic connections. The simultaneous fixation on, and erasure of, the border in respondents' minds also contributes to the defense bridge called selective enforcement. This bridge equates undocumented status and Mexicans through the race consciousness of others. Because of the power of Latinos, the United States fails to enforce immigration laws for Mexicans. Therefore Mexicans become the problematic undocumented population that leads to lawlessness. All three strategies serve to connect Mexican migration and criminality in the contemporary moment, a lasting impact from the movement beyond Proposition 187.

We can understand respondents' actions in support of the measure and the legacy of Proposition 187 only when we understand these bridges between illegal migration and criminality. The bridges are essential for three reasons. The first is to understand why the measure focuses on social services. Only through the connections between illegality and criminality can we see why immigration enforcement through denial of services, as opposed to a range of other options that focus on the act of crossing, became the target of this movement at this time. Criminal character is being punished, not just an illegal act. Second, uncovering the bridges is necessary to understand the role of color-blind conservatism and the role of race in mobilization for this measure. The bridges highlight how notions of the law were used effectively in conjunction with the others used in the battle over Proposition 187, how concerns over a raced criminality were transformed into an effective mobilizing message while still maintaining a connection with fairness. Third, revelation of the bridges is vital if we want to understand the changes in the racial terrain that resulted from the passage of the measure. The campaign around Proposition 187 created bridges between undocumented migration, Mexicanness, and criminality. While the connections between other mobilizing schemas explored in subsequent chapters are constructed during the campaign and then altered in the aftermath of Proposition 187, the bridges between illegality and criminality prove more durable. The connections between illegality and criminality are useful for reading the court action that comes after the passage of the measure. As such, we gain insight into the legacy of the project by seeing how these bridges allow respondents to read judicial intervention in this matter as evidence of increased lawlessness.

To explore how this happens, I first look at the schemas of illegality and criminality as expressed through history, the campaign, and respondents. I then turn to the three bridging strategies evidenced by respondents. Finally, I consider the legacy of these twin schemas. State action is read through the nexus of criminality and illegality. In the post–Proposition 187 world, criminality, not simple illegality, is highlighted by restrictionist forces. The potential danger of criminal immigrants becomes central. This focus is readily picked up in the aftermath of September 11, 2001.

Illegality

The crux of the immigration debate since the Immigration Reform and Nationality Act of 1965 has been about undocumented immigration. Those who were not under state control are identified as problematic migrants. Legislation in both 1986 and 1990 attempted to bring immigration back under the control of the state through various devices. Proposition 187 continued this emphasis on illegal immigration. This was understood as being race neutral. Proponents of Proposition 187 answered accusations of racism or of being anti-immigrant by focusing on the distinction between legal and illegal immigration. Their support of the measure was merely support of the law, as the measure addressed only those who had violated the law to enter the country. Proponents threw up their hands in dismay and disbelief as they talked about those who opposed the measure. Opponents were defined as "pro-illegals." Proponents believed that one's political leanings should not affect one's stance on the measure; immigrants without proper papers had violated the law and should therefore be punished, not rewarded.

Propaganda supporting the measure drew sharp distinctions between illegal and legal immigration. The first question on a question-and-answer sheet distributed by Save Our State in 1994 asks what the measure is about. The response: "It's about our immigration laws. Will we have laws that are actually enforced, or will we have open borders that are unrestricted?" The next seven answers address consequences and implications of the measure. In responses to accusations of racism, immigrant bashing, and concerns over disease epidemics and increased crime from kicking kids out of school, proponents' responses always included a retreat to the primacy and the immutability of the law. The measure would enforce the law, and enforcement was understood as a good in and of itself to be defended. The emphasis on illegality as a mobilizing strategy can be seen in the argument in favor of the measure in the voter's pamphlet as well. All capital letters are used every time the word "illegal" or "illegally" appears.

Pete Wilson came to rely on the distinction between legal and illegal. His first forays into getting money from the federal government to offset the budget deficit included requests for reimbursements for all federal mandates. He then moved into asking for money to offset the cost of California's integration of newcomers. As late as May 1993, Wilson was still making speeches about the costs of assimilating newcomers in general (e.g., Wilson 1993c). In August 1993, he began to focus exclusively on state money used for the undocumented, not just immigrants in general. He issued an open letter to President Clinton that month, which Wilson discussed in a speech titled "Closing the Door on Illegal Immigration." Wilson voiced concerns about assimilation, quality of life, use of social services, and impact on jobs, issues he had previously raised in the context of immigration more generally, but now he focused on the undocumented.[1]

Respondents also used this schema of illegality, which combined concerns about violations of immigration laws with the rule of law in general. The measure was seen as a referendum on enforcing laws or allowing lawlessness. Twelve of the interviewees raised concerns about lawlessness.[2] These respondents' support of the measure stemmed from a desire to support "the law." When asked about possibly supporting a similar measure in the future, Kyle, currently a TV journalist and previously a state legislative aide, said: "It all depends on what is right and what is wrong. If statistically people are still coming here illegally, then that's wrong. That very basic level is wrong. If there are laws against something and you're caught, there should be repercussions. A country should try to enforce against the break- ing of those laws." Respondents described opponents of the measure as supporting lawlessness. By opposing the initiative, people were in fact defying current law:

> People should obey the law. And those who are arguing against Prop 187 are essentially saying we shouldn't abide the law. They weren't saying we shouldn't change the law and say that no matter how you get here, once you're here, you're entitled to all this stuff. They weren't saying that. They were just saying we shouldn't enforce the law. Now, we've had this same debate about other things, like about marijuana. Should we change the law? Well, we did. It got struck down.

As opposed to initiatives to change laws regarding drugs, here the supporter understood a new law as essential to preserve the rule of law and the con- cept of citizenship. The constructive nature of the proposition is masked under a support of the status quo.

Supporters argue for enforcement as a universal ideal, not for a particular law or against a particular group of immigrants, and therefore understand their action as supporting a color-blind society. In doing so, however, they ignore how history, culture, and politics produce immigration laws, migra- tion patterns, and enforcement of the law. Similar to other color-blind conservative projects, through universal and transhistorical premises of equality, supporters of this measure are able to understand themselves as color-blind and their opponents as race conscious. Nicholas De Genova (2002) points out that as a result, "the inequalities generated by the law's apparently uniform application among asymmetrically constituted migra- tions from distinct sending countries tend to be naturalized" (424).

Supporters of the proposition were not merely supporting existing law, as they suggested, but were struggling to create a *new* law. The tactics of the movement and supporters' additional concerns show that proponents were not concerned with simply enforcing current law. Supporters did not question that an initiative at the state level creating new legislation was the right tactic. In fact, many suggested it was the only way, since legislators were too scared to do what was "right." That the "right" move required legislative activity at all illustrates supporters' intentions of creating a new order, not enforcing the status quo.

Supporters could avoid questions about the social and racial implications or morality of the initiative by portraying their support as being about the rule of law. Respondents felt that enforcing the law was an unquestionable good: "No, I thought it was a good measure just because—I mean, for me, it's just obvious that if you're going to have a law, you have to follow through on it, I mean, why have it, then?" Supporters placed the justness of immigration laws that define citizenship outside the realm of debate when discussing the illegality schema. By doing so, supporters deny how "illegal alienage is not a natural or fixed condition but the product of positive law; it is contingent and at times it is unstable" (Ngai 2004, 6).

Through the schema of illegality, citizenship appears to be a presocial or natural state of being. This is in part evidenced through the use of a family metaphor to describe citizenship. David, an educator from southern California who did not like to talk about politics, became extremely animated when discussing the benefits of citizenship. Instead of seeing citizenship as a contract, he suggested, "A country is like a huge big family. We start out with a little family, a community of family; the states are a family, so is the government. That's nationalism, love for your country, your family." As Rogers Smith (1997) writes, this is part of a history of "efforts to mythologize nations or peoples as somehow 'prepolitical,' as families or primordial kinship groups" (10–11). Through the naturalization of immigration laws come serious dangers to liberal principles, according to Smith: "The greatest threats come from profound political and psychological tendencies to treat such communities as natural, in ways that seem to legitimate both oppressive internal hierarchies and harsh injustices toward outsiders" (10).

Supporters talked about other immigration issues besides Proposition 187, revealing a vision of reconstructing citizenship around a perceived notion of community, not reaffirming current legal interpretations. Almost every supporter interviewed and most supporting groups argued for more restrictive immigration policy and against current legal interpretations of birthright citizenship. While they defended the current legal system—that is, the rule that those who did not have documentation by the government were illegal—they called for reform of the institutions that distributed citizenship. They wanted to deny citizenship to children of the undocumented born on U.S. soil. In calling for reform of the citizenship clause of the

Fourteenth Amendment, supporters were not simply highlighting the current divisions between legal and illegal but in fact attempting to transform that line and the meaning behind the divisions. Despite consistent constitutional interpretations by the courts that children of the undocumented born in the United States are entitled to citizenship, supporters questioned the fairness of this system, and many expressed support of a constitutional amendment. The rule of law is important to the extent that it provides for fairness. Supporters had a vision of fair immigration laws that sometimes worked in conjunction with enforcement of the status quo, but sometimes fairness trumped concerns about current laws.

The schema of illegality is embedded in the metaschema of color-blind conservatism, as evidenced by the centrality of fairness and concerns with treating everyone equally. Allowing individuals to use services after breaking the law was unjust and unfair to the rest of the nation and to other immigrants. It was unfair to let some break the law and get the benefits of being in this country while others had to wait for long periods of time or even be denied entrance after they had followed the proper immigration procedures. Enforcement of the law is key to maintaining fairness: "We hire people to enforce the laws and protect them, and then we restrict them on what they can do and let other people break them—we don't even treat everybody alike, that's not constitutional, it's against the preamble of the Constitution." The rule of law is essential to preventing discrimination and hence to ensuring equal treatment and fairness.

Proposition 187 would therefore correct the unfair situation described by respondents and in propaganda. Lack of enforcement was unfair to both citizens and immigrants. The 1994 question-and-answer sheet put out by Save Our State responds to an accusation of being "mean-spirited": "If enforcement of our laws is being 'mean-spirited,' then this 'nation of laws' is in deep trouble. . . . We cannot tolerate the abandonment of whole sections of law, nor can we tolerate discrimination against our own citizens and legal residents." Supporters echoed the same sentiments concerning fairness to legal immigrants: "And I especially resented it because I had a number of students and others whose families came from other parts of the world that were trying to legally obey our laws and were being denied left and right. And the ones who broke our laws got anything they wanted." The movement to pass Proposition 187 understood itself as returning fairness through enforcement and return to the rule of law, even while its aim was to enact legislation.

Many social movements use notions of holding ground or returning to a better time as a mobilizing narrative. People respond to maintenance of the status quo much more easily than they do to change. People understand their use of schemas as maintaining tradition or upholding the law, not recognizing the creative act in which they are engaged—reconstructing new narratives from old, recombining schemas, and reapplying schemas to new situations. In this case, people are using the notion of transgressing immigration laws and combining it with the idea that criminals forfeit their rights. That is, where previously the transgressors of immigration law were threatened with deportation, now they also must consider whether they will have schools for their children. Therefore to understand the full strength of the claim of illegality in relation to Proposition 187, we need to understand the construction of Mexicans as criminals. The struggle over Proposition 187 was a battle over constructing the undocumented immigrant as illegal *and* criminal.

Criminality

The American imagination has historically connected Mexicans with criminality. Beginning with the Mexican Revolution, Mexicans became linked with unrest and violence. Fear of the unstable border and the war occurring on the other side translated into fear of Mexicans, particularly expatriates. Mexican Americans mobilized to counter the stereotypes they faced of being criminal and violent (Rosales 1999). During Prohibition, smuggling across the border further entrenched the relationship between Mexicans and crime (Ngai 2004, 62; Rosales 1999, 72–73).

These ideas about the innate criminality of Mexicans were reified by a U.S. criminal justice system that disproportionately incarcerated Mexicans in the 1920s. Police preemptively arrested Mexicans lest they engage in criminal conduct or become public charges (Rosales 1999, 78–80). Judges exhibited prejudices about the violent and criminal nature of Mexicans, which most likely contributed to high rates of conviction among Mexicans. In some places, that rate was twice as high as other "nationalities" (Rosales 1999, 125). The higher rates of arrest and incarceration, combined with publicity of these facts, perpetuated the link between criminal conduct and Mexican origins.

The trope of the criminal Mexican is part of the American racial terrain and was central to the mobilization around Proposition 187. Groups supporting the measure, elites, and respondents talked about violations of a variety of laws, not just immigration laws. This is evident in discussions about the number of undocumented migrants in prison and about changes in safety of Californian communities wrought by Latino immigration. Propaganda supporting Proposition 187 connected the undocumented and criminal activity.

Pete Wilson, in his calls for the federal government to reimburse California for the presence of illegal aliens, widely publicized the estimated costs of keeping illegal aliens in prison. Wilson stressed the criminal nature of the migrants by focusing on the amount of money spent to incarcerate the undocumented and said that illegal immigration is "endangering . . . the safety of too many California neighborhoods" (Wilson 1993a, 6). Wilson suggested that the criminal activity by undocumented persons led not only to Californians' decreased safety but also to a host of other problems as well. It is not Mexicans' violation of immigration laws alone that is causing the budgetary problems, but their criminal activities: "And the budgets for our parks, beaches, libraries, and public safety will continue to suffer while we spend billions to incarcerate enough illegal aliens to fill 8 state prisons" (2). The same day that Wilson delivered his speech "Closing the Door on Illegal Immigration," he issued a press statement on I-5 stressing the "public safety hazard created when thousand of illegal aliens clandestinely slip into California every day" (Wilson 1993b, 1). Wilson stressed the multiple dangers to the body and the body politic from the illegal and criminal activity of undocumented migration. While the bodily integrity of the state was in danger through uncontrolled migration, the bodily integrity of the citizenry was threatened by the criminal behavior of the undocumented once they were here.

The groups authoring and campaigning for the proposition also stressed the criminal and dangerous nature of the people to whom they were attempting to deny social services. Section 1 of the proposition itself reads: "The people of California find and declare as follows: That they have suffered and are suffering economic hardship caused by the presence of illegal aliens in this state. That they have a suffered and are suffering personal injury and damage caused by the criminal conduct of illegal aliens in this state." The fact sheet put out by Save Our State comments on this finding section by declaring, "And the people, who are now victimized by the nearly 18,000 illegal alien felons now in prison (with tens of thousands more on our streets) can no longer afford to provide an open invitation to crime across an open border." The undocumented are described as not merely "illegal" but also criminal. The notion of a border out of control is used to conjure up images of chaos and danger.

In early internal meetings to generate funding for the measure, organizations used a statistic on the criminality of the undocumented. One supporter reported that he was told that one out of four people arrested in the Los Angeles riots was an illegal immigrant. He said that the information was not used in the public campaign because of the overall restraint strategy used by those in charge to reduce racial conflict. Here we see a construction of the undocumented as criminal and that criminal behavior as being central to racial discontent in the form of the 1992 riots. Racial realism is expressed in concern over invasion and danger to the body.

The schema of criminality grounded in racial realism worked in conjunction with the schema of illegality grounded in color blindness. The schema of illegality successfully mobilized individuals because it intersected not just with conceptions about immigration law but with broader conceptions of lawlessness, disorder, criminal activity, and danger. Supporters connected these two schemas in various ways around a raced notion of behavior. In doing so, they used and reconstructed the trope of Mexican criminality. I lay out three patterns that emerged as respondents discussed issues of illegality, criminality, and Mexicanness, which provide insight into the mobilization and the legacy of Proposition 187.

The Culture of Crime

The first way that supporters use notions of criminality and illegality together begins with the racial characterization of Mexicans as being more prone to criminal activity. Because of their connection with criminality, they are then understood as the problem immigrant group who will break the law to get here. Therefore the undocumented become raced as Mexican. Initially, Mexicanness is associated with criminal behavior by respondents through a connection with corruption, gangs, and drugs.[3]

Supporters point to individual criminal behavior of Latinos. Here supporters used media images of Mexicans associated with gangs, which become central to the criminalization of Mexicans. Twelve of the respondents brought up gangs in two contexts. In the first, respondents talked about gangs when pressed about the impact of immigrants on the area or changes that have occurred since the respondents have been living in the area. In the second, respondents mentioned gangs when answering questions about tensions that have resulted from the demographic shifts. Gangs were seen as racialized tension, but always between minority groups. Here racial realism comes to the fore while respondents maintain a personal distance from racial conflict and hence feel a commitment to color blindness. Racial conflict exists, but the central manifestation is between people of color. The use of gangs as the primary example of interracial conflict shows whites as being on the periphery of racial tension, at least for now. This provides a way for respondents to portray the presence or activities of other racial groups as a reason for society failing to be color-blind. Therefore the measure, which addresses the problematic, criminal, and dangerous race-conscious minority group, addresses the possibility of a color-blind society.

The media provides resources essential for the construction and maintenance of the criminalization of the Mexican. Leading up to the formulation of Proposition 187, the *Los Angeles Times* featured stories about the threat to the body, specifically on the border, from immigrants. This included stories of rape and murder associated with the undocumented,[4] border patrol chases resulting in the death of agents, immigrants, and citizens, as well as stories on Latino gangs. A *Los Angeles Times* poll in October 1993 reported that crime was the number one concern among more than half of the residents in Orange County, the heart of Proposition 187. In the same poll, 50 percent viewed Latinos as "more inclined to violence" than others (Di Rado 1993).[5]

A general sense of threat through criminal activity emerged from respondents. Three respondents independently suggested that I go into downtown Los Angeles if I wanted to understand what they were talking about. Respondents were suggesting that only those living their reality could understand the truth of the situation. The conclusions they reach are understood as a result of apparent fact; the apparent facts are demographic shifts and an attendant sense of threat that can be *felt* in Los Angeles. One respondent suggested I go on a Sunday morning when everyone is sleeping because downtown has been taken over by criminal and dangerous elements. Maria and her friend "go to downtown LA. . . . Over there you don't see one single white American. All you see is poor homeless blacks and full of Central America. I feel like I'm in one of those countries." Through her suggestion that I go to Los Angeles to understand the problem, she connects danger and race: "Go with someone who is safe to go with, with your husband or with someone that knows the area. Don't go alone. I don't go alone. I go with my friend who knows all the alleys and corners and here and there. And you'll feel like you are in a foreign country.... When I go there I feel like, gosh, we just crossed the border." Those "foreign countries" are understood as dangerous places.

Mexicanness is criminalized through connections with the political system of the home countries. During the Mexican Revolution, a fear developed about Mexican militancy in general (Romo 1983, 89–111). Today the dominant image of corruption contributes to a perception of criminal immigrants from Mexico.

Some supporters cited corruption in Mexico and Central American countries and then transposed those characterizations onto individuals coming from those countries. Mexicans as a racial group are perceived as functioning in a shady way. Jack, a white man in his seventies originally from Iowa, suggested that one of the reasons immigrants come from Mexico is because of the corruption there. While he knew more about the corruption in Mexico, he felt fairly certain that the same was true of other Latin American countries as well. Later in the interview, Jack talked about the experience of living in a corrupt country as an impediment to integrating in society. Jack told the story of a former employee of his at his small furniture manufacturing company. Juan, although he had been in this country a long time, had never been to a bank. This was evidence that "they do things the underground way. That's a mind-set that they have." Mexicans become racialized as criminal through a connection with corruption in Mexico. Corrupt politics or officials become conflated with private lawlessness.

Mexicans are criminalized, and criminal behavior in other areas suggests that Mexicans will be the most likely to violate immigration laws. The undocumented therefore become raced as Latinos or Mexicans. The presence of Latinos becomes illegitimate through supporters' notions of racialized proclivities toward crime. The undocumented therefore are criminals undeserving of the rights of membership, including social services.

The Border

A second way in which supporters connect race-neutral notions of law enforcement inverts the first two steps in the process described in the previous sections. That is, the undocumented are understood as Mexicans; then, since Mexicans are more likely to violate immigration law, they are understood as displaying a tendency toward criminality. Mexicanness becomes criminalized through a conflation with the undocumented. The initial connection between Mexicanness and undocumented migration that has been developed in the last half of the twentieth century rests in part on a fixation on the border as a site for migration and conflict.

Mexican border crossing was characterized by informality until the Immigration Act of 1924. While the national origins quota act exempted countries in the Western Hemisphere from numerical limits, the 1924 act established a formal process of immigration control focused on visas and border control. This "regime of paper and quotas," with a focus on proper documentation, created the illegal immigrant, and by the late 1920s, Mexicans made up the largest illegal immigrant population.[6]

Subsequent immigration action and reform only served to tighten the connection between illegal immigration and Mexican migration. The Bracero Program in 1942 was an attempt to control Mexican migration. Their temporary presence for work sanctioned residence within the borders, which was otherwise seen as illegitimate. The Bracero Program, however, also created a more intense immigration regulation system and more illegal immigration. Operation Wetback in 1954 led to the forcible repatriation of thousands of Mexicans and Mexican Americans and left the question of the legitimacy of their presence at the forefront. The Immigration and Nationality Act placed numerical limits on immigration from the Western Hemisphere for the first time in 1968. This allowed for an increased focus on the illegality of Mexican migration. The next major legislative act addressing immigration, the Immigration Reform and Control Act of 1986, dealt almost exclusively with illegal immigration—and the discussion was about undocumented Mexican migration.

The conflation of the Mexican and the undocumented (explored in chapter 2) is a result of the "legal construction of 'illegality'" surrounding Mexicanness (De Genova 2002). This construction, which rests in part on the use of the border as a site for conflict, is amplified in border states. After the Immigration Act of 1924, "walking (or wading) across the border emerged as the quintessential act of illegal immigration" (Ngai 2005, 89). De Genova shows how the selective enforcement of immigration laws has focused attention to the Mexican migration experience as illegal. He notes that the focus on border enforcement as opposed to interior enforcement serves to naturalize the connection between undocumented migration, "illegality," and Mexicans:

Overstaying a visa—the rather discrete act by which very significant numbers of people become un-documented migrants—is, after all, not terribly
dramatic. Hence, it is precisely "the Border" that provides the exemplary
theater for staging the spectacle of "the illegal alien" that the law produces.
The elusiveness of the law, and its relative invisibility in producing "illegality," requires the spectacle of "enforcement" at the U.S.–Mexico border
that renders a racialized migrant "illegality" visible and lends it the common-
sensical air of a "natural" fact. (436)

The undocumented are raced as Mexicans, and Mexicans become characterized as illegal, regardless of immigration status. Central to the racialization
of Mexicans in this country is the construction of illegality surrounding
their presence:

> One of the consequences of this history of selective border enforcement
> is that the sociopolitical category "illegal alien" itself—inseparable from
> a distinct "problem" or "crisis" of governance and sovereignty—has come
> to be saturated with racialized difference and indeed has long served as a
> constitutive dimension of the racialized inscription of "Mexicans" in the
> United States. (433)

The processes of naturalizing immigration law and using the border as
the site for contention informs supporters' views. For respondents, it is an
unquestionable and unchangeable fact that undocumented migration is
Mexican. Therefore supporters understand themselves as merely stating
the facts when they note that the undocumented are mostly from Mexico:
"I think there was some illegal Armenian immigration, and other groups
too, but overwhelmingly it was, you know, south of the border people
coming across, 80–90 percent." Another respondent notes, "It [the propo-
sition] was anti–illegal immigration. It became known or discussed as being
anti-Mexican. The reason being that the majority of the illegal immigrants
were and are Mexicans." Respondents suggest the proposition comes from
a place of realism, not racism, by stating that Mexicans compose most of
the "illegals" in this border state: "I don't think it's just because I'm preju-
diced against them, it's an actual fact!"

Supporters of the measure then criminalized the raced, undocumented
population. Transgressing the law in one realm, supporters argued, means
a higher likelihood of violating laws in other realms.[7] Richard, a school-
teacher who has worked with kids of all kinds, thinks that there is a substantive difference between immigrants who are documented and those

who are not: "Those who come illegally. You get a better grade of people, better quality of people that come from normal routes." Lots of gardeners, Jack reported, are illegal because it is an easy business to get started in. Jack mentioned that he "saw" lots of undocumented immigrants because he would walk by a lawnmower repair shop almost daily. He reported his observations of the repair shop: "I'd see a lot of them [undocumented migrants], they'd come to the shop. And I'd see how they'd flaunt the laws of this country. They'd have four men in the front seat, and they'd be lucky if the driver had a seat belt; they didn't care about things like that. And their vehicles would have various things wrong with them, violating the vehicle code." Jason grants that immigration in general stems from a desire to better one's life. Willingness to break the law for a better life is a slippery slope for Jason, however: "But I think today it's sometimes a better life translates to more money and more money at any means possible, so that equates to illegal activity including drugs, drug smuggling." The undocumented are not just seen as violating immigration law but are established as a criminal group. If Mexicans are undocumented and the undocumented are criminal, Mexicans become associated with criminality.

The border serves as a crucial conduit of this association bridge. Proximity to the border generates increased fear for the bodily integrity of the person and by extension to society and the state. Northern and southern California in this respect seemed to generate different compelling narratives for support of Proposition 187 and other restrictionist agendas. None of the nine respondents from northern California brought up the issue of gangs. The contrast between northern and southern California also appears in letters to the editors in the *Los Angeles Times* and the *San Francisco Chronicle* during 1994. It is no great surprise to note that Proposition 187 or the issue of illegal immigration appeared more often in the *Los Angeles Times,* or that more letters were written in favor of restrictionist agendas, given the well-known proclivity toward liberalism in the Bay Area and the editorial boards of each paper at the time (although it is interesting to note that both papers, while coming out against Proposition 187, did support Wilson). Looking at the sorts of arguments used to support the measure, we see not only that letter writers from northern and southern California were using different arguments but that the editors targeting different audiences were selecting very different sorts of arguments as well. Notions of crime, invasion, or physical danger to people were evident in 42 percent of letters to the editor negatively portraying illegal immigration or immigration that appeared in the *Los Angeles Times* from September 1993 until election day in November. In contrast, similar letters make up 10 percent of those that appeared in the *San Francisco Chronicle*.[8] As one moves closer to the border, stories of the danger associated with criminal or dangerous undocumented migrants adopt a more personally threatening aura; people begin to feel on the "edge" of safety. Proximity to the border in this case provides fertile ground for transposing schemas of a porous border and threats to the bodily integrity of individuals or society.[9] Connections between Mexicans and the "problematic group" are intensified as well. The closer one gets to the border with Mexico, the more natural the connection appears as the Mexican border becomes part of the everyday subconscious—the intersubjective lived reality and the unnamed frame of reference.

Selective Enforcement

A third way that supporters negotiate the race-neutral notion of law enforcement with a racially specific notion of lawbreakers begins with the race consciousness of others. In this defense bridge, the undocumented become raced as Mexican because *others* fail to be color-blind. Because others in society are race conscious, certain racial groups, according to supporters, are privileged. Latinos are among the privileged racial groups. This suggests to supporters that the government fails to enforce laws for those south of the border. Through a perception that Latinos enjoy a privileged status in society, supporters racialize the undocumented as Mexican. Then, in a similar pattern as seen earlier, the racialized category of illegal immigrants becomes criminalized as well.

To show that Mexicans are privileged in our system of immigration, supporters contrast Mexicans with other immigrant groups. This is a process of triangulation whereby respondents draw contrasts between the white native experience, privileged Mexicans, and other racialized groups. These other racialized groups are still clearly foreign but are used as a sympathetic contrast to the unsympathetic, powerful Mexicans. Immigrants from other countries such as Vietnam or Africa are understood as victims because they follow immigration laws:

> Yeah, I don't hear many complaints towards the Asians anymore. I did a little bit at first about the Vietnamese. You don't hear much about Japanese. All you ever heard about 'em was hardworking, industrious. Chinese, same thing. And the Vietnamese and Chinese came here . . . whether or not they

liked the laws. . . . [They] all came under the law. . . . They did it by the law. And even they, when I talk to some of them, they resent the fact that how come they can't get their relatives here, but if you're from Mexico, you can.

"Line-jumpers" from Mexico are permitted unfair access to the United States because of the privilege Latinos have in this country. This was expressed by a professor in California, who suggested that if the Chinese were entering our system at the rate that Mexicans were, we would have tanks on our borders (see chapter 2). Latinos are understood as one of the politically powerful minorities that are granted special rights and considerations.

This perception of advantages given to Mexicans through lax law enforcement means the current situation violates fairness through color consciousness. The law should be color-blind: "You're going to have a law, you have to follow through on it, I mean, why have it, then? I mean, why Mexicans have it easier than Africans? Why do they get special treatment? Why don't we just let them all in? Why don't we let people from Russia just come in without making them go through the process?" Proposition 187 is raced only because it is an attempt to rectify the color consciousness of opponents who support disproportional enforcement of the law. The geographic realities are ignored—from a fixation on the border to an erasure of the border—in an attempt to generate a raceless world.

Like those fixated on the border, however, proponents concerned about racially selective enforcement draw a connection between documentation and criminality. Therefore the racialization of the undocumented leads to a criminalization of the race. If Mexicans are equated with undocumented migration, then Mexicans are naturalized as transgressors of the law. They become not just illegal but criminal and dangerous in their proclivity toward violating the law. Proponents continue to use a triangulation with various "foreigners" to create the Mexican undocumented migrant as criminal and dangerous. These other immigrants, who are still clearly not understood as being "American," are used to further illustrate the ways that undocumented migration is connected with danger and destruction. Referring to the technology boom and skilled visas, an interviewee depicts Indian immigrants as desirable and documented:

These Indian people come over, and they're the *best*. They come over here, and they learn, and then they go back, or they get a job and stay. But they're legal. And so legally I think we're fine. But when illegal immigrants come in, [they] destroy the system.

The respondent uses another set of immigrants to distinguish documented, desirable immigrants from Mexican, dangerous immigrants. Because of their power, Mexicans can violate a range of laws and change the system. Minority privilege means the end to the rule of law.

Conclusion

As supporters connect racialized notions of criminality and the notion of a nation of laws, they are mobilized to act on Proposition 187. Laws are universal and abstract. Support of the law is therefore a way to support a color-blind and fair society. Supporters explain the apparent "truth" that most undocumented immigrants come from Mexico with the attendant notions of Latino power, a fixation on the border, and a criminalization of the Mexican. This allows supporters to maintain their feelings of support for a color-blind world while "seeing" racial differences in the world around them.

Passage of the measure was an attempt to institutionalize connections between illegality and criminality by declaring that Mexicans qua criminals have forfeited their rights. If Mexicans or Mexican Americans are criminals, they are not perceived as having the rights or privileges of formal, cultural, or economic citizenship. The measure signifies this distancing of the undocumented (read: Mexican or Mexican-appearing) from the rights and privileges of being part of society by denying social services. The schema of criminality also led restrictionists to believe it would be right to deny this group a range of other rights associated with full membership: the right to own property, protection by the Constitution and other legal protections, consideration when governing. Denying the benefits of membership to the undocumented by denying them social services would have instantiated the connection between criminality and undocumented migration through legislation. The racial project would have been incorporated by the state. Passage alone, however, gave power to this notion.

While the measure was not enforced, the state response was read through the nexus of documentation and criminality. The court injunction was not understood as merely an example of an overactive judiciary getting in the way of citizen politics, a dirty trick by opponents, or a failure of the system. Many interviewees felt that the court injunction and subsequent mediation were evidence of lawlessness that was prevailing. The criminal elements were taking over, and the power of minority groups to ignore the law had increased. The loss of the rule of law meant the border was an even greater danger. The border becomes chaotic, and respondents describe the situation as "out of control at the border" and "uncontrolled movements" of people.

As the world becomes increasingly insecure, the criminal Mexican becomes an increased focus. The criminal element would cross the border, run drugs, and aid terrorists. Criminality and danger overtake concerns about fairness and documentation in the restrictionist movement in California. The connections established between criminality and migration are readily adapted in post-9/11 America. Eleven respondents discussed immigration as a national security issue. The criminal, undocumented Mexican plays an important role in the threat to security. In a post-9/11 interview, one respondent reported that the Mexican security minister announced that he knew they have active Hezbollah cells in northern Mexico. The border, central to the construction of the criminal Mexican, becomes dangerous because of the access it provides to another set of dangerous foreigners. The criminal tendencies of Mexicans are emphasized to explain the danger: Mexicans will guide the terrorists across the border into the United States. Yet another respondent worried about the Mexican consular ID cards being distributed to Arab terrorists: "Now, Mexican smugglers already admitted that they have escorted people from suspected Mideastern terrorist groups across our southern border. You're gonna tell me they're not going to walk in [and give them an ID card] and for their, I mean, they'll probably float them a hundred bucks.... They get these Mexican smugglers to bring them across the border. I mean I'm talking thousands of dollars. So you think they're going to walk into the Mexican consulate and they're going to argue with them, not for a minute. So we are importing not only smugglers, drug smugglers, the drugs, of course, the criminals, and now terrorists; that's exactly what we're doing right now." The schemas of illegality, criminality, and Mexicanness, reconstructed through the Proposition 187 campaign, are used to understand this new terrorist threat to national security.

CHAPTER FOUR

Economic Citizenship: Dependency and the White American Work Ethic

I met Sue, a woman in her forties, in a fast food restaurant in northern California to discuss her support for the Proposition 187 campaign. She was wearing no makeup and had her blonde hair pulled back into a ponytail. She had recently left the city because of a fear of crime and entered into the farm business. Sue reported her disgust at Mexicans who abused the welfare system and created economic problems for Californians. Mexicans were out to take advantage of the system and were bankrupting the state. As we talked, Latino workers occasionally passed our table in the back corner. As a Latino worker changed the garbage immediately behind our table, Sue offered a different narrative about Mexicans and the economy. Lots of Mexicans work and live on the ranches where Sue lives. Many people who own farms around her say they will only hire Mexicans because they are hard workers. She also personally knew this to be true; in the 1970s, she worked side by side with Mexicans in a tomato sorter. Mexicans, she told me, are willing to take lower wages. Sue suggested that the problem is that Americans will not start at reasonable salaries. However, these jobs are understood as beginning jobs for Americans, who will work their way out and advance into other positions. For Mexicans, there is no discussion of advancement, and as such, Sue still understood Mexican workers in America as a problem. Sue's two divergent depictions of the relationship between Mexicans, the economy, and work highlight the multiple ways a notion of a white work ethic combines with concerns over the economy and labor in the struggle over Proposition 187. These narratives show that Proposition 187 was an attempt to redefine the borders of economic citizenship.

Proponents, opponents, and scholars alike shared in portraying Propo-

sition 187 as a measure designed to ease the burden on taxpayers. The measure, according to this common reading, was about a cost-benefit calculation
and was passed because illegal immigrants were seen as taking from the
pot more than they put in. This color-blind conservative schema stressed
the issue of fairness to taxpayers. Proponents and opponents addressed
the measure at times as if it was a policy attempt to save the citizenry money,
to help balance the California budget at a moment of tight economic resources. A materialist understanding of movements or nativist responses
would also depict this measure as a response to the economic recession in
California in the early 1990s.

However, to really understand why services were central to this measure,
and what that meant to supporters, one needs to understand an attendant
notion of a raced work ethic. Services to the undocumented were to be cut
off not because they didn't contribute tax revenues but in an attempt to
define the undocumented out of the community and as part of the undeserving poor. A recognition of the racial realism central to mobilization
allows us to see that the passage of Proposition 187 (re-)created Mexicanness as lacking a white work ethic and therefore existing outside the community. Mexican migrants lacked a legitimate claim to services, according
to proponents, not because of their legal citizenship status or even because
of their failure to put enough dollars into the collective pool but because
of their perceived inability to fulfill the criteria for economic citizenship.

Materialist accounts of mobilization cannot access this story; only by
acknowledging the role of agency from below, and the centrality of reconstructing race during mobilization, is this revealed. To highlight the short-
comings in materialist explanations for mobilization, I first consider the
idea that economic explanations are sufficient for understanding mobilization behind Proposition 187. While economic factors certainly help us
understand why *some* political activity happens, it is not a sufficient answer
to explain the timing of the initiative, nor does it get us very far in explaining why the undocumented were the target and why services were at the
center of the debate. Extra attention is paid to the economic argument,
since this is a central way scholars understand nativist movements. This
discussion also highlights the inability of standard social movement theory
to understand the legacy of Proposition 187.

To explore how individuals constructed notions of economic citizenship through mobilization around the measure, I turn to the role taxes and
fairness played in the minds of supporters (a cost-benefit calculation and

concern over the citizen-taxpayer grounded in the broader schema of color-blind conservatism) and a notion of a white work ethic that underpinned the campaign (the racial realist sister schema of Mexican dependence). I then turn to three bridging strategies supporters used. They used conceptions of dependence to connect racialized concerns over a work ethic with race-neutral discussions of fairness to taxpayers. As opposed to the other conceptions of citizenship considered in this book, proponents did not use a defense bridge when considering economics and immigration. Here, however, there were two different versions of a racialization bridge. This is in part because of the historically schizophrenic way in which the Mexican worker has been characterized, both as lazy and as a pliable, hard worker. In the first racialization bridge, then, "Mexicans as takers," Mexicanness is connected with acquisitiveness and the lack of a work ethic. Here, similar to the "welfare queen" of the 1980s, Mexicans are understood as only being diligent in their attempts to get whatever they can without wage labor. Mexicans are therefore dependent on the state. In a second racialization strategy, however, dependency is understood somewhat differently. Mexicans may be hard workers, but they lack a sense of autonomy or self-governance in their work habits. Because of their docility, they fail to be able to meet American economic citizenship requirements, resulting in the exploitation of Mexican workers.

Respondents also used an association strategy, focusing at the outset on documentation status and *then* turning to race, which I label "magnets." Here the system of social services is to blame for attracting a particular type of person. Those who cross the border illegally are understood as looking for services. The conflation of Mexicans and the undocumented is therefore evidence that Mexicans lack an independent white work ethic. Here, as in the other two strategies, Proposition 187 is a guard of American economic citizenship, keeping out of the system those who fail to display an independent American work ethic. The notion of economic citizenship constructed by passage of the measure is used by politicians and individuals to channel resource distribution in the wake of Proposition 187.

It's Not the Economy, Stupid

Deteriorating economic conditions have long been understood as contributing to nativism (e.g., Burns and Gimpel 2000, 202; Alvarez and Butterfield 2000, 169; Higham 1988). This notion, however, has recently been challenged by scholars who find "that anti-immigrant nativism has had as much to do with the social strains of urbanization and industrialization as with anxieties associated with economic contraction" (Skerry 2000, 61). Peter Skerry points to two of the best-known and most intense nativist moments in American history, the Know-Nothings of the 1850s and the immigration restrictionists of the 1920s, and notes that both occurred during periods of economic growth. He suggests that more opportunities during economic growth can also lead to more conflict. Economic downturns can cause nativism, and so, it seems, can economic growth. Proposition 187 is an important contemporary example in which to consider the role of the economy in generating nativist movements.

Proposition 187 has been understood by others as proof of the economic-threat thesis; the appearance and passage of the measure have been seen as a result of the recession in California in the early 1990s. Not only did many in California explicitly see their economic woes as a result of the influx of illegal immigrants, but, so the argument goes, renewed nativist attempts are made during times of economic crisis. Michael Alvarez and Tara Butterfield (2000) argue that "voter support for Proposition 187 is an example of cyclical nativism and that the impetus for this nativism was the sagging California economy" (168). Using exit polls from the 1994 election, they conclude that the poor economic conditions "caused" the nativist reaction (176). Their study places the racial component of the measure in the back-seat by claiming that "history shows us that nativism is not race dependent. The differentiating factor has been simply immigrant versus native status" (170). By placing race in a secondary role to economic and nationalist considerations, they must rely on inconsistent logic to explain the outcome of different populations voting for the initiative.

This can initially be seen in Alvarez and Butterfield's contradictory interpretations of economic interest. They state that the strongest indicator of whether someone would have voted for the initiative is the person's perception of the overall California economy and that the perception of his or her own personal economic situation in comparison had a negligible impact (175). Yet, to explain differences among voters by class and race, the authors state that those who perceive their personal finances to be threatened by illegal immigration voted for the measure. They point to the number of blacks and less-educated voters of all races (except Hispanics) who voted for the measure.[1]

An economic explanation using data from a single point in time, such as exit polls, is misleading in this case. When one considers the timing of the initiative in relation to people's perception of the change in the recession, an economic explanation becomes harder to defend. As people saw hope for the future of California's economy, they maintained that immigration was one of the most important issues facing the state and supported restrictions on services to illegal immigrants.[2] Concern with illegal immigration and their perceptions of the economy did not covary leading up to the election. Immigration and illegal immigration came to concern citizens more than the economy. An explanation that relies solely on economics cannot explain why, given the length of this recession, a renewed nativist movement found fertile soil right at the time people perceived the situation to be turning a corner.

Additionally, an economic explanation does not really help us to understand the content of the measure and what happened with Proposition 187. If economic troubles cause people to search for someone to blame or fear, then we don't need to take supporters of the initiative who said race had no role to play at face value; race could enter the debate through felt economic difficulties. But this still leaves us with many questions as to why Proposition 187 took the form it did and why it gathered such mass-based support. Why was the focus on the undocumented and not on immigrants in general, or certain groups of immigrants, as has been the reaction by Californians in the past (e.g., the Chinese Exclusion Act, the "Anti-Okie" law)? And even if we can understand why illegal immigrants may have been the target, why did public services become the center of the debate and not border control or employer sanctions, especially when opponents of the measure showed how it could potentially cost a lot more money than it would save?[3]

Kitty Calavita provides a more sophisticated interpretation of how economics impacted the production of this movement by looking at the particular political-economic shifts that were occurring. To understand the people's reaction, we need more information than the existence of an economic downturn; we need to understand the particular history of the economic moment and how it was experienced. Calavita suggests that the nativism of the 1990s in general and Proposition 187 in particular are unique in their focus on the costs associated with immigration. She explains the measure's emphasis on the fiscal impact of immigrants by looking at the political-economic landscape. This focus on services is an expression of balanced-budget conservatism that developed out of America's post-Fordist crisis. Much of the policy discussion therefore took place on the grounds of a cost-benefit analysis. The arguments frequently were about whether or not immigrants or the undocumented were an economic benefit or an economic strain. Did they use more services than they paid for?

The Taxpayer-Citizen

Many Proposition 187 proponents attempted to portray the struggle in just these terms. California simply could no longer afford to support illegal immigrants, who were a huge strain on the economy. The measure would therefore exclude illegal aliens from public social services, publicly funded health care, and public elementary, secondary, and postsecondary schools. Governor Pete Wilson and other politicians supporting Proposition 187 clearly painted the initiative in this light. Wilson repeatedly defended the proposition and other moves to restrict undocumented access to social services by arguing that there was not enough money and legal residents were being turned away. Wilson issued a series of public letters and then lawsuits in an attempt to get the federal government to reimburse California for mandated services first to immigrants in general and then illegal immigrants. The state was unable to balance the budget, according to Wilson, because of money spent on illegal immigrants. Services such as providing dental care to poor women and the elderly, treatment for drug-addicted pregnant women, and prenatal care in general would need to be cut because of the costs associated with illegal immigration (Wilson 1994a, 3–4). In a letter to the *Los Angeles Times,* a state representative wrote: "Prop 187 doesn't demonize immigrants, nor stigmatize anyone. The question is simple: Should illegal aliens be entitled to free education, housing medical and other government benefits?" (Rohrabacher 1994).

Nonelite supporters also attributed anti-immigrant sentiment to economic concerns. In January 1994, a resident of Malibu wrote:

> The majority of the cost goes to "Joe and Jane Sixpack Taxpayer" whose state and local income taxes are going to pay for the social costs of these immigrants and who get nothing but inferior schools, diluted law enforcement protection, strained sewer, water and other services. . . . [Many of the new arrivals] are not paying taxes and sending money to their home countries to the detriment of revitalizing the Southern California economy. ("Debate over Immigration," 1994)

Proposition 187 was designed to protect not simply residents or citizens but those considered economic citizens. Supporters talked about the importance of taking care of "our own" first. Citizens' interests were to come before others.

I asked interviewees about the privileges and responsibilities associated with citizenship. One nearly universal sentiment was the obligation to support yourself. In addition to knowing "the" language and occasionally a mention of military service, almost all respondents suggested that citizenship required one "be responsible," meaning to "support yourself and your family." This included "raising your own baby." Economic citizenship was the central recurring theme in respondents' definitions of citizenship in general. I asked the question on the rights and responsibilities of citizenship after a long discussion of Proposition 187, so that respondents were defining citizenship with their feelings about the measure in the forefront of their mind; thus they offered insight into what components of citizenship were important to their mobilization around this measure. Additionally, respondents frequently used this question as a segue to the relationship between the new immigration and the intent of the measure. In their support of the measure, people attempted to reinforce notions of economic responsibility and tie these firmly to economic citizenship. Proponents used social services to define the boundaries of economic citizenship. Those who could access services were economic citizens; those who would be denied services were not. Proposition 187 was a struggle to define economic citizenship.

Part of the definition of economic citizenship that mobilized individuals to support the measure was "citizen as contributor," or as taxpayer. Vivian, a white retired preschool teacher, talked about a zero-sum perspective on services: "But by the same token it's taking money that's spent on them and on *people who have never contributed anything to the economy* where there might be other people who have been in the area for a long time but they can't get the same benefits" (italics mine). The grassroots activist core I interviewed in Costa Mesa discussed dual citizenship as another way in which the U.S. government was failing the citizens. Bernie, an elderly female respondent, said, "In other words, our government has betrayed us." The chorus around the table responded by repeating the word "us." Bernie continued to describe the "us": "citizen taxpayers, we are betrayed." The term "American" or "citizen" was frequently coupled with "taxpayer" in letters to the editors and in Wilson's later speeches immediately before and after the November election. "Taxpaying citizens are saying with Proposition 187 that the time has come to fix the crisis. . . . I will vote for Proposition 187 and for candidates who recognize they are elected to serve taxpaying citizens first and foremost" ("Debate over Immigration," 1994). Wilson, after the election, reported to the Heritage Foundation that the 1994 election was a victory for "people who work hard, pay their taxes and play by the rules, and who raise children to play by the rules" (3). Here Wilson is referring to his victory, the Republican takeover of Congress, and the passage of Proposition 187. Californians passed Proposition 187 because they thought "it wrong when health care was denied working poor California mothers while the same care was being given to illegal immigrants" (5). Those on the other side, whose interests the measure challenges, are nontaxpayers. As one respondent irate with the press's coverage of the measure stated: "And they [the newspapers] didn't state the obvious, which was that all it was doing was upholding the law. I mean these people are illegal, they are not taxpayers, so you know they didn't go into that so much." This distinction between taxpayers and nontaxpayers was understood as being a color-blind concern as expressed in a letter to the editors of the *Los Angeles Times:* "Why is it that when an American citizen, who has worked so hard, in many cases for a lifetime, and wants to keep what little they've managed to accumulate are labeled racist for speaking up in their effort to do so?" ("Debate over Immigration," 1994).

Calavita highlights this "subtle semantic shift from 'citizen' to taxpayer as the central unit of civic life" as a component of balanced-budget conservatism. Calavita suggests that this is evidence that Proposition 187 is symbolic. It is symbolic in that it did not emanate from a belief that the measure would have a real impact on the economic conditions, but addressed this shift in definitions. If we take Calavita's challenge seriously, to interpret the measure as neither instrumental nor symbolic alone, we see the measure is about capital, defining citizenship, and defining outsiders. The measure was not *grounded in a shift* from citizen to taxpayer; the struggle over the measure was to define the content of those categories. Economic citizenship is a very real resource associated with tangible goods. Proposition 187 was a struggle to define this powerful capital, economic citizenship. Fairness to taxpayers was only part of the struggle and can only be understood in conjunction with racialized notions of dependence.

Mexicanness and Dependence

Motivation for supporting this measure stemmed not only from the economic conditions but also from the racial terrain. Supporters were mobilized to act as they connected notions of work ethic and race with the idea of citizen-taxpayers. Proposition 187 was a racial project attempting to enforce a racialized notion of the American work ethic.

Economic citizenship is central to American citizenship (Shklar 1991/ 1998; Smith 1997), and racial dimensions have been fundamental to economic citizenship since the founding of the United States. The ideal of the American work ethic consists of a willingness to work hard and an ambition grounded in individuality and freedom. These categories have been associated and disassociated with race in various ways across time. Free labor was clearly initially denied to blacks through the institution of slavery. But after emancipation, blacks were still restricted from American economic citizenship. Through an association with laziness and a lack of self-control, blacks were understood as permanently excluded from American citizenship, even if legally granted the rights to participate. European immigrants, attuned to the struggle for economic citizenship, went to great lengths to ensure they were identified as white and therefore as workers (Roediger 1991).

In a different tactic for excluding racial others, Asians were associated with diligent, almost unconscious and involuntary labor. At the height of the controversy over Asian immigration in the late nineteenth century and the early twentieth, Asian laborers were compared with machines. Though tireless and hardworking, they were thought to be inhuman because of the conditions they would accept. They were foreign because they lacked independent will in their work ethic.

Still another variation on racializing American economic citizenship can be seen following the Mexican-American War. Here the Mexican elite were associated with an affluent but lazy lifestyle. As such they were deemed to lack the ambition and drive of the American work ethic. Taking their land and denying them economic citizenship were therefore justified by the depiction of rancheros as failing to fulfill this white "American" work ethic.

Proponents of Proposition 187 were able to draw on a wide range of available schemas to reconstruct an American work ethic that excluded the contemporary Mexican immigrant. The centrality of a white work ethic in the campaign for Proposition 187 becomes evident when we look at the construction of categories on each side of the native-foreigner dichotomy and in the intent of the measure itself.

Maria, the respondent from Guatemala, clearly displays that whiteness is connected with a work ethic and Mexicanness is understood as a contrast in this campaign. She repeatedly stated her qualifications as a hard worker to distance herself from other Latino immigrants and align herself with people who belong in the United States. Defending her status as an American, she said, "You know I wasn't born here but I never been in, I have never collected, I haven't used, I always worked all my life." Her husband, an American "mutt" who doesn't know his background, reminded her that she had collected unemployment. Quickly she told me that she had collected once, explained why, and said that she had immediately reentered the workforce: "One time when I got laid off from [name of company]. And I got back to work because I went straight to learn computers, straight to do what I had to do to get myself a better job. And I did, I went to work for [name of company] and I swear I got out. I retired from there. But unfortunately you know people of my own culture they don't have that." Here Maria uses others within her culture as a contrast to her own work ethic to illustrate why she is different, why she is, as she said about other hard workers throughout her interview, "truly American." "Truly American" means having a *white* work ethic. Maria told a story about a man without insurance who had to pay for his care while lying side by side with a man who bragged about coming to the United States to get free medical procedures: "But anyway, so this guy worked for—never been on welfare, just like Bob, you know, engineers very, truly American okay." Bob chimed in, "Pay-their-way kind of people, yeah." Maria continued: "I always call them tall gray hair blue eyes."

Jack, a furniture manufacturer, also illustrates how Mexicanness is being defined out of the possibility of economic citizenship. For Jack, a lack of ambition combined with a desire to abuse the system defines Mexicans out of the realm of economic citizenship. Central to his interview was his ambivalence over helping a man from Guatemala become a U.S. citizen. Jack hired the man not knowing he was undocumented. Jack, however, does not see his actions to help this man obtain citizenship and his support of Proposition 187 as contradictory because Proposition 187 was about punishing those without a proper work ethic. Jack helped his Guatemalan employee because "he's one hardworking person, and his family always conduct themselves in an honest fashion. . . . He wasn't asking for hand-outs. When he worked for me, he worked for a restaurant five hours a night, too. He managed to bring his family here and support them, and he wasn't looking for handouts. He was anxious to learn anything I could teach him and very soon became indispensable to us. And then he got a better job with a new furniture company." Jack explained away any seeming inconsistency by contrasting the person he helped with the majority of Latinos, those who don't belong because they lack the white work ethic: "Some of my friends think it looks contradictory how we helped this one fella, doing one thing with one hand and another with the other. I guess it's just because he was ambitious, that's the only reason. And I don't see that in a lot of Hispanics. A friend of his came to work for us, and he just takes every opportunity he can to chew the government. He only deals in cash, so he doesn't have to pay taxes."

Proponents of the measure connect the idea of Mexicans' lacking a work ethic with the idea of fairness to taxpayers. While taxpaying is used occasionally as a proxy for economic citizenship, this shorthand misses the role of dependency central to the construction of "economic citizenship." We run the risk of returning to a debate over cost-benefit calculations and missing the import of the roles of work and money in this measure if we don't unpack the shorthand and note how the color-blind category of taxpayer worked in conjunction with a raced notion of dependence. This happens in three ways. First, Mexicans are initially raced as takers; the system therefore needs to be corrected to prevent abuse. The measure's color-blind attempt to rectify the unfair situation will address those who abuse the system who are understood as being Mexicans. Second, Mexicans, even understood as hard workers, fail to meet the criteria of American economic citizenship. Mexican laborers are understood as lacking independence, which is anti-American. Therefore the measure is in fact designed to save these dependent laborers from exploitation in the American system. Third, services attract those who lack the work ethic and also create the lack of a work ethic. The predominance of Mexican undocumented immigrants indicates their racial distance from a white work ethic, and the system intensifies that tendency. All three of these strategies are used, sometimes by the same respondent; each mobilized respondents to act on Proposition 187 and provides insight into the measure's legacy.

Mexicans as Takers

A central strategy connecting raced and unraced concerns about economic citizenship begins with a set of racial characteristics that proponents attach to Mexicans. This strategy initially racializes Mexicans and a work ethic and then addresses the system and the ways to rectify it to achieve fairness to taxpayers. Mexicanness is characterized as lazy, but also as shiftless or underhandedly acquisitive. These associations have been central to depictions of Mexican Americans since the Mexican-American War. In addition to the "happy-go-lucky shiftless lover of song, food, and dance," Mexicans have been depicted as "conniving, treacherous *bandido*[s]" (Delgado and Stefancic 1992, 175). Respondents drew on this tradition by portraying Mexicans as out to get what they can from the system. This is done through a contrast with other immigrant groups as well as immigrants from other time periods. Mexicans therefore violate standards of American economic citizenship. A campaign to deny services to the undocumented (read: Mexicans) attempts to distinguish between residents within the borders by constructing this racial group as failing to emulate the white American work ethic.

Triangulation is used to depict the Mexican as lacking the proper American work ethic. This triangulation highlights how economic citizenship is grounded in a *white* work ethic. Other sympathetic immigrants, though still foreigners, are used to illustrate the lack of drive south of the border. Ed, a professor in southern California, discussed experiences with immigrants from many different countries. The sympathetic groups include Russians, Africans, and Asians. He distinguished the sympathetic Asian immigrants from white citizens, though, as he depicted Asians as having a hyper–work ethic. According to Ed, Asian immigrants are different from whites because they work harder, value education more, and have a different communal life and set of cultural norms. In his narrative, this hyper–work ethic caused Asians to appear threatening to whites because if "we" let too many of "them" in, there would be no room for "us" at colleges and universities. While he used Asians to highlight the laziness of Mexicans, the desired work ethic still belongs to whites.

Supporters used previous eras of immigration as a contrast to the era of "new" Mexican immigration to explain the connections between a white work ethic and a good citizen. A supporter from the Bay Area used her childhood background from Pennsylvania: "That's a little difference: there is the fact that when immigrants came here years ago they had skills, and they came and they got work, where so many of them come now and expect to be taken care of, and they are to a great extent, as far as getting different kinds of aid." These new immigrants are outside the contours of who can belong because they do not exhibit the proper work ethic and do not have the same motivations for entry and for life. Therefore they are undeserving and should be defined apart from the deserving or the American citizen.

Latinos or Mexicans did not just come here and get services but came intentionally to take advantage of the system. "They come here, they get food, programs, prenatal care, birthing care, and postnatal care and a new citizen, and they go back to Mexico and apply and they get a check every month." Some respondents, viewing their experiences through a lens of racial realism, used personal narratives as proof. Someone who would occasionally hire illegals "inadvertently" reported: "In a way we were forced to do that [hire illegals] because they would accept lower wages. We did try to give them raises when we could. We did find they would take advantage of certain things. Like of any free service they could get."

Two stories were repeated almost identically throughout numerous interviews. One is an eyewitness account—or a recitation of a friend's eyewitness account—of illegal women coming to give birth to babies in American hospitals. Another personal experience used to explain supporters' stance, which provides insight into the respondents' racial realism, is a description of the scene in hospital emergency rooms. "They [immigrants] would go to the emergency room when they got sick because of course they had no medical insurance. This meant a few things, like if you really needed emergency service, you'd have to wait and wait and wait because there'd be lots of Hispanics in line in front of you with stuff that could be treated by a normal doctor in his office." If one of the interviewees or a family member went to the hospital, he or she would find long waits and many nonwhite faces. This was in part because the services were known to be free, and people without insurance would go for any little thing, including headaches and other common ailments (why they would want to wait for hours to get a headache treated was never addressed). This problem, which is a function of illegals using services, was "evident" through people's lived experiences:

You may come up from Mexico and you may earn minimum wage, you may pay some payroll tax, even some sales tax, probably no income tax. Um, and by and large these people were not so much on welfare where you actually go down and get checks for you not working. But what they were getting was access to public parks, public schools, medical care, and those costs were relatively high. It is still the case. My wife had some kind of stomach upset this past week. Still don't know what it is, but had to take her down to the emergency at [name of the hospital], which is a private hospital. If it was a county hospital it would be even worse. As it was, we had to wait two hours to get in. But what I noticed was that out of maybe fifty, sixty people waiting, there were three or four Caucasians, and the rest were all Hispanic and a couple of Asians.

Here we see how supporters' racialized ideas of work ethic and illegality combine to allow them to "see" the problems the measure is supposed to address by denying services to the undocumented.

One supporter went further by stating that "illegals" would decide *which* hospital in California to go to based on what free services the hospital offered. He reported his son "seeing illegals" (read: Latinos) at a private hospital, which they would birth at because it was well known in the "Mexican community" that the hospital provided champagne and a steak dinner for each new father. There is a clearly developed feeling that Mexicans have a sophisticated network, which is tuned into finding out about various services and how best to take advantage of the system. A woman reported reading a newspaper story in which "a Latino lady about eighty-five years old [arrived on an airplane in] San Francisco. All she had in her hand was a piece of paper, 'Natividad Hospital.' So they finally got her down here to the hospital.... They checked her out.... They found her a retirement home. Well, sure, there were people waiting in line to get a spot in the retirement home. But her people were very astute, and they figured it all out.... So they sent a dear old lady with the paper and they got help." And those who do take advantage of the system in fact brag about it both to Americans and to others. One respondent retold a friend's story of the man lying next to him in the hospital, who said that he came to the United States to get his heart worked on because it was free. Another respondent said that Proposition 187 would have prevented people from coming here to get services and "then go home and say, 'Oh, I took advantage of those Americans.'" These stories come firsthand, secondhand from relatives, passed through a long train of friends, and even interpreted from snippets in the newspaper. Respondents use these stories, from the serious to the frivolous, from heart surgeries to steak dinners, to show that Mexicans communicate about how to get all they can from the system.

Respondents believe that Latinos are out to use America and Americans, and not just through government services. It is reported that Latino immigrants want to do as little as possible to get as much as possible. One interviewee had helped an employee by giving and transporting an old washer-dryer set to the employee's mother:

> Generally when you do something like that, you're not expecting any kind of lavish thank-yous, just some recognition. But it was never spoken, never any acknowledgment that we had done anything! It was just take. And that sort of characterized the attitude of the people who come from especially

Mexico. We were always having to be a go-between with them and the law, saying this is what you have to do here, this is the law. But you could tell by the kind of things they were doing that they were trying to get whatever they could from the government. And it always really bothered me that they just don't seem to care about this country! And so that's my story.

While Mexicans hold the central role of takers in the many personal experiences or secondhand experiences reported, occasionally other racial or ethnic groups will be portrayed as takers as well. Sometimes this is done consciously to illustrate that despite the stories and the language used to describe the problem migrants, it is not *all* Latinos. Maria gave an example of a European au pair who had a baby here and wanted to stay and be taken care of by her host family: "So you see, there's a lot of that. It's not just the Latin American people. The Russians are the worst. Uh, they know all the tricks." Maria's husband laughed uncomfortably and said, "Oh, we're going to bring the Russians in, okay."

Other racial or ethnic groups have appeared in the role as taker when the local racial terrain is a significant factor in the construction of the racial realism of the supporter. Where Sue lives, Ukrainians and Russians have formed a community. She reported that the Ukrainians come over here and get on assistance right away. She contrasts this with her hardworking immigrant great-grandparents. For one interviewee, it appears that 9/11 altered the social and racial terrain significantly enough to alter his understanding of what it means to take advantage of the system: "You can't stop all the immigration, and yet we've found we have many, not from the Latino countries but from Saudi Arabia and Iran and these places, in here really taking advantage of this country. They get their schooling. We have all kind of people who come here from those countries and get their schooling, and then some go home and some don't and then some stay here, and they've got these fanatic ideas and that's where we have our trouble."

The problem immigrant, the one who takes from the system, was the central target for Proposition 187. Through a conflation of the undocumented and the Mexican, supporters understood the proposition as targeting the appropriate population. The measure was about a raced notion of economic citizenship, not a cost-benefit calculation or a concern over legal status per se. When presented with a counterargument about the economic contribution of the undocumented, Sue stated, "If they have a job, then they are not part of the problem." When asked about the possible increases in infectious diseases that might have resulted from the denial of health care, Sue responded, "Then let's not let them in. We need to send them back. If they can't support themselves, they should be returned, because it's not up to the government to pay health care.... If they can't get health care, they need to go back to their country of origin." Notions of independence and individual responsibility are central to Sue's responses to a range of counterarguments. Policy arguments about a cost-benefit analysis are less important to her support for Proposition 187 than notions of a strong work ethic. However, the desire to correct the system to support this sort of work ethic is informed by racialized depictions of Mexicans as takers.

Diligent and Dependent

The racialized category of Mexican contains multiple and sometimes competing characterizations; each, however, appeared in the campaign to distance this racialized group from obtaining economic citizenship. Mexicanness, in addition to tending toward abuse of the system, is also understood as lacking a strong individualism. Mexicans were understood both as failing to work and living off the government and as hardworking. Even as workers, though, Mexicans lack an independence and motivation for betterment that is crucial to the white American work ethic. This depiction has roots in the time after America took control of the Southwest, when the new white landowners saw the need to distinguish between themselves and the Mexican workers who were still present. Delgado and Stefancic (1992) write: "Anglos living and settling in the new regions were portrayed as Protestant, independent, thrifty, industrious, and interested in progress; Mexicans, as traditional, sedate, lacking in mechanical resourcefulness and ambition" (175). This image is used today to illustrate how Mexicans are unable to succeed economically in America.

Supporters use this image to suggest that the measure was in fact a protective device to stop the exploitation of workers. Because Mexicans and especially the undocumented lack autonomy and strength of independence, when they do work here, they are treated poorly. They are exploited and cannot flourish in this society because of racial incompatibility or employers' racialized perceptions of Mexican employees. The measure, by drawing firmer lines around economic citizenship and making life more difficult for these dependent, exploitable hard workers, is understood as a way to discourage these workers from being here. Supporters argue that it is in the interests of these workers to deny them services.[4]

The racialization of Mexicans as hard workers emerges from the interviews. Sometimes this characterization is noted as an exception or as applying to distinct groups of Mexicans, and sometimes it is expressed as characterizing the whole race. Eleven respondents had positive stories regarding hardworking Mexicans. Frequently the same respondents who characterized Mexicans as takers also described them as hardworking. Sue is an example of a respondent who demonstrates how individuals can hold both visions of Mexican workers, as takers and as diligent workers. For Sue, however, Mexicans, even as diligent workers, become a permanent entry-level worker, or permanently childlike.

Another respondent also suggested that Mexicans are stand-ins for young American workers. Scott, a retired worker, said that whereas current immigrants come here without skills and some therefore expect to be taken care of, others, also without skills, will work: "Well, at the same time there are many of them that are doing jobs that—I don't know what the young white people do anymore around here. I don't care where you go, you're lucky to find two or three working at this place or that place. It's all immigrants that are doing all of them, the fast food places, the yard work, the brick work, repairs on homes, uh, they've taken. I mean, they'll do anything to make money." Three other respondents used the image of the hardworking Mexican to decry the lack of a work ethic among young (white) Americans today.

Each of these stories suggests that Americans will not work these jobs because they are low paying and do not provide benefits or opportunity for advancement. Mexican workers are willing to accept conditions and dominance that American workers will not. This description is sometimes used by defendants of more liberal immigration policies. However, these respondents understand this as a reason for excluding Mexicans from American citizenship, both economic and legal.

As hard workers, Mexicans still fail to meet norms associated with the white work ethic: Mexicanness is associated with docility and peonage. This association troubled politicians when discussing Mexicans' fitness for citizenship in the 1920s. The historian Mark Reisler notes: "To Americans, who defined Mexicans by and identified them with the work they did, the servile peon was antithetical to the rugged, self-reliant yeoman who had made their nation prosperous and progressive. The peon could be directed and used to perform the lowest class of labor, but he was incapable of carrying on independent projects in pursuit of progress" (quoted in Sheridan 2002, 15). Sheridan reports that at the time, people understood "the 'full purport' of maintaining 'American standards' was that achieving economic independence meant not being beholden to any man. This was necessary to attain autonomy in political life and to be truly equal citizens."

Using similar understandings of economic citizenship, respondents suggest that denial of services makes sense even if we understand Mexicans as hard workers. Supporters understand the initiative as protecting workers who would inevitably be exploited by employers if they came to the United States. When justifying their support of this punitive measure against hard-working people, supporters frequently said that it was for the good of the undocumented; by targeting social services for the undocumented, Proposition 187 would reduce the number of illegals and therefore also their exploitation. Donald, a libertarian from northern California, suggested that this was the flip side of his concern over people taking advantage of the system: "That's the other way I was looking at it: the same people were getting exploited who we were supposed to be helping! They were working long hours, doing backbreaking work; they weren't legally getting any retirement or social security. The whole thing, it doesn't make sense that people would support that. Especially people who care and say they have to have social services, but then they're just keeping them doing this shit work for low wages. It's just so contradictory."

Bob suggested that his primary concern was the exploitation of illegal immigrants. He suggested that if people understood the issue more clearly, then the sides would in fact have been reversed. If the connections between the well-being of immigrants and the measure were understood, those who supported the measure might not have, and those who thought they wanted to help immigrants would have switched from opposition to support. "If you are one of those bandidos and you come here, so where does that leave you. You're a second-class citizen, I mean you are not a citizen, period. You have certain rights, and yeah, we're fighting over some benefits. First thing you got to do is get a fake social security number. What does that entitle you to do? It entitles you to pay taxes—that you can never collect. The IRS collects money from you, the social security people collect money from you. It entitles you to pay taxes and to work. You can't ask for citizenship exactly, but you can ask for a social security number." This, he suggests, turns them into a "slave class." People who want to help immigrants should not be "for keeping the collection plate going or the collection rou-tine going because they're being taken advantage of. It's simple. You're pay-ing and you don't have any right to collect." It was his sympathy for the un-documented, dominated Mexican that caused Bob to support the measure.

Bob and other respondents employed this bridging strategy that con-nected the raced, dependent worker with the unraced notion of economic citizenship while simultaneously using the strategy of connecting Mexi-canness with being a "taker." Sometimes respondents suggested there were two different populations that crossed the border: hardworking Mexicans and takers. For these respondents, the proposition to deny social services could be seen as beneficial for both populations. The unfairness of the sit-uation for the hardworking Mexicans was a function of businesses exploit-ing racial differences. Through this secondary racialization bridge, the measure could be understood not as an enactment of racism but as a salve to racial injustice.

Magnets and Mexicans

The last central bridging strategy, the association bridge between the racial-ized campaign over dependence and color-blind understandings of fair-ness to taxpayers, revolves around services as magnets. People without the appropriate work ethic are attracted by services and will come here with-out documentation. The illegal, problem immigrants were precisely those who were attracted by the services; therefore the fact that the undocu-mented are understood as Mexicans is taken as evidence that Mexicans lack the ability to be full economic citizens. Mexicanness becomes associ-ated with a lack of independence central to the white work ethic through the conflation of "the Mexican" with those attracted by services.

The explicit intent of the measure was not just to save the state and the American taxpayers money but to stop illegal immigration. The arguments supporting Proposition 187 in a voters' pamphlet discuss the financial strain but also suggest that providing services is causing "social bankruptcy." The undocumented are not just receiving services but getting the "royal treat-ment," and these benefits are the "magnets that draw these ILLEGAL ALIENS across our borders" (*California Voter Information* 1994, 54). Further argu-ments for the measure in the pamphlet draw the distinction between Ameri-cans using government services and illegal aliens. The needy American citizens are described as the "aged and the mentally impaired," and those worthy poor go without services because of the illegal immigrants (55).

Repeatedly billed as an attempt to end the "tidal wave" or "flood" (or any other catastrophic water metaphor) of immigration, Proposition 187 did not directly address the entry of people into the state but dealt only with the presence of the undocumented by assuming that services were the reason for their residence in the United States. The suggestion was that if services were cut off, people would cease to cross the border. Respondents remembered the main purpose of the initiative as being to "hold down the population," "curb illegal immigration," "prevent the inflow of illegal aliens," "reduce the number of immigrants," and "discourage people—illegal immigrants—from coming to California." Every respondent talked about the measure as a way to alter the number of illegal immigrants residing within the border.

Benefits and social services were understood as reasons for migration. One respondent, explaining some of his ambivalence about the harshness of the measure, said: "The social services, the welfare and so on, again, you didn't want to cut it off, but . . . if that's what's drawing people, that's what's pushing them out of Mexico." Others suggested that families are more motivated by services, drawing a distinction between the old image of the single worker immigrant and the new reproductive immigrant family.[5] Providing services is a magnet that draws the undocumented to California, according to supporters: "But these people come over the border and receive all this help just by showing up! Hispanics—let's say illegals, don't necessarily have to be Hispanic—can receive free medical care at this clinic up the road. And what that's saying is, 'Come on up! Bring your relatives!'"

Ed explained that free services only attracted a certain type of immigrant: "I've just resented so much of what we've done, that we single out some people and in fact we've held them back and we've attracted them. They come here seeking benefits rather than opportunities. Not everybody—there are a whole bunch [who are] hardworking, save their money, and work their way to the top." From a wide range of examples given, Ed showed that the hardworking ones include legal *and* illegal Asian, Russian, and African immigrants. Immigrants from Mexico ("Mexico, that's a metaphor for anything south of the border") appear as the culprits who are attracted by services. The system, in fact, is being blamed for attracting people who have tendencies toward dependence (i.e., Mexicans) and in doing so further accentuates that characteristic in Mexicans, to their detriment. The offering of services not only attracts Mexicans but also prevents them from being forced to find other ways of supporting themselves. The ease of access brings out the dependent tendencies in Mexicans, according to this schema.

The centrality of services as a magnet suggests that reading the measure as a cost-benefit calculation misses much of what Proposition 187 was really about. Supporters were concerned with separating those who did not belong here from those who did. And those who did not belong were those who were attracted by social services. Free services alter the behavior of people only if they fail to have the appropriate work ethic. Those who do not have such a work ethic were being *defined* as illegals, and as Mexicans. As opposed to the previous strategy where Mexicanness is initially noted as lacking the work ethic, here the connections between Mexicanness and dependency arise as a result of the conflation of the undocumented and Mexicans. For supporters, it is evident that Mexicans lack the appropriate work ethic, since they are attracted to illegally cross the border by the promise of services.

However, it is through the mechanism of a magnet that supporters reconnect their racialized notions of work ethic and illegality with their color-blind concerns over the taxpaying citizen. The question-and-answer sheet put out by the Save Our State initiative denied immigrant bashing by focusing on a distinction between persons based on economic responsibility. The document states: "Illegal aliens are not immigrants." Immigrants are those who come here legally, "assuming responsibility for themselves and their families." The mechanism for distinguishing Americans from others based on work ethic, however, is filtered through the intervening variable of race. Arguments for the initiative based on work ethic, and even the proposition itself, could not be understood if one considered legal status alone; the concern over a magnetic lure of services did not rely on citizenship per se but relied on an intervening variable of race.

Conclusion

Racial realism informed "color-blind" arguments about a cost-benefit calculation to construct this measure. Such a reading highlights *how* arguments about jobs and services impacted individuals' support of the measure. The measure defined the category of economic citizen by excluding Mexicans from the white work ethic in a variety of ways that generated fairness to taxpayers and to Mexican workers. The measure was about the social capital of belonging, citizenship, and services. The very real impacts of this can be seen in events that occurred despite the court injunction.

After the initiative passed, some local charities in Orange County began seeing donors specify that their donations go to legal residents only. Since some of the organizations refused to ask about legal status but still wanted to accommodate these donors, workers at these charities "had to find someone white and English-speaking, a Bob Cratchit family, because that was [the donor's] comfort zone" (Berkman 1994). Both donors and workers, who might personally disagree with donors' requests, clearly understood the implications of enforcing such requests. A donor's request that whoever received the gift not be an illegal alien meant that a worker had to give the donation to a white family. This illustrates that "illegal alien" was not a covert code word. The actions display the intersubjective reality constructed by the racialized struggle at the time. Others also made specific requests that their donations help English-speaking or non-Latino families. One group who was adopting a family for Christmas declined a family with a Latino surname (Berkman 1994).

Two years after the passage of Proposition 187, the federal government limited legal immigrants' access to services through the Personal Responsibility and Work Opportunity Reconciliation Act. This act prevented noncitizens from receiving most federal means-tested assistance. Proponents, opponents, and scholars attribute the inclusion of this denial of services to immigrants to the impact of Proposition 187. Notions of economic citizenship, not tied to documentation status, created during the struggle over Proposition 187 helped lead to this national policy shift.

The 1996 welfare reform act, however, did not lead to a decline in the use of services by immigrants relative to natives in most places in the country. This was because "both state governments and the immigrants themselves responded to the new political landscape by altering their behavior" (Borjas 2002). There was an increase in the rates of naturalization, and many states provided services to those who were cut off by the new federal rules. California also provided many services to those who were to be excluded under national guidelines. However, California is the one state that experienced a precipitous decline in the rates of immigrant use of services.[6] Steve Camarota (2002) of the Center for Immigration Studies reports: "California is one of the most generous states in offering benefits to otherwise ineligible immigrants. Thus there appears to be no measurable factors that can explain the significant drop in immigrant welfare participation in California. The California experience may indeed reflect a 'chilling' effect—but the chilling seems to be related to the passing of Proposition

187 in 1994 rather than welfare reform." Almost 60 percent of the electorate voted in favor of Proposition 187, generating a new definition of economic citizenship in California and radically altering the lives of many migrants in the state.

Seeing the struggle over defining citizenship and belonging through the lens of a white work ethic explains why the measure was so contentious, mobilized so many, and left such a lasting legacy. The capital at stake was very important, including, but not limited to, the distribution of services. This struggle was about the range of resources that come with inclusion in the community. This is evidenced in the other schemas central to the struggle over Proposition 187. The struggle was about defining not only economic citizenship but also cultural and political citizenship, the focus of the next two chapters.

CHAPTER FIVE

Assimilation and Civilization:
Language, Trash, and Power

And we just resented the fact that, hey, we don't want to be taken over by somebody who doesn't share our values. You know they came over here, we didn't invite, they came over here on their own free volition, they weren't forced to come here. Okay.

—Jack, respondent

American citizenship helps to form American culture; it is not just a by-product of a preexisting or somehow more fundamental culture.
—Charles R. Kesler, "The Promise of American Citizenship"

Whites can be most secure in their Americanization: it appears to be the least contingent and the least apt to fluctuate in value and social meaning.

—Juan F. Perea, *Immigrants Out!*

Immigration policy has long been understood as a central means to engineer a desirable culture.[1] In the United States, immigration debates have raged over the impact immigrants were having on American culture. Were immigrants assimilating? What was the best way to encourage Americanization? Can a society function with multiple cultures? In the battle over Proposition 187, arguments about culture played a key role in the minds of proponents. While the most public propaganda and the highest level politicians avoided addressing cultural arguments head-on, low- and midlevel activists as well as more informal propaganda used arguments about culture as a basis for supporting a measure that denied social services to the

undocumented. These arguments mirrored the "English Only" movements in the late 1980s and early 1990s. According to proponents, concerns
about assimilation were color-blind; the particulars of the immigrant group
were not the focus. Rather, it was the acceptance of American values and
language that mattered. Proponents understood their version of American
culture as race neutral. Some went further in defending their color-blind
credentials and argued that assimilation to *any* culture was what mattered.
For society to function, proponents argued, there needs to be a single culture, but the content of that culture was not important to them. However,
when one looks at the connections between cultural concerns and people's
support for this particular measure, one finds that these concerns are not
race neutral but in fact rely on racial realist schemas about Mexicanness and
cultural invasion. Mexican immigrants bring with them uncivilized ways
that are dangerous not simply because they are different, according to proponents, but because of their content. The cultural traditions of Mexicans
and Americans are at war with one another. To coexist or merge is not an
option, as to do so would mean the destruction of the power of white American culture. This racial realist fear that American culture is losing the battle
was connected to race-neutral ideas about the importance of linguistic,
moral, and cultural homogeneity to maintaining a functioning democracy.

Proposition 187 was a struggle for cultural citizenship, which has implications for struggles over jobs, political power, and formal citizenship as well.
The lines of the battle were about who could legitimately determine the
culture of the country. This involved defining Mexicans as being outside
American culture. Supporters were mobilized to act as they connected color-
blind notions of assimilation to raced conceptions of Mexican culture.

After exploring how the struggle over cultural citizenship in Proposition
187 was grounded in color-blind conceptions of assimilation and racial realist notions of cultural invasion, I explore the three central bridging strategies that connect these mirror schemas. The first two strategies characterize
Mexican culture as uncivilized and American values as unraced. In each,
the cultural power of the problematic population prevents respondents
from being able to live in a "civilized" color-blind society. In the racialization bridge ("color-blind society"), Mexicans are initially raced as backward,
and the conflation of Mexicanness and undocumented migration provides
reasons for supporting the measure. In the association bridge ("allegiance
and documentation"), the undocumented are seen as unable to assimilate,
and since Mexicans are associated with the undocumented, Mexicanness

becomes permanently foreign. For both, support of Proposition 187 is understood as a way to define the culture of the community, and supporters believe they are creating a raceless culture. In the third strategy, "intent on invasion," supporters suggest that there is a set of race-conscious individuals determined to wipe out white American culture. In this defense bridge, the undocumented are a tool in the cultural battle initiated by others. Despite respondents' desire not to act with race consciousness, they are forced to act defensively to prevent cultural takeover. Finally, I turn to the ways that racial realism and concerns over invasion have come to the fore in the nativist movement in the aftermath of Proposition 187. The first bridge that proponents construct is difficult to maintain in the face of the state response to the measure. The court injunction and the failure of the measure to be implemented are understood as evidence of invaders' success. The second and third bridges become the most politically relevant. Self-defense or not, the cultural war is on, and concerns about a color-blind society become less important. In the interviews conducted following the attacks on September 11, the connections between culture and loyalty become intensified, and cultural citizenship becomes a national security issue.

Assimilation as a Race-Neutral Proposition

According to proponents, the undocumented in California are problematic because they have not assimilated. This leads to practical problems, from functioning on a daily basis on the streets and in the market to maintaining a viable democracy. Proponents suggested that a society needs to share a culture to get along. Examples ranged from little cultural rules such as walking single file when approaching others on the sidewalk and not cutting in line at the grocery store, to aesthetic preferences that may affect neighborhood appearance, to the mother of all cultural rules, language. A single, shared culture is important for people to get along in society, to prevent economic, political and social balkanization. In making these claims, respondents suggested that culture generally is changeable and contingent. Respondents relied on pragmatism and individualism to make this claim. This notion of assimilation was therefore embedded in the color-blind conservative meta-schema, as values of individualism and equality were universalized and any other cultural markers, especially those with a racial connotation, were viewed as constructed and therefore malleable and of little relevance.

Sharing a similar culture is key to a functioning democracy, according to proponents. This includes both language and values. Self-governance becomes difficult without a shared linguistic tongue and a moral language, according to one respondent: "Yeah, and I don't think that leads to healthy functioning of democracy. I think that a common language is a critical function to have a healthy, free society. How can people vote on issues when they don't even understand what the candidates are saying? To me that's nonsense, and I don't care what anybody says." Here we see the proponent of the measure preempting those who disagree by a reliance on common sense, a tool used to naturalize the culture and language of choice.

Philip, a conservation scientist, emphasized that his concerns over culture are not about American values but

> just about *a* consistent set of values. I don't think American values are any
> better, but they're my values. There was a big tempest in San Francisco over
> the fact that Chinese people were selling live animals on the street for food,
> including some cuddly things. And people got really angry and, um, there
> was a lot of back and forth about the rights of the Chinese community, and
> I thought we shouldn't even be having this argument. In the American set
> of values, it isn't acceptable to sell live animals on the street for food. It
> doesn't matter that that's a completely arbitrary cultural value. It makes
> people feel nauseated. And if the Chinese want to come here, they're going
> to have to adapt to that. And I don't like the idea that there would ever be
> enough Chinese to outvote me on that, either. To me that's just being prag-
> matic. I was raised here. If I was raised in France, I'd support French values,
> probably.

Philip believed that his insistence on American values is simply a pragmatic stance. He took for granted, however, that there is a consistent set of values that we can call "American" and suggested the propagation of those values so that "we" can get along. Those wanting to enter into the "we" have the obligation to adopt those values. He also expressed a fear that if those entering don't do that, the "we" may be overrun. Values and culture here were understood as constructed and therefore changeable. Pragmatism, however, the guiding value behind his claim, was understood as a universal goal, not a culturally specific American value.

When respondents raised these concerns, they often asserted their color-blind credentials in the same breath:

> In my unsophisticated opinion, I don't think that free societies function
> very well when they have groups of unintegrated cultures. I guess I'm not
> a multiculturalist anymore. I don't think—I developed this feeling when
> I was on a school board, because even in my little community, which was
> mostly white, there were some issues where people just couldn't agree what

day of the week it was! 'Cause they came from just completely different value constellations. And I guess I've come to the surmisal that when you have low rates of immigration, people integrate into the culture. And by the way, I'm the child of an immigrant.

Here we see the respondent assert that cultural differences are problematic to democracy. For this respondent, cultural heterogeneity caused the problem, not any particular culture, and he therefore understood his complaint as a race-neutral concern. He emphasized that he came to these antimulticultural stances from experiences in a white-dominated political setting. To stress further that he was not coming from a racial or nativist standpoint, he added his credentials as a child of immigrants at the end.

An immigrant from Poland used his own history as a contrast. Milton connected cultural assimilation with citizenship. He argued that he was not evaluating one culture as better than another. He stressed the voluntary nature of a person's decision to migrate:

Nobody forced the Koreans or the Mexicans to come here. They decided, "I want to go to the United States because it will give me a better life." That's why I came, and I feel once you make the decision, you kind of say, "Yeah, I lived over there and I still have a sentimental attachment to it. On the other hand, I made a decision to come to this country." That means I've got to, number one, speak the language. Number two, pick up their habits. And be a good citizen.

According to Milton, cultural citizenship is an obligation when a person chooses to live in another country. Again, the cultural content is depicted as being beside the point. And here values of individualism and free choice, central to the color-blind conservative schema, come to the fore as culture becomes a choice that individuals make. Other respondents echoed this color-blind conservative theme, arguing that in choosing to leave their countries of origin, immigrants made the commitment to assimilate.

Other proponents also suggested that they were not concerned with maintaining American values per se but simply wanted a unified culture. In the abstract, culture clash causes problems: "Oh, more cultures come, where they meet is where you get the problems. Okay. You don't have a problem if in [the] middle of nowhere in a big population you take two, three percent of somebody else. That's not going to be a problem, generally. Well, they'll absorb, and everybody looks after the people next door. You don't have a problem. It's where a large, two large segments come together, where those borders happen is where you get [problems]." Cultures, like races, are social constructions whose only power comes from what we attribute to them as individuals; culture is malleable, and people can pick and choose cultures freely. Assimilation is a matter of individual choice to embrace a new society. Respondents used values of individualism and pragmatism as universal values to stress how assimilation is a color-blind concern.

Civilization and Culture

Respondents, however, held conflicting views on culture and assimilation. While they were concerned with homogeneity in the cultural abstract, they also portrayed Mexican culture as being a particular threat because of its perceived power and because of its failure to have the appropriate values of individualism and pragmatism. Supporters were concerned about the introduction and possible takeover of Mexican culture, which they understood as especially problematic and offensive. Supporters, by drawing on notions of Mexicans as backward and uncivilized, portrayed the struggle as being between Mexican culture and unraced humanity, not between Mexican culture and American culture.

Contemporary manifestations of racializing Mexicans as backward or uncivilized are evident in the other schemas explored thus far, as well as in further connections drawn by respondents between dirtiness and Mexicans. Proponents expressed these racialized notions of culture and civilization as realistic assessments based on their experience in the world around them. While color-blind notions of assimilation rested on a combination of philosophical arguments, common sense, and evidence, personal narratives and news stories played the largest role when respondents were constructing their raced notions of culture, thus reemphasizing the distinction between an idealism of color-blind assimilation and a realism of raced cultures.

Mexicanness becomes raced as backward in part through the lack of a strong work ethic and strong sense of individuality, as explored in chapter 4. This connection between individualism and civilization emerged when respondents discussed the crowded living conditions of the problem immigrants. The notion of collective or more communal living arrangements is associated with an earlier stage of civilization, with tribes or bands of people as opposed to the modern differentiated human. Respondents contrasted Mexicans' tendency to live communally in apartments with Americans' desire to own a home. Living situations with multiple families in one abode provide additional evidence of a culture lacking a normatively positive notion of individualism.

Crowded living conditions, understood as a cultural phenomenon attached to Mexicans, are also evidence of the danger of Mexicanness through crime and disease, again evidence of an uncivilized culture. Such living conditions, even if a function of being poor, suggest to one respondent that "there are just more problems, violence, drugs, people not going to school, and on and on," and he believed that "there were studies to prove it." The criminalization of Mexican immigrants is central to their exclusion from cultural citizenship as well. As we saw in chapter 3, proponents suggest that the politics of Mexico are uncivilized because of corruption and their inability to take care of their people, and this is then transposed onto the individuals; corruption and underground dealings, proponents suggested, are a part of Mexican culture. The perceived choice of housing conditions was associated with Mexican danger through disease as well. "There's another thing, you'll see a small house, maybe three small bedrooms and one bathroom with maybe twenty people living in it, and apartments with five families living in 'em. There are about 200,000 illegal garage dwellings in Los Angeles County where maybe ten men are housed. Um, this, we have TB in this state, in this country. When I was a kid, TB was wiped out."

Lack of hand washing and general cleanliness, attributed to Mexicanness, was also noted as giving rise to an increase in diseases. The interview with the activist core illustrates how they depict Mexicans as failing to have a civilized culture:

FRAN: They bring [disease] in and nobody stops them.

KATHY: They work in our restaurants.

BERNIE: That's right.

KATHY: What's that disease? Hepatitis C. They don't use our sanitary methods. They don't wash their hands.

Disease was associated with the uncivilized practices of the Mexican migrant that threaten the host country. The activists continued by associating lack of cleanliness with violence through a notion of being uncivilized as they described scenes of people crossing the border:

JILL: I just heard reports from people in Arizona who said that the people running across have trashed the trails with dirty diapers, they just leave wherever they drop them.

KATHY: Slicing their watchdogs' throats.

JILL: Slicing the throats of their cattle . . . cutting their water lines.

FRAN: What we are talking about is an invasion of barbarians.

BERNIE: You're right.

FRAN: Literally barbarians.

When describing border crossings, at least three other respondents raised the issue of trash being left along the way. Others also noted the uncivilized nature of Mexicanness by pointing to the literal garbage they bring. Trash was understood as a condition south of the border and a part of the culture of the problem immigrant. Here, Jack connected failure to learn the language with the bringing in of a trash culture:

> We used to laugh and say it appears that Hispanics don't feel comfortable unless there's lots of trash in the street, 'cause I'd have to go every morning and sweep the street in front of my shop, because people would park there and not bother to use trash cans. I'd pick up their trash, including their cigarettes, and go over to them and say, "Oh, you dropped this." Many times, unless you were talking to the boss, who always drove the car, they didn't speak English, but they would get the picture. What it does is it demonstrates an attitude. Here they are, for the most part they've been accepted by this country. And in this country we try to keep our streets clean! I don't know if you've ever been south of the border? We were downtown in Mexico, we saw the *real* Mexico, trash and everything. I guess that's one reason why Hispanics don't really notice trash here. But you'd think that they would recognize we are a fairly civilized country here. A country that takes care of its poor people, its disadvantaged people, like they are.

For this respondent, Latino culture's perceived propensity toward garbage is evidence of the uncivilized nature of the invading culture. Mexicans are not civilized because the country they come from is uncivilized, not only in its perceived lack of sanitation but in the way it fails to take care of people. (Jack does not recognize the irony that, in fact, his support of Proposition 187 attempts to alter precisely the characteristic that he says indicates a civilized country—taking care of those in need.)

Respondents portrayed American culture as being raceless while simultaneously racing the invading culture. The level of government support in the United States was understood as a neutral benchmark for being civilized. Additionally, respondents pointed to a general rudeness in immigrants that precludes them from cultural inclusion. Respondents pointed to cutting in line and failures to abide by pedestrian rules or norms of greeting. Rudeness was understood not as a failure to abide by specific cultural rules but as an inherent failing in the individuals, an uncivilized nature. Here we see an equation of white American culture with civilization. Those who fail to follow the rules, Mexicans as a race, are not failing to assimilate but failing humanity.

While a race-neutral concern over assimilation focuses on the ability of society to function and get along, a racialized fear of Mexican culture is a fear of invasion. The racial realism undergirding the depiction of Mexicanness connects culture with allegiance. The politics of language central to the cultural struggle are about preventing overthrow of the current political order. We need a common language not only to function smoothly but to prevent sedition: "You know, my wife comes from Hungary, and she thought it was funny that there's American flags all around and we're waving it all the time. They don't do that in Hungary. A lot of that probably is for cohesion. The Pledge of Allegiance, she thought it was funny to have before every game, you know, but maybe you need that because you don't want pockets to pop up that they want to secede or rebel or be totally isolated, you want people to come here and learn the language, read the Constitution." Learning the language and the political culture is essential to maintaining the political order.

For supporters of Proposition 187, immigrants' failure to assimilate indicates a lack of allegiance to the host country. A midlevel female activist connected Mexicans' lack of assimilation with Mexico's failure to provide troops for American campaigns after September 11. "They don't want to assimilate, they don't want to learn our language, they don't want to become citizens because they don't want to fight for this country; they've already made that statement." Loyalty was connected specifically with learning English. Another respondent worried about pride in Mexican culture and political allegiance in times of war: "I think that's a very simple question: whose side are they going to fight on during the next war? That's it. Mexico or America. The rest is BS. You can fill pages of newspapers. That's the basic bottom line, and that's what we're talking about. Are these people going to— where are their hearts, in Mexico? 'Oh, we're proud Mexicans.' Okay, if you are proud Mexicans, go back to bloody Mexico." Central to the racial realist understanding of assimilation was a connection between the culture and allegiance.

These concerns about cultural invasion are the sister schema to the race-neutral concerns about homogeneity and democracy discussed in the previous section. In the color-blind conservative schema, culture is unraced, highly contingent and flexible, and about individual choice. The focus is on the culture of the receiving country. The racial realist schema races Mexican culture while deracing American culture. American culture, in fact, is unmarked, as the focus is on immigrants' culture. Here culture appears less malleable and inherent to groups of people. These competing concerns over an invasive, uncivilized Mexican culture and a color-blind, culturally homogeneous society work together. Proposition 187 served as a bridge between these competing conceptions of culture in three ways that mirror the bridges constructed between the metaschemas of racial realism and color-blind conservatism.

To Achieve a Color-Blind Society

The first strategy that respondents used to combine concerns over the uncivilized nature of an invading population and color-blind notions of assimilation begins with the racing of Mexicans as uncivilized. Since respondents identified the undocumented population as Mexican, they used Proposition 187 to deny the uncivilized population cultural citizenship. Once these problematic populations are excluded, a color-blind society can function. Through naturalizing American culture and values as civilized, proponents were able to see their racialization of Mexicanness and the attendant desire to exclude as a step toward a culturally homogeneous, smoothly functioning society.

Language was used as a central source of evidence of the inability of uncivilized Mexicans to assimilate. Initially, a connection was drawn between "foreign" languages and the culture of trash. Charles reports: "You drive down Broadway in Los Angeles, which used to be the most beautiful street in the city—it is a mess. Even on Sunday mornings it is a mess . . . and everybody trying to sell things. Everybody jabbering in some language you don't understand. You know. When you hear that expression 'third world country,' that's what Los Angeles has become." A particular characterization of the invading culture emerged in Charles's description of downtown Los Angeles. "Mess" and informal commerce are two of the characterizations of the transformations of American culture that appeared in others' narratives of support for Proposition 187. Mexicans are bringing an undesirable, unassimilable third world culture. Since the undocumented were raced as Mexican, the undocumented were understood as being racially uncivilized and unable to assimilate.

Mexicans, and therefore the undocumented, are unique in their inability to assimilate, as evidenced by schoolchildren and language. Sam, a low-level activist who donated money and engaged in fax activism (the campaign took place before an expansive Internet), connected Mexicanness, assimilation, and documentation by grounding intelligence in race. Sam, like other respondents, had also supported United We Stand and Ross Perot. He was also a fan of the book *The Bell Curve*, which posits a racial difference in IQ scores. Mexicans, according to Sam, fail to assimilate and learn the language because of a lack of intelligence:

> I could be wrong, but I think that the thing [Proposition 187] was completely undone by the federal judges in Texas who decided that the children of illegal aliens were entitled to an education. I'm very much of the opinion that the only thing you're entitled to is to be deported. Now, I would be perfectly willing to educate Chinese children, Japanese children, and Philippine children. But I see no point in educating Mexican children when they are incapable of learning. I mean, California had absolutely wonderful schools—in fact, the best schools in the country, if not the best schools in the world—when I came here in 1956. And now because of the high concentration of stupid aliens, the average percentile on standardized tests in Los Angeles County is 26 percent in mathematics and 31 percent in English. . . . It's just utterly collapsed.

Later in the interview, Sam continued to contrast Mexican immigrants with Chinese immigrants. He suggested that the Chinese have done very well despite the "language difficulties" and discrimination. This was evidence that if Mexicans fail to learn English and do well on SATs and incorporate themselves into American life, it is a function of being Mexican. Documentation status, Mexicanness, and inability to learn the language were connected through a racialized notion of intelligence.

Even for respondents who do not put intelligence at the fore, Mexicans were still understood as being the problem immigrant group that does not learn the language and therefore does not become incorporated into society. One respondent used his grandson's school, which has "quite a mix" of students, as evidence of the particular problems Mexicans pose. This school has students from India, Japan, Korea, and Pakistan. He reports: "And those immigrants really get into it. They speak it, they learn it, they're good at math, they go to—they get a large turnout at the school for programs and things. This school where he goes, there's about 1,500 children in that school. . . . That's a big school. And I would say three-quarters of it is Asian. But the kids get along fine, and those kids pick up English, it's unbelievable. So they're finding that by doing that, their children are getting better scores on the SAT." Even with a large school, and a large immigrant population, the school is able to function at a high level. Immigrants are succeeding academically, kids are getting along with one another, and there is a sense of community to the school. This experience was contrasted with schools that are predominately Latino, where there is no comparable success or assimilation. According to the respondent, Latino culture hinders the assimilation process and the success of Latinos and of society to function at a high level. The respondent used this as evidence that because of Mexican immigrants, bilingual education should be stopped. Bilingual education was seen as furthering the problem for Latinos. While other immigrant populations may be able to work with a system that provides instruction in their native language and still learn the new language and achieve success and friends, for Mexicans the system needs to coerce assimilation.

Respondents viewed Proposition 187 as a tool either to coerce assimilation, to remove the unassimilable, or at least to question the cultural citizenship of problem immigrants. By focusing on the undocumented and excluding both the undocumented and their children from schools through strict monitoring, the measure would alter the ability of these immigrants to threaten the culture through their failure to assimilate to educational and linguistic norms. Mexicans (the undocumented) threaten cultural invasion, and the measure was part of a struggle to deal with that invasion.

Mexican culture, through its unassimilability, threatens to break down a single, uniform culture that is necessary for society to function. Milton suggested that it is these racial differences that cause problems for society and *prevent us from being color-blind.* He illustrated this idea by making an example of Japan:

> Remember one thing: United States is an experiment, all right? Now, nobody has the guts in this country to go back and say, hey, let's look at the other side. The opposite point of this country . . . and this area . . . is greater diversity and multiculturalism and blah blah blah. Now look at Japan. One nation, homogeneous, lives together forever, know exactly how they behave, they

don't need any lawyers, whenever there is a case, nobody stands up and says, "Racist, racist, I've been discriminated against." They're all Japanese. There is no crime, very low crime. There is very low venereal disease. Nobody sprays, no crime, no any of that stuff. Yet that is a nation 120 million people. It is the second-largest economy in this world. How did they do that? You know what, because they didn't waste their time on 70,000 lawyers who will grab at anything that basically smacks of—they will make a racial case out of something that has nothing to do with it, you know. So there is something wrong with the system.

The only way to achieve a color-blind society is through a homogeneous society. Proposition 187 was one way for proponents to attempt to create a color-blind society by declaring the nonhomogeneous, nonassimilating members to be outside the community; the measure produced a bridge between a racialized other and a color-blind society.

Allegiance and Documentation

A second way in which proponents understood the measure as an attempt to achieve a color-blind, functioning democracy revolves around an initial connection between the undocumented and Mexican culture. That is, the undocumented are particularly problematic and the least able to assimilate because they are underground and because they are the most bound by their culture. The undocumented therefore display a lack of loyalty to the United States, and their restriction is the key to stopping the cultural invasion. Since Mexicans are undocumented, according to proponents, the targeted problem immigrant becomes Mexican, and the invading force is Mexican culture.

The undocumented were understood as being uniquely unwilling to assimilate. Their lack of documentation was understood as a failure to begin the assimilation process. Becoming a citizen is the first step: "When you decide to make the move, you gotta say, okay, well, I'm going to leave where I've been, I'm going to go to this country, I'm going there for a better life, I'm going there to become part of that country. You look and see what [you] need to do. First of all, do it legally, and then decide, okay, I'm going to try to support myself. If I can't support myself, if I don't have a real good idea how to do it, then I won't go. If I want to become a citizen, a permanent part of the country, then I have to do some things that conform to the country as a whole." Lack of documentation was seen as a lack of commitment. One respondent encouraged a reporter to "write a story and find out why these people have been here for ages [and] have never bothered to become citizens. You can't have your feet planted in two different areas. You know. Do or get off the pot, as they say."

According to supporters, the undocumented are a clear example of the problem Mexican immigrant who does not want to assimilate. Problem immigrants have not accepted that they have left Mexico and want to maintain cultural and political ties with their country of origin. Documentation status was used as an indicator of a person's desire, willingness, or ability to assimilate into American society: "There are two kinds of Mexicans: there are Mexican Americans, and there are Mexicans who live here who really want to stay Mexicans. Unfortunately, it's probably pretty close to fifty-fifty. The illegals fall very heavily on the Mexicans who want to live in America for a lot of reasons but really want to stay Mexicans." These problem immigrants threaten invasion because they fail to generate allegiance to their new country. For another respondent, the undocumented are an extreme example of the way that all Mexicans, citizens or not, don't want to join: "They don't seem to want to join in being a citizen in this country. And they of course never vote. Even the ones that are citizens. They don't participate in the community, they don't contribute anything, all they do is take." Mexican undocumented immigrants, and Mexicans more generally, were perceived as not having accepted that they had left their country of origin. This lack of commitment to the United States is in tension with a vision of Mexicans wanting to take over the country. Both, however, represent a rejection of American culture, and both indicate a lack of allegiance.

Mexicans are not loyal to the United States, according to respondents, and this lack of allegiance is manifested culturally in symbols such as food and flags. Maria suggested patriotism to an immigrant's country of origin was connected with a failure to assimilate and succeed in the host country. Her daughter was recruited by fellow Latino students to work on a campaign, and her daughter refused to carry the Mexican flag: "And so this group of Mexican students were so upset, and they wanted to make a big issue about it, and she said no. She put her foot down. She said, 'The reason we are getting an education is because we are in the United States. You guys, at least you should carry an American flag, just to say thank you, instead of a Mexican.' That's the thing, you see: they have this patriotism that don't let them get away, don't let them grow. They need to accept the fact that if they left their country to look for better horizons, accept the culture that they are going into." Later in the interview, Maria wanted to draw a distinction between maintaining pride in a native culture while assimilating and becoming loyal to a new country, and failing to become a member of the country one chose to enter. Here she demonstrated a complicated connection between identity and the broader category of culture and food:

> You know, people should always be proud of the land or the people or the soil [where] you were born; that is your own ethnicity. You never should get rid of that. But you need to accept the fact that if you make a choice to go live in a foreign country, you have to absorb that culture, you have to learn that culture, and you have to excel in that culture. Learn the language; you have to learn how those people live. But you still can carry your own ethnicity; don't get rid of that, that's part of you. That's the beauty of not— being bicultural. But don't, don't, don't move to a foreign country and bring your tamales and your tortillas. You know? Because there is something else that you can try that tastes probably better. And it's okay, too.

For Maria, while one may have pride in another culture, there is a basic notion of allegiance, which is accessed through key cultural symbols including language, flags, and food.

During the struggle over Proposition 187, the Mexican flag was displayed in marches and rallies opposing the measure. Newspapers and supporters both pointed to the use of the Mexican flag as a major factor that mobilized people to vote for the measure. The use of the Mexican flag generated further resentment and served to confirm the notion that Mexican migrants resisted assimilation and were threatening invasion. The Mexican opponents of Proposition 187 were understood as its target, regardless of their documentation status; they were the people the measure was trying to define out of cultural citizenship.

The second bridging strategy shows how Proposition 187 connected a race-neutral notion of assimilation with a raced notion of invasion. Allegiance and loyalty of the populace was understood as central to having a functioning society, the color-blind concern. Undocumented Mexican immigrants, however, displayed a lack of loyalty through a lack of assimilation. Mexican culture appears to be uniquely intrinsic to the group, not an individual choice, as in other cultures. The undocumented Mexican was depicted as unwilling and unable to conform to a race-neutral American culture. Proposition 187 addressed this problem by promoting a loyal, homogeneous populace.

Intent on Invasion: The Color Consciousness of Others

The third strategy, a defense bridge, relies on the color consciousness of others to connect color-blind concerns about culture and raced notions of cultural invasion. This bridge begins with the notion that some immigrants and other minorities in society actively prevent assimilation. Immigrants and others who promote a nonassimilationist agenda are understood as promoting a color-conscious society. By naturalizing and deracializing American culture, respondents saw others who do not accede to the dominant culture not only as foreigners but also as intent on invasion or uprooting the natural order. Invasion was understood either as multicultural, which is detrimental to the functioning of a society, or as an invasion of Mexican culture at the expense of colorless American culture. This is seen clearly in the struggle over language. If English is the naturalized tongue of America, those who were understood as refusing to speak or learn the language are subversives.

Discussion of language emerged in every interview and brought some of the most passionate responses from the respondents. English was seen as essential to getting along, but more than that, English was seen as central to maintaining America. Only two respondents did not care about the debates over bilingual education and seemed nonplussed at the emerging Spanish infrastructure.[2] Every other respondent felt it was critical to maintain English as the dominant language and seemed offended by an emerging Spanish infrastructure. Current immigrants' lack of desire to learn English was understood as subversive. Here previous rounds of immigrants are contrasted to contemporary Mexican immigrants who are subverting America through their use of Spanish. A couple who discussed the contrast between the European immigrants they encountered growing up in Pennsylvania and the Mexican immigrants in southern California stressed assimilation as one of the biggest differences. The wife began by talking about language acquisition: "They [European immigrants in Pennsylvania] learned the language. They wanted to fit in. They didn't want to have their—they had their culture, but they didn't want to be like it was in their homeland. They came here because they wanted to better themselves, and they learned the language, and they wanted to fit in." Her husband more firmly extended her argument about language to culture: "A lot of what we see now... they're into their own little culture, and you're expected to go along with it. So there's a big difference between immigrants now, what we see here in southern California and what we ever saw back east. There's no comparison."

Sue also used the politics of language to contrast the current immigrants with previous immigrants around the issue of assimilation. She repeatedly talked about how immigrants today refuse to learn English, thus forcing "native" Americans to learn Spanish instead to make society function. As a citizen, Sue thinks she should not have to learn someone else's language. She blamed this in part on immigrants' refusal to stop talking Spanish at home, so that the children of immigrants are not learning English. She contrasted this with her relatives who would never have spoken German in the house. Maybe a few songs were taught in German, but her grandparents refused to teach her the language. Her grandparents, in fact, took pride in not sounding or looking German, and her grandmother at times refused to admit she was German. Sue reported this with pride.

Other respondents suggested that powerful Latino leaders and groups like La Raza and MALDEF (Mexican American Legal Defense and Educational Fund), understood as being both race conscious and dangerous to the United States, were promoting the maintenance of Spanish culture and threatening invasion. They suggested that this can be seen through the struggle over bilingual education. Some suggested that it is a powerful minority of Mexicans who are promoting the importance of speaking Spanish and cultural rights. Respondents talked about sympathetic Mexican migrants who simply wanted to succeed and get along in American society. These sympathetic Mexicans were depicted as being thwarted or led astray by the powerful, race-conscious Mexicans. The undocumented are especially vulnerable and are used as tools by these forces. This is illustrated by one respondent's discussion of the current state of bilingual education in California. California passed an initiative shortly after Proposition 187 ending bilingual education; however, parents can still request that their children receive bilingual education: "[Parents] can sign a waiver, and the parents are being pushed by seditious groups, MALDEF, LULAC [the League of United Latin American Citizens], the whole ball of wax, so they can overcome that as much as they possibly can; so it's another piece of the power taking, the power to push these people to do that. Because when these seditionists scream blue, the illegal aliens move." These groups and leaders *are* powerful, according to proponents, and their race-conscious agenda is succeeding and threatening American culture.

Respondents cited the growing Spanish infrastructure as evidence of a takeover in America resulting from the race consciousness of others. Areas of concern included language used in the workplace, for commerce or advertising, and in entertainment. As Spanish is spoken in public spaces, America begins to be lost. This is evident, as we saw earlier, when respondents worried about America becoming like a third world country when immigrants continue to use their own languages (here we see that the problem immigrants are defined as being from the third world). The Spanish information infrastructure is evidence of the immigrants' desire not to assimilate and of a successful takeover. The presence of Spanish newspapers, radio stations, and television programming serves to remind supporters that Spanish culture is not integrating with American culture. The availability of public documents in languages other than English also served as a doorway connecting Proposition 187 with the English Only movement. In the group interview, respondents discussed with disgust how public documents are available in a large variety of languages. While this challenges the supremacy of English, the real evidence of the takeover came when discussing Spanish. The frequency with which Spanish is provided for as an option on most public or commercial customer service telephone systems was indicative of seditious activity:

> JILL: You know, when you call a civic office, they have "press one for English."
>
> BERNIE: Oh yeah, that's another thing.
>
> JILL: You have that in Oregon?
>
> BERNIE: Always "press one for..."
>
> TONY: It's endemic here. To the point where sometimes, in fact, the gas company changed; several California gas companies, they answer the phone in Spanish and ask you to press a number for English.
>
> JILL: Really? Oh, God.
>
> TONY: Yes, they changed it, but they did it.

The inverted ordering of languages during an automated telephone call served as an indication of the edge on which American culture is perched. Respondents understood language as a key site in the cultural battle by race-conscious minorities and as the central evidence of minority power.

Culture and Allegiance after Proposition 187

The cultural battle is of central importance to respondents because they view cultural unity as necessary for a functioning democracy, both on a daily basis and through solidifying allegiance and preventing seditious forces. Assimilation is about getting along and preventing invasion. In the post–

Proposition 187 world, the fears of invasion take center stage. Again, the failure of Proposition 187 is not read simply as a policy failure or even as the result of an interfering judiciary; rather, it is evidence of the power of the invading forces. The cultural struggle is being lost, and racial realism comes to the fore. It is no longer a matter of not getting along but one of invading forces through cultural reproduction. Globalization appears to threaten culture and sovereignty as people migrate easily across borders, bringing their cultures with them. As the world becomes increasingly insecure, the equation of culture and allegiance intensifies, and the restrictionist movement emphasizes the unassimilable Mexican.

The connections between perceptions of cultural power and a focus on invasion are evident in a video produced by the California Coalition for Immigration Reform titled *Attack on America*. Recorded in 1996, the video depicts the main themes in the constructed cultural invasion central to the California restrictionist movement after Proposition 187. One sees both the power of Latinos and an emphasis on their cultural differences. Latinos are depicted as foreigners through an affiliation with communism and socialism, as well as through images of the savage. The Hispanic as savage is emphasized in footage of brown-skinned protesters wearing indigenous costumes and performing dances to drumbeats. The classic "Indian" is portrayed. Savagery is also portrayed by close-up shots of posters made by Latino demonstrators. The camera zooms in on the posters' images of revolutionary violence and bloodshed to highlight the uncivilized nature of the "opponents" and the intent of their presence. Finally, the intent of the tape is to show the violence that is enacted on the "American" protesters by the invading forces. Clips of protesters swinging at the restrictionist activists, and particularly at old, white Americans, are highlighted along with pictures of the aftermath of the confrontation: bloodshed and police coming to the aid of "Americans" who had violence acted upon them by a culturally alien force.

Advocates of immigration restriction in the post–Proposition 187 world perceive themselves as losing the cultural battle, a battle that becomes even more important following September 11. The second bridging strategy gains more salience as a way of understanding the world because of the central place of allegiance. If culture is understood as a sign or a mechanism to achieve allegiance, the current state of world affairs makes tolerance of multiculturalism even more dangerous. Milton talked about the losing battles in the language war: "There is a city right on the border, you read about it?

Where the people are not allowed to speak English. You know, you speak English, and you're fined immediately. And that's inside the United States. I mean, come on, what is this, are we chicken or what? I mean, this is unbelievable. And this goes on all under the law of, the heading of First Amendment law, you know, tolerance. Hey, there is no good thing as tolerance, especially after September 11. Even before that there shouldn't have been tolerance." Following 9/11, respondents suggested that it is even more important to be vigilant in the cultural struggle against Mexicanness. One respondent pointed to the Spanish infrastructure as a sign of the out-of-control immigration situation, whose dangerousness was highlighted by the events of September 11:

> But I think that especially after September 11, you see more and more people who think we should rein in the amount of immigration that we're doing and make sure we know where people are that are in the country. Because we've been caught with hundreds of thousands of people here and they don't know where they are. We see around all over you have billboards in Spanish, you have publications in Spanish, you have five or six or seven channels in Spanish. And my feeling is, it keeps them from learning English, because you go out and all you hear is Spanish. They make no effort to learn English, many of them.

He continued to suggest that those who learn the language and try to assimilate are not part of the problem, or dangerous immigrants. Because of the second bridging strategy, the threat of cultural invasion is stronger in the aftermath of the terrorist attacks on the United States.

Proposition 187 was a struggle to define those problem immigrants as being outside the community and therefore to limit their ability to alter American culture. By creating American culture as an unmarked category and racializing Mexicanness as uncivilized, links between assimilation and democracy, and between assimilation and loyalty, are constructed. As proponents constructed these links, they were mobilized to support the measure. They read the passage of Proposition 187 and the subsequent court injunction through the lens of those links. The failure to implement a measure that had been passed by a majority indicated a further breakdown of the democratic process because of the powerful minorities. The threat is increasing as the power of these groups increases and, as we shall see in the next chapter, as the numbers of these seditious forces increase as well.

CHAPTER SIX

Population and Hyperreproductivity

I was scheduled to meet Dean at his country club for breakfast. Because of heavy traffic, I arrived twenty minutes late for the interview. He was very understanding and said this was typical. He pointed to my experience as a key example of how population growth in California was overwhelming the infrastructure and harming the quality of life. For Dean, a white man in his fifties who had owned an advertising agency and dabbled in political campaigning, population growth from immigration was a concern because of quality-of-life issues, but also for political reasons. As we sat in the well-appointed (and at that time in the morning on a weekday, nearly empty) dining room with large windows overlooking the manicured golf course, Dean talked about the conflict he foresaw arising as the Latino population grew in California. According to him, a power struggle was coming because of the growing Latino population. A growing immigrant population would lead to a growth in Latino political power. This in turn would balkanize the political system along racial lines, Dean continued (as a crew of neatly dressed Latino workers performing upkeep on the golf course passed by our window), and whites would be on the defensive. His two concerns over population growth—quality of life and unequal political power—were key factors that led him to support Proposition 187.

Concerns about growth and population played a central role in the struggle over Proposition 187. Quality-of-life issues and environmental concerns were at the forefront of people's minds in the early 1990s.[1] The measure was seen as a way to control population by making immigration less tempting. Denial of schools, health care, reproductive services, and other government programs targeted immigrant families in particular. Having and raising children without access to those services would be more difficult. Proposition 187 therefore was a mechanism to limit growth of immigrant families in California. Proponents argued they were concerned with the sheer numbers—unraced, unspecified numbers—of people entering the country and the state; it was the quantity, not the quality, of the immigrants, that supporters of Proposition 187 hoped to limit. Population arguments can be seen as being grounded in color-blind conservatism as proponents focused on quality-of-life issues that result from any population growth.

However, to understand why numbers mattered, and specifically why such arguments would compel people to vote for a measure that focuses on social services for the undocumented, one has to investigate the description of the contemporary problem immigrant as a hyperreproductive Mexican woman, the racial realist twin schema. Fears of racial invasion emerge at the juncture between the racialization and gendering of the immigrant. The immigrant is understood as female, a characterization that distinguishes this moment of nativism from previous debates over Mexican immigration. Mexican women are depicted as reproducing at an exceptionally fast rate, further threatening whites. Latinos gain more votes and more clout to direct the future of the country as their population grows. Increases in population are understood as part of the race war over political control in the United States, not a simple quality-of-life concern.

Proposition 187 bridges race-neutral concerns over population and racial realist fears of political invasion through hyperreproduction. This is accomplished by providing a population control mechanism that addresses a particularly problematic population: the undocumented. However, these bridges collapse in the face of the state's response to this racial project. Supporters find the racial realist schema provides a better framework for understanding the invalidation of the measure than any of the bridging strategies. In the end, alliances between race-neutral environmental concerns and electoral takeover break down, and the threat of political racial invasion through population comes to the fore.

In this chapter, I begin by looking at the connections and disconnections between environmentalists and immigration restrictionists in this latest round of nativism. This provides further insight into the political terrain into which Proposition 187 entered, as well as the competing schemas of race neutrality and racial realism. I then turn to the proponents of Proposition 187 and their accounts of color-blind population concerns. Quality of life and the environment are threatened by numbers of generic, unraced people. I then turn to proponents' racial realist fears of being overrun by a racialized, hyperreproductive other. I highlight how the bridging strategies connecting the twin concerns over environmental exploitation and quality-of-life issues with the fear of political invasion at the ballot box mirror the bridging strategies used throughout. These bridges, however, collapse in the post-187 world. In the political aftermath of the measure, as an increased polarization of the politics around immigration and race becomes evident, color-blind conservatism takes a backseat to racial realism in the restrictionist movement. As a result, the movement loses allies and becomes smaller and more extremist in the late 1990s.

Environmental Nativism

Concerns about population and the environment are a distinctive characteristic of this latest round of nativist sentiment. Looking at the recent history of the environmental movement and immigration politics sets the stage for understanding the debate over population in Proposition 187. These earlier groups and discussions provided narratives and central schemas used by proponents of Proposition 187. These schemas are creatively bridged through action on the measure. And those bridges are then given back to the larger political terrain to be used by groups and actors not explicitly involved in the campaign. Therefore, to understand the mobilization and legacy of Proposition 187 on the issue of population requires us to investigate how population concerns entered immigration politics.

The entrance of environmental concerns into the contemporary immigration debate is marked powerfully by the founding of the Federation for American Immigration Reform (FAIR) in 1979. John Tanton had been active in the Sierra Club, Zero Population Growth, and Planned Parenthood. Frustrated with the direction of these organizations, Tanton formed FAIR to address specifically the problems of increases in American population resulting from immigration. Others who helped FAIR get off the ground included Tony Smith from the National Parks and Conservation Association and activists whom Tanton and Smith had met through Planned Parenthood, the Environmental Fund, and Earth Day rallies.

While the founding members of FAIR came from squarely within the environmental movement, FAIR is now the strongest immigration restrictionist group in the country. FAIR claims an official membership of at least a quarter million people, which does not include the numerous local organizations affiliated with the group. Congress has asked FAIR to testify twenty-two times in the last five years. The organization does not limit its arguments to environmental concerns. FAIR uses cultural, economic, and security arguments to push for reduced immigration levels and "stronger enforcement" of current laws. FAIR may have been founded by individuals dissatisfied with the environmental movement's reaction to the immigration debate, but the organization has come far from its roots and is now concerned foremost with immigration restriction. The environmental argument is just one of many tools in their toolbox.

Restrictionists claim that environmental priorities are a clear example of the racially neutral motives behind their activity. Organizations and individuals concerned with population and immigration argue that they are concerned only with numbers and therefore are "color-blind" regarding their activism. Negative Population Growth (NPG) is a national membership organization founded in 1972 that focuses on achieving a sustainable population in the United States. NPG focuses on immigration control as a primary mechanism for reaching a "sound population policy." "Immigration, as it relates to population, is not a racial issue; it's about numbers, not race or ethnicity or skin color" (Negative Population Growth 2003). SUSPS, a network of Sierra Club members who want immigration reduction included in the club's platform, argues: "[Immigration control] is not a racist issue, but one which addresses the population-environment connection of unrestrained mass immigration and increasing U.S. population growth" (Elbel 2001). The SUSPS Web site includes a long disclaimer regarding the connections between race and environmentally driven immigration restriction.[2]

However, those involved in the issue of population and immigration restriction have become active with other groups for which the racial implications are not far from the surface. John Tanton, cofounder of FAIR, also started a national group called U.S. English, which focuses on making English the official language while avoiding the issue of immigration. The connections between these two movements serve to illustrate the very real racial implications of the population arguments:

> Privately, Tanton believed the two issues were "inextricably intertwined," but as a tactical matter they had to be kept separate. To charge linguistic minorities with refusing to assimilate and simultaneously to propose limiting their numbers smacked of ethnic intolerance, a return to the old nativism. It would reveal an impolitic analysis—shared by several (though not all) leaders of FAIR and U.S. English—that the problem was not merely

the *quantity* of new immigrants, but the *quality:* too many Hispanics.
(Crawford 1992, 153; italics in original)

Alliances between a variety of restrictionist groups and overlapping membership among activists are clues to the racial implications of the population argument despite race-neutral language.

Traditional nativist groups are eager partners in these alliances, as they
happily include arguments about population and the environment in their
repertoire of restrictionist arguments. Groups that are explicitly concerned
about an invasion from Mexico and the battle against a white American culture find population arguments to be quite useful. Glenn Spencer's American Patrol is focused on preventing America from being "reconquested"
by Mexicans, a plot Spencer attributes to Mecha, La Raza, and even California representative Loretta Sanchez. In arguing against NAFTA, American Patrol's Web site includes information on the environmental squalor
caused by the operation of maquiladoras on the border next to warnings
about NAFTA contributing to "North Aztlan." Spencer's mention of Aztlan
references the Chicano movement in the 1970s, the goal of which was pur-
portedly to create a Mexican state north of Baja California. His use of the
inflammatory historical reference is a clear example of the racialized use of
environmental concerns for nativist goals.

Funding relationships also provide insight into the racial nature of the
restrictionist groups that emerged from the environmental movement.
The Pioneer Fund, a eugenics foundation, supplied FAIR with a good portion of its working budget for years. The foundation was originally incorporated in 1937 for "racial betterment" and to aid people "deemed to be de-
scended primarily from white persons who settled in the original 13 states
prior to the adoption of the Constitution of the United States." In 1985 the
organization minimally reworked its primary goal to be "conduct[ing] or
aid[ing] in conducting study and research into the problems of heredity and
eugenics in the human race generally." The organization has funded many
projects exploring the connections between race and intelligence, including
Murray and Herrnstein's *The Bell Curve* and its forerunners, some who advocated sterilization for "intellectually inferior" blacks and saw desegrega-
tion as the destruction of the school system. The Pioneer Fund gave FAIR
over $680,000 between 1982 and 1989, a sign that decision makers at the Pio-
neer Fund found FAIR's goals consistent with the foundation's goals.

The claims that environmental concerns are race neutral get lost in moments when leaders let their guard down. This is most clearly demonstrated by the now infamous Tanton memo. When this internal document written by FAIR's John Tanton became public in 1988, it revealed racial concerns as being central to some environmental immigration restrictionists. Tanton's memo asked: "Will the present majority peaceably hand over its political power to a group that is simply more fertile? ... Does the fact that there will be no ethnic majority in California early in the next century mean that we will have minority coalition-type governments, with third parties? Can *homo contraceptivus* compete with *homo progenitiva* if borders aren't controlled?" Here we see not only the suggestion that the newcomers are different, and therefore problematic, but also the naturalization of their difference. Ethnic or racial groups are identified with pseudoscientific classifications indicating they are in fact separate species. The differences are portrayed as stemming from biological variation. The result is not just environmental degradation but political takeover by these biological "others."

Racialization that occurs with other elements of the immigration reform movement is replicated by those focusing on population. This is evident, in part, in the easy alliances formed between more general nativist groups and population activists, exemplified by the Alliance for Stabilizing America's membership. This alliance includes not only groups that initially entered the debate because of concerns over population levels but also more traditional nativist organizations. Individuals and organizations active in the passage of Proposition 187, including the California Coalition for Immigration Reform, attended the most recent national meeting of the ASA. We can begin to understand the seeming disjuncture between how those using environmental arguments for restrictionist purposes understand themselves and the racial realism embedded in their arguments, alliances, and policy goals by investigating the use of population arguments in the struggle over Proposition 187.

Population and Color-Blind Conservatism in Proposition 187

Proponents of Proposition 187 suggest that their use of arguments about population demonstrates the color-blind nature of their political activity. According to proponents, population growth is important to understanding mobilization around the measure because immigration in general, and illegal immigration in particular, have led to increases in population that threaten both the natural environment and quality of life. Some respondents explicitly pointed to the population problem as uniquely motivating them. The interview respondents included former and current members of the Sierra Club, Zero Population Growth, and Californians for Population Stabilization (CAPS). Asked if he would vote for Proposition 187 again, Michael, a teacher who was the least active and the most ambivalent interviewee who voted for the measure, responded: "Probably, for the same reason. I think that I would vote for it because I am probably for anything that will hold the population down." Gary, a park service employee, describes himself as an "ardent conservationist" in explaining his support for the measure. According to Gary, there are too many people in the world and too many people in California. He saw the proposition as one way to hold down the "gobbling up of the [California] landscape." He is also the only respondent who suggested that he would *not* vote for the measure again. He has decided that a more global view is the only way to address the population problem. He believes that political forces will not allow Californians or any local groups to establish their own controls, and therefore a holistic approach is needed. Because population control should be dealt with globally and because another version of the measure would be doomed to failure, Gary would not support such a move today.

When discussing the question of population, proponents exuded a calmness and confidence unmatched in their other reasoning in support of the measure. While questions about the economic impact of immigration led to ambivalent, modified, or contradictory responses from proponents, questions about population seemed to provide a clear and strong basis for their support. Dean suggested that economic criteria alone will hide the true effects of population increase brought about by immigration: "Heavy illegal immigration . . . was an incredible drain on the resources of the United States, not just the state of California. . . . People like to say, well, economics work out in the end; they really don't work out. And . . . what people don't mention is what this additional population does to the incredible drain on our natural resources." Dean went on to talk about water and power shortages and connected these with the inability of the infrastructure to handle the large increases in population that he attributed to undocumented migration.[3]

Individual supporters credited the problems they see in their daily lives to an increasing population resulting from immigration. From overcrowded schools to long lines in post offices, immigration is the culprit. A prominent concern is traffic in California. Traffic congestion came up in almost every interview, frequently as "small talk" before the interview, then later as an example of the problems caused by immigration. Some respondents illustrated their frustration by contrasting Oregon and California or by asking about my experiences on California highways. Proposition 187 was understood as offering a solution to traffic, to overcrowded schools, and to the pushing and shoving of everyday life in California.

Respondents, however, made no distinction between illegal and legal immigration in their race-neutral accounts of population. Other schemas, such as economic drain, cultural concerns, and criminality, relied in part on an initial distinction between illegal and legal immigration, even if that distinction was blurred during mobilization and bridging. Immigrants in general drain services, but it is unfair to allow the undocumented to do so. Immigrants tend toward criminal behavior, but the undocumented have already *expressed* their proclivity toward crime. Immigrants from Mexico do not want to join or assimilate, but the undocumented are an extreme. However, proponents made no such distinctions when talking about population. That is, increases in population, regardless of status, are damaging. In a race-neutral approach to the issue, the undocumented are portrayed as using natural resources or infrastructure such as the highways, or crowding schools, in the same way as legal immigrants.

Respondents suggested they are concerned with numbers, not types, of people. Because of the neutral stance embedded in an argument about numbers, population concerns are appealing to people in contemporary liberal America. Michael argued that population, unqualified, is the problem: "And the more people come in, the worse things seem to get. I can't think of a place in southern California that improved because the population grew. I see big population as a big minus." Respondents were confident in talking about population because they perceive concerns over population to be evidently race neutral and therefore above the fray of much of the rest of the debate over immigration.

Some proponents were drawn to the measure because of a race-neutral concern about population. This color-blind schema involved an environmental critique of increases in population and a resentment of growth in California. Unraced newcomers were causing a much-bemoaned decline in the quality of life. However, this schema alone cannot account for support of a measure that focuses on social services to the undocumented. To understand why these supporters acted, we need to understand the racial realist schema that addressed population. The racial realist schema posited Mexican population as threatening political invasion.

Population and Racial Realism

Population increases resulting from undocumented migration prompted proponents to discuss a racial invasion. More than one respondent, echoing discourse heard from more radical organizations, discussed the problem with undocumented immigration as being "beaten at the cradle," a racialized struggle for cultural and political power being waged through reproduction. For some, talk of invasion is a metaphor for being overwhelmed by population and by the problems associated with the increase in population, in terms of both absolute numbers and the specific characteristics of the immigrant population. Respondents talk about the "takeover" as the result of being "swamped" by Spanish-speaking people. This damages the environment and the quality of life and causes white Americans to lose political power as politicians cater to the increasing Hispanic population.

One respondent, who lived in a heavily Republican area of southern California but has since moved out of state, suggested that support for the measure stemmed from people seeing racial changes in their midst. He said that increases in nonwhite populations were a problem for those around him: "It was mostly a question of feeling overwhelmed. Whereas at one time you had nine people who looked like you and one who looked like someone else, there were now six people who looked like someone else, and four who looked like you, and it was beginning to get a little scary." Supporters used visual cues and conflated race and immigration status to make judgments about population shifts and racial invasion.

Because of the racializations explored in previous chapters, the rapid increase in the Latino population frightened some respondents. It was understood as an invasion by a criminal, dependent, uncivilized race; the other racialized schemas were used in conjunction with a concern over population and invasion. For example, Maria noted:

Oh, there is an invasion of uh Central Am—you know, when I go with my friend from Nicaragua, she is like me, hardworking woman. Worked for years. Got her retirement, her daughters are doing great, now she doesn't work so we go out and play. And that is okay, we earned it okay. If somebody says, "Why don't you work," hey, I used to get up at four in the morning, do my shopping at five in the morning, okay; so did she. We go to downtown LA. We walk over there, you don't see one single white American. All you see is poor homeless blacks and full of Central Americans.[4]

Here the invasion is a racial invasion dependent on the characterization of Latino immigrants as lacking the American (white) work ethic and independence. Maria also suggested that because of this invasion, downtown Los Angeles is a dangerous place to be; the criminal element is part of the invasion resulting from the rapid demographic changes.

For others, the term "invasion" was used quite literally to mean intentional displacement or a planned domination. In chapter 2, we saw respondents refer to Reconquista, a centerpiece of restrictionist radio talk shows. Reconquista is the name given to a supposed plan by Mexicans to take back the southwestern portion of America, called Aztlan. Racial realist concerns over invasion were grounded in certain racial characterizations of the Mexican immigrant. The other schemas explored thus far can be seen as being used to depict the threat of the invading force. The negative characteristics associated with Mexicanness become more threatening as the numbers of Mexicans increase. These characterizations and the concern over invasion worked with race-neutral concerns about the environment and quality of life to mobilize individuals to act in favor of Proposition 187. It was also during the mobilization, as supporters constructed bridges, that the meaning of the measure was created.

Hyperreproductivity

For many, the circuitous route through which Proposition 187 reduces population and the unexplained targeting of some over others were not a large concern. Respondents did not feel the need to explicate a pathway of influence between the denial of social services to the undocumented and a reduction of population, in part because not a single respondent cited population as the sole problem. Even those who made it clear that it was their primary reason for supporting the measure spent very little time in the interview talking about problems generically related to population; they talked mostly about a range of other themes, such as cultural conflict. The confidence exuded by proponents when discussing population was unmatched by the amount of time they spent on the issue.

In part, this is because color-blind arguments about population proved difficult for respondents to connect with Proposition 187. However, under-

standing how respondents thought the undocumented uniquely threatened the quality of life and the environment illuminates the first bridging
strategy. This strategy begins with a regendering of the Mexican immigrant
in America as female. The Mexican female is then characterized as hyperreproductive and dependent. The conflation between the undocumented
and Mexican therefore means the undocumented uniquely threaten the
environment and quality of life through their propensity to reproduce.
Cutting services becomes a solution to the problem of the perceived dependent nature of these fecund Mexicans. The gendering and racialization
of the immigrant as a dependent, hyperreproductive Mexican female and
the racial realism through which supporters view the world connected many
of the schemas we have seen so far. While proponents understood population concerns to be race neutral, to understand why *this* measure should be
considered, one must draw on characterizations of immigrants as uncivilized (chapter 5), recalcitrant (chapter 3), and dependent (chapter 4). When
supporters suggested they were concerned with "sheer numbers," to connect this argument to Proposition 187, they needed to explain why a focus
on the undocumented should be the answer to the population problem. In
that moment, many respondents lost the coolness associated with their
views on population as the racialized and gendered image of the problem
immigrant emerged.

We gain insight into the bridging strategy that proponents employ by
their attempt to use color-blind concerns over the environment to explain
their support of Proposition 187. In attempting to connect their concerns
over population with a measure focused on the undocumented, proponents
found it necessary to deal explicitly with race. In explaining why he voted
for the proposition, Michael tried to handle this conflict between the measure's focus on the undocumented and the logic of population arguments:

> I don't think that I was strongly compelled to vote for it, but I wasn't com-
> pelled to vote against it either, so the reason would be that, and it probably
> boils down to what I said before about the population. Many of the prob-
> lems here are due to the people, the sheer numbers. So why allow people
> in here illegally and then on top of that to have to support them. I'm not,
> I'm not, ah, ethnocentric, I'm not racist.

This justification led him to connect concerns about population with the
depiction of the problem immigrant as dependent, as seen in chapter 4. As
Michael talked through the connection between the undocumented and
population, he found it necessary to deny racist intentions.

Grounding their stances in concerns over the environment, proponents of Proposition 187 needed to argue in the same moment that their concerns were color-blind. Jim emphasized that it was just numbers: "It's just that there's so many of them, you know. If there were Swedes and French and Finnish people coming in, in the numbers that these are, I would be just as upset. It's just that the quality of life is going down the tubes. And they're so poor. And pregnant women come across the border." But it is as respondents talk through the connections between their color-blind concerns about population and the measure that other schemas are revealed. At the end of Jim's statement, he illustrates that it is not just the quantity of the immigrant but the quality: fertile, poor, female.

When discussing population, respondents depict the problem immigrant as a woman, a gendering of the Mexican immigrant that is new to this latest round of nativism. Historically, the Mexican immigrant was envisioned as a single man coming to find work and then, at best according to the restrictionists, returning home. National debate on Mexican immigration beginning in the wake of the 1924 National Quota Act focused exclusively on men and centered on issues of labor and fitness for citizenship.[5] Mexicanness was associated with docility and hard work. These characterizations connected the Mexican to a system of peonage that was both un-American and a threat to American labor (Sheridan 2002). Issues of labor and employment continued to dominate the national debate regarding Mexican immigration, which was understood as a male phenomenon, as evidenced in debates over the Bracero program (1942–64) and subsequent repatriations.[6]

Proposition 187 is indicative of a shift from traditional nativist economic concerns, which focus on job competition and the male immigrant, to a focus on the female immigrant and the immigrant family. As discussed in chapter 4, concerns still center on labor, but the Mexican immigrant is depicted as being dependent and lacking a work ethic. Chang (2000), in her book on the global economy and migrant women laborers in the United States, notes that the focus on the drain of social services by immigrants "signals an implicit shift in the main target of anti-immigrant attacks. Men as job stealers are no longer seen as the major 'immigrant problem.' Instead, the new menace is immigrant women who are portrayed as idle, welfare-dependent mothers and inordinate breeders of dependents" (4).[7]

Nicholas De Genova (2002) points out how this shift to the image of the female immigrant threatens the nation-state uniquely through takeover and reproduction; it is precisely this regendering of the immigrant that characterizes the contemporary restrictionist movement:

> What has been insufficiently explored is how the historical production of the racialized figure of "the Mexican," as male "sojourner," has been rendered synonymous with migrant "illegality." This linkage has become more readily visible with the increasing equation of undocumented migrant women with permanent migrant (family) settlement.... The pervasive presumption that "a natural relationship between babies and mothers [blurs] lines of rights and responsibilities mapped by the state between two categories of people (citizen and alien)," such that "women's fertility [multiplies] the risk to the nation." (436)

Other immigrants at other times have been depicted and attacked because of perceived dangers resulting from their sexuality. From the Chinese prostitute of the late nineteenth century to the Filipino male who threatened the purity of white women in the 1920s and 1930s, sexuality and reproduction have been at the heart of restrictionist movements. A look at one moment when sexuality was racialized to address the immigration issue shows how the particular racial and political terrain transforms the meaning of the schemas as people adapt them to new settings. And the transformation of the schema has real political and policy implications.

In the nativist movements at the beginning of the twentieth century, the hyperreproductive female immigrant was also a central image. However, the racial terrain of the late 1800s and early 1900s led restrictionists to draw different conclusions about the threat of immigrant women. Eugenics, or scientific racism, which dominated the discourse, led to a focus on the biological threat to the existence of the white race. Katrina Irving (2000), exploring the feminization of the southern European and Irish immigrant in her book *Immigrant Mothers,* notes how the female immigrant was perceived as the site of danger: the immigrant woman "functioned along with her male counterpart as a villain whose take-over of Anglo-Saxon space threatened the Republic's very existence, [and] she was also singled out as a particular locus of eugenic concern" (40). The woman was understood as being nearer to the ideal type of the race and was the site where racial characteristics were transmitted. The immigrant woman was also depicted as containing a "preternatural fecundity" (41). This hyperreproductivity, cited alongside the low fertility rates of native-born Americans, threatened the racial suicide of the Anglo-Saxon population.

The altered racial terrain of the 1990s works with similar gendered descriptions of the immigrant to illuminate a different danger—loss of political, not biological, power. The contemporary struggle is understood as being about racialized political power, not racial purity. Grounded in the eugenics of the era, immigrant females at the beginning of the twentieth century threatened a biological invasion. The racial realist schema of the 1990s, where race is understood not primarily as a biological category but as some permanent groupings based on culture, suggests the hyperreproductive raced immigrant woman threatens to unleash a political invasion. Threats of political invasion are important for understanding mobilization for Proposition 187.

To understand how color-blind arguments about population and political invasion are connected and led to support for a measure that denies social services to the undocumented requires understanding the particulars of the racialization of Mexicans as fecund in the mid-1990s. The pregnant Mexican woman crossing the border to give birth on U.S. soil was the central image that emerged from the interviews. Respondents were eager to explain the conditions in California to a perceived outsider. Almost every interviewee had either seen or had accounts from friends and relatives who had seen pregnant women coming from Mexico to give birth in the United States to gain citizenship and services. Respondents describe Mexican women as hyperreproductive with phrases such as "breeding like cattle" or statements like "they love to have kids." Maria suggested that I drive through "Latin areas" to see the problem for myself: "All the girls, they, I think the moment they reach 110 pounds they start having babies. There is one in the stroller, two on each side of the mommy and there is one in the stomach. Hmm. That's true."[8] Pregnant, hyperreproductive Mexican women play a central role in their narratives of support.

This fear over the entrance of the hyperreproductive immigrant woman is about quality of life and the environment but also intersects with the other schemas explored thus far to create concerns about racial cultural struggles. These problem immigrants contribute to an increasing Latino population, who, as explored in the last chapter, are raced as impenetrably different from other "Americans" ("whites"). This fear is further intensified by the ongoing publicity about the impending moment when whites will no longer be a majority in California.[9]

Supporters also fear invasion and dominance of one race over another, a perceived political power struggle stemming from a racial realist perspective.

The metanarrative of racial realism presents this increase in population as particularly threatening in a republican form of government. The hyper-reproductive Mexican immigrant threatens to overturn the electorate. Milton suggested that Reconquista can only happen through female migrants' reproduction capabilities:

> They can't do it by force. So they are doing it in a very simple way. By putting a lot of, by bringing in a lot of illegal immigrants who breed like rabbits, okay, and then get representatives, and eventually the whole legislature's gonna be Latino, and they'll be, you know, some president at some point in time probably twenty years down the pike. We'll have a hell of a problem. We may have a little guerrilla war here, you know.

The electoral system is the site of invasion for the hyperreproductive immigrants. The ultimate danger of the population increase resulting from immigration is a political takeover. In this story, Hispanics are understood as having a unified set of interests in opposition to white interests. This schema relies on a conflation of the documented and the undocumented and between immigrants and hyperreproductive Mexicans.

Hyperreproductivity is understood as both a conscious tactic by Mexicans and an uncontrollable part of their nature. Milton's comments suggest that reproduction is a calculated step toward reconquest. As we will see in the next bridging strategy, supporters also suggested that reproduction by Mexican immigrants was a conscious move to get services and citizenship. On the other hand, Maria's comments earlier indicate that young Latino women simply can't control themselves. Respondents used animal references (e.g., cattle and rabbits) to talk about Latino reproduction. This uncontrolled version of hyperfertility contributes to the characterization of Mexicanness as uncivilized or animallike, as we saw in the previous chapter.

The population issue and the hyperfertility bridge are unique in that they draw on the other racializations central to the campaign. Proponents are concerned with sheer numbers as they affect quality of life and the environment. Mexicans pose a unique danger as they are raced as hyperfertile. To address environmental concerns, then, one needs to address the problem of hyperfertility. Mexicans are understood as composing the undocumented population; therefore a denial of services to the undocumented, a reduction in incentives to cross the border, will have a drastic impact on population. Mexican hyperfertility, however, is also an indication of other problems associated with the population, like intentional attempts to gain power and a large population of uncivilized, dependent criminals. Hyper-fertility therefore serves as a powerful bridge between racial realist concerns about the quality of the population and color-blind concerns about the quantity.

Documentation and Control

A second strategy used by proponents to bridge race-neutral concerns over population with raced concerns over invasion begins with characterizing the undocumented as particularly problematic for concerns over the environment. Because the undocumented are understood as being out of control, they appear more threatening. Notions of invasion emerge in the context of a population out of control. Additionally, supporters understand the undocumented as coming here precisely to reproduce. Because of the tradition of birthright citizenship in the United States, proponents suggest undocumented migration followed by reproduction is understood by immigrants as a way to get services and citizenship. As the undocumented become raced as Mexican, Mexicanness is equated with reproduction and invasion.

For supporters, the undocumented pose a unique problem for population control given the uncontrolled nature of the movement. The use of weather and nature metaphors to talk about the undocumented during the campaign illuminates the connection between lack of control and undocumented migration. Governor Wilson tapped into public frustrations and made quality of life a central theme of his speeches, beginning in an August 1993 speech titled "Closing the Door on Illegal Immigration" (Wilson 1993a). Alongside the economic impacts of immigration, which had been placed at the center beginning with his failure to balance the budget, Wilson repeatedly warned of the inability of the California infrastructure to handle the "flood of illegal immigration": "And make no mistake, our quality of life is threatened by this tidal wave of illegal immigrants" (2). Others picked up on this language, and water became a central metaphor.

Water was used to describe invasion, physically and culturally. Milton talked about being an "island" and getting "swamped." Five respondents used the word "flood" to describe the immigration situation. Four used the idea of a "wave" of immigrants. Four talked about the "flows" of immigration. Four talked about the "influx." Water metaphors appearing seven years after the passage are remnants of the struggle over the measure. Otto Santa Ana performed a study of the language used to talk about immigration and immigrants during Proposition 187. Using a metaphor analysis, Santa Ana found that dangerous water (e.g., floods, tide) was the dominant metaphor to describe the process of immigration. The second most commonly used metaphor to describe immigration was war (e.g., invasion). As the undocumented were understood as Mexican, so too were the "flood" and the "invasion."

Proponents also understood the undocumented as an immigrant population who had unique incentives to reproduce. Birthright citizenship in the United States conveys citizenship to anyone born within the territory of the United States. Respondents portrayed citizenship and the services the citizen children of the undocumented received as motivating reasons to cross the border and reproduce. The image is borrowed from the welfare debates in the 1980s and 1990s, when government largesse was depicted as a motive for becoming pregnant. According to proponents, the undocumented intentionally cross the border and have children, called "anchor babies," to secure services and ultimately citizenship.[10] Four respondents connected the idea of anchor babies explicitly to the 1965 changes in immigration law that placed citizens' immediate family as a top priority when considering what immigrants to admit. Respondents believed the undocumented would intentionally have citizen children to secure citizenship for themselves and their families. The undocumented (read "Mexicans") become understood as hyperreproductive in order to attain services and documentation. This, proponents believed, could be addressed through a denial of services, including reproductive care.

In this association bridge, the undocumented are perceived as being hyperreproductive for instrumental reasons. Therefore the undocumented are perceived as an important site for action on the population problem. Mexicanness, however, is implicated as hyperreproductive because of the conflation of the undocumented and Mexicans. Therefore this provides a link to the racial realist concerns over invasion. Both invasion and environmental concerns could be addressed, then, through a measure that targets the undocumented, that is, Proposition 187.

Increasing the Power of Race

Respondents' belief in the detrimental race consciousness of others shapes the ways that proponents link concerns over population, invasion, and their support for Proposition 187. First, respondents suggest that environmental organizations are too scared to take on the immigration issue because of the race consciousness of the groups and the power of minority groups; therefore a citizen initiative is needed. Second, *because* of the race consciousness of politicians and the power of minority groups, the changes in population will result in a political invasion; as others racialize the political process, shifting demographics become dangerous. Therefore, the measure is understood as an attempt to make color-blind the electoral system and interest group politics.

Because of powerful race-conscious minority groups, the environmental movement and lobby will not address population as it should be discussed, according to proponents. Sam, a former Sierra Club member, pointed to this as a reason for leaving the organization. He stated that if environmentalists were concerned with population, as they profess, and not with race, then such organizations would take on the issue of immigration. John, a member of Zero Population Growth, also expressed the same set of concerns with the organization and suggested he had tempered his activity in the movement because of the group's fears of accusations of racism.[11] The race consciousness of these environmental organizations prevents them from addressing immigration, according to respondents.

Because respondents believed that lobby groups and minority voters act politically with race at the forefront, they felt that politicians are also forced to be race conscious. And because politicians are forced to be race conscious, they will respond to large demographic shifts. This is the racial political invasion feared by respondents. As a defensive reaction, white citizens must also become race conscious. As we saw in chapter 2, Dean argued that the California political landscape could be understood as a variety of ethnic and racial blocs. In reaction to these color-conscious blocs of minority voters, white males began to form their own voting bloc, resulting in political balkanization, according to Dean. In responding to the electoral pressures of the growing minority voting blocs, another respondent notes that the parties have also become color conscious: "I think the Democratic Party thinks of the illegal immigrants as an additional ten million potential voters. And, uh, so they'll, they'll never do anything about it. And the Republicans are, some of them are afraid that the Hispanic vote, the Mexican vote which is what it is primarily, will be too much for them on a local or a statewide basis." Because of increases or perceived future increases in the Mexican population, political parties will cater to the needs of Hispanics. According to these respondents, parties function with a racial realist mind-set, which in turn means white citizens must as well. Population is critical

to a racial political power struggle in a democracy. Respondents fear finding themselves on the losing end of this racial struggle forced on them by
color-conscious Latinos and political parties, and they fear they will lose
because of population growth through undocumented immigration.

This defensive bridging strategy suggests that because of the color consciousness of others, whites need to be concerned about racial invasion. Out
of self-defense, whites need to be aware of the racialized political power
struggle. Color-blind concerns over population take on a different meaning here than in the previous two strategies. Here whites can see their activity on Proposition 187 as an attempt to make politics appropriately color-
blind once again by removing the incentive, a growing Latino population,
for politicians to act in a race-conscious manner.

Invasion in the Post–Proposition 187 World

The aftermath of Proposition 187 highlights how the bridges on population concerns are used to read the state response. The first two bridges do
not help to explain the state response. However, the third bridge provides a
useful schema for reading the court's intervention. The failure to implement
the measure was read by supporters through a concern over a powerful
race-conscious minority; schemas about environmental concerns had little
to contribute to interpreting the court injunction and subsequent mediation. The state response to the measure led to a decline in the importance of
concerns over natural resources. The first two bridging strategies collapsed,
leading to an increased focus on invasion and a weakening of the alliances
between environmental activists and immigration restrictionists.

This coalition destabilization is evident among both individuals and
organizations. Gary is a good example of the split between environmental
concerns and immigration restriction. He is the only respondent who would
not support the measure again, and he is the only respondent who continues
to claim environmental concerns as his central motivation. Environmental
groups have distanced themselves from the immigration issue in general
and Proposition 187–type policies in particular. In 1998 the Sierra Club
asked its members to vote on whether it should lobby to reduce immigration. The measure threatened connections with the Latino community and
was voted down. This can be attributed to the political and racial terrain
generated by Proposition 187. Harry Pachon of the Tomas Rivera Policy
Institute talks about Proposition 187 as one of the reasons the Sierra Club
measure generated such a response: "I think it really raised some eyebrows.

It was like, you too are joining the fray against the Hispanic community. Because you have to take the context of the period in which the vote was taken. It came within four years of Proposition 187, the restriction on immigrant assistance" ("The Politics of Population," 2003).

Respondents' narrative structure reveals that the concern over political invasion has come to the fore since the passage of Proposition 187. The plotline focuses on the conflict between political parties and politicians doing what is right for the republic (again, read "white population") and what is "demanded" by the invading forces. The story is of the downfall of the Republican Party. It begins with the Republican Party's endorsement of Proposition 187. The rising action contains the mobilization around the measure where countermobilization forces, "pro-illegals," attempt to intimidate and defeat the righteous fighting on the sides of law and order and color blindness. The Republican Party was on the side of the righteous during this struggle. The Republican Party was a strong supporter of Proposition 187. Three of the more active respondents remember getting involved in the campaign for Proposition 187 because of information provided by the Republican Party. Others involved in organizational work remember contacts with various local Republican groups. And others remember receiving literature or first being informed of the measure by Republican candidates or by the party. The measure was passed despite pressure from the color-conscious forces. The central conflict presents itself at the climax of the story, when the measure is kept in the courts and declared unconstitutional. The falling action includes the mediation by Governor Gray Davis in court, and the tragic resolution is the abandonment of the restrictionist cause by Republican leadership. Respondents suggest that those politicians or political groups would not support a similar measure today. This leads not only to the moral downfall of the Republican Party but also their political downfall. A respondent who used to work for a state Republican politician suggests that the impact of the passage of the measure was not about whether it got implemented or not: "Propositions will always be challenged, and now it's become an accepted way of life. The message had been sent. The Republican Party now thinks that might have been a mistake politically, so they've run away from any criticism of illegal immigration. . . . I know politically it's off the table, and the question is, is that the right thing?"

With that moral downfall comes the party's political downfall. By not standing strong in the face of opposition, the Republican Party lost its moral strength and its base, and that, according to supporters, is why Democrats ran California until 2003. As the Republican Party fails to uphold what is right, the parties lose their significance and begin to blend. Charles's friend, whom he meets at McDonald's to talk over coffee about how the world is changing around them, echoes Charles's concern with disappearing citizenship: "I don't feel like my vote even counts. Let's take the immigration [issue], for instance. The Republicans want it at the federal level because they get lobbied and everything for immigrants to come. And the reason being cheap labor. Democrats want it because it's a surefire vote." This blurring of agendas leads to the political downfall of the party. One respondent, who donated money to the campaign and worked with a local organization behind the scenes to mobilize support, explained:

> In fact, I think the Republicans have made just a horrible mistake because they said they lost out so much because of the terrible people like me who were in favor of 187 and alienated the Hispanics. I think all they've done is alienate the white base and turn themselves from being the party of respectable white people to the Mexican party of the United States. I really don't have, don't want to have anything to do with Republicans anymore. It may be that they're right and there will ultimately be more Hispanics than whites, but I think that they say the reason they've done so poorly in California of late is because they've alienated all the Hispanics. I think the reason, the reason they've done so poorly is because they've alienated all the whites who just stayed home and haven't voted.

Proposition 187 is noted by its proponents as being the last time Republicans were able to stand up to the political invasion. President George W. Bush and Washington Republicans in particular are the focus of the respondents' angst. State and local politicians and parties are understood as being hamstrung by the pro-immigrant stances of the federal politicians and organizations. President Bush is perceived as catering not just to Hispanics but to Mexicans and the Mexican government. Interviewees mentioned his amnesty plan, as well as his perceived tight relationship with President Vicente Fox. "And you ask me what was the goal of coalition [to pass Proposition 187]. It's really very simple. Enforce our existing immigration laws which includes deportation. We have a federal government, talk about the word, depraved, and Bush is leading the parade right now. Selective enforcement." President Bush and other "treacherous" Republicans are the target of venomous descriptions because they are perceived as catering to minority interests ("selective enforcement"). Respondents suggested that it is not surprising that Democratic politicians will ignore the rule of

law, but the entire system is corrupt or "depraved" now that Republicans
have abandoned their defense of the country. The California Coalition for
Immigration Reform issued a petition addressed to national politicians, but
foremost to President Bush, warning of policies that "will end U.S. sovereignty." The petition asks Bush to oppose "the bogus 'guest worker' program" and an amnesty that would allow "racist, pro-illegal alien groups" to
fulfill their vow "to control our government by 'sheer numbers,' using the
VOTE if possible." The national party is understood as preventing local Republican politicians from being able to represent their own views and the
will of the people.[12]

The invasion in our governing institutions has begun. The story is one
of the people's voice being lost. This is evident in the failure of responsible
parties:

> I used to be [a Republican] but now I'm very confused about what's going
> on out there. And, uh, I'm for the way it used to be. And now I can't hardly
> even, talking about free speech, if I say I'm a patriot and I believe in the
> Constitution and the Bill of Rights and the Declaration of Independence
> and I'm a Christian person. And all of that, it's getting to be almost so you
> don't say that. . . . I guess you used to call that a conservative but now they're
> all the same. The Republicans and the Democrats, there's no difference. If
> you get to the bottom of what they're doing, they're all working for the
> same thing. It's become very polluted, very corrupted. And it no longer
> expresses the voices of the people.

There is little difference between the two parties as both become color-
conscious and abandon tradition and the people. This is the failure of
democracy.

Additionally, respondents pointed to the legal aftermath of Proposition
187 as an indication that the voice of "the people" is no longer being heard.
After the court injunction was placed on the measure, the measure took a
number of years to work its way through the federal court circuit until it
was finally mediated when Governor Gray Davis came into office. Davis
and the judge who declared large portions of the measure unconstitutional
became the two villains. The respondents talk with passion about the judge
and her actions. While many couldn't remember the name of politicians in
their area or statewide leaders from the time of the campaign, this judge
left quite an impression. One respondent said after spelling the judge's
name, "I'll never forget that name." And another said "Somehow her name

is burned into my memory." Respondents vilified the judge because they perceived her to be thwarting the will of the people.

Governor Davis is also responsible for democracy's failure. Henry states passionately: "But Davis, Gray Davis, who is now governor, decided not to represent the will of the people. So he dropped the suit. So we have a governor who decided not to pursue the wish of the people." Governor Davis is identified as a traitor because he subverted the will of the people, abandoned his campaign promise to uphold the vote on Proposition 187, and embraced liberal positions on immigration policy in general. During the group interview, the idea of Davis as a traitor emerged a number of times. Kathy said, "I think it's somewhere around eighty thousand babies are born in California alone annually to illegal alien mothers and they are instant citizens and Governor Gray Davis in his first budget he set aside $76 million to cover prenatal and birth and postbirth care for illegal alien women." Fran added, "Talk about aiding and abetting the enemy."

Davis's actions are evidence of the "enemy," alternately immigrants, Hispanics, and Mexico, gaining ground. According to Milton, Governor Davis was elected because of the "enmity" Wilson garnered by his strong stance on immigration. Latinos voted Democratic, and in turn "the first thing Governor Davis did was go and visit Mexico. Well, first of all, Governor Davis is the governor of a state. It is a federal issue. So you know, he goes over there to Mexico, promises them all kinds of things, tells them to come across here [and] break—come across the border, no problem." The electoral power of an increasing Hispanic population threatens the integrity of the country as politicians feel the need to cater to Mexico's needs: "Whether Davis will [sign a bill allowing people to get driver's licenses without documentation of citizenship] or not, I don't know. He's another one who wants to cozy up to Vicente Fox in Mexico thinking it will bring jobs, and all it's going to bring is more illegals here, but you know he must see something down the road where he thinks he'll get an economic benefit, maybe votes, who knows."[13] As people understood their power to be waning and the power of color-conscious Latinos to be increasing, themes of invasion became more prominent in the restrictionist movement.

This racial realist stance is also evident among immigration restrictionist organizations. The California Coalition for Immigration Reform and Voices of Citizens Together were coauthors of the measure and were central proponents. Both groups currently place invasion at the center of their work. The president of Voices of Citizens Together has founded the American Border Patrol, which has basically taken over VCT.[14] Central to the American Border Patrol in the late 1990s was uncovering and stopping Reconquista, the name given to a supposed plot to reclaim the American Southwest for Mexico. Today Glenn Spencer, president of VCT and American Border Patrol, has moved to Arizona to be on the "front lines." American Border Patrol now uses videotaping and reporting to attempt to stop border crossings. Current articles highlighted on the organization's Web site discuss damage done by crossings and by the undocumented once in the interior, as well as the activities of sympathetic politicians and policies.

CCIR also now focuses on the notion of invasion through political channels in the aftermath of Proposition 187. An audiotape made in 1997 and a centerpiece of CCIR mobilization today is titled "The Takeover of America."[15] This tape and its accompanying booklet are "composite[s] of statements by college professors, pro-alien activists and elected representatives whose goal is to control our government and YOUR lives 'by the vote if possible and violence if necessary!'" The phrase "by the vote if possible" appears repeatedly throughout CCIR's mobilization literature, including their newsletters. Highlighted in this tape are politicians who support "pro-illegal" policies and others who talk about or attempt to mobilize the political power of Latinos. Vice President Al Gore is quoted in a speech arguing against Proposition 187; a state senator is cited saying that people will "make sure that we re-elect a president who . . . opposes CCIR" and the Californian initiative to end affirmative action; and a member of the Los Angeles Board of Education is quoted as being adamantly opposed to the end of bilingual education. These statements are presented as self-evidently treasonous.

Statements about Latino solidarity are also highlighted. Attempts to politicize the Hispanic population count according to this group as part of the "invasion." Former U.S. ambassador to the United Nations and U.S. secretary of energy Bill Richardson is put on the wall of shame for his quote "Illegal and legal immigration are being unfairly attacked. . . . We have to put aside party and think of ourselves as Latinos." A Hispanic professor's argument that the classroom is a place to organize, and another professor's discussion of how to avoid white backlash while still increasing political participation, were clear evidence of these educators' desire to "control the government and your lives." A Los Angeles County supervisor is targeted for saying, "We are politicizing . . . those that are becoming citizens of this country." The focus on invasion is a response to the perception of the growing power and increasing politicization of the Hispanic population in the wake of Proposition 187.

The actions of the Bush administration since 9/11 have served to intensify this idea of representative democracy opening the door to invading forces. Restrictionists believe that politicians responding to the perceived political imperatives of shifting demographics are not concerned with the best interests of (white) America and will enact pro-immigrant policies. The March 2002 CCIR newsletter is subtitled "Will March 2002 be 'Handover America' Month?" The question at hand is the Bush amnesty plan that was circulating before September 11, 2001. Because Bush was traveling to meet with President Fox in late March, the organization asks, "Will Bush Sell Our Sovereignty for 'Immigrant Vote'?" In an accompanying cartoon, we see a man in a sombrero with a menacing look saying, "We, the majority, demand *special* rights." This man is displaying the power that stems from the size of the Hispanic population as he says, "We, the majority." He will use this power to circumvent liberal individualism through the "demand" of "*special* rights" for a group of people intent on complete control. We see President Vicente Fox persuading President Bush to enact an amnesty by holding out the promise of more votes. Elsewhere in the newsletter, CCIR states that those who support the amnesty are the "'Abolish America' Committee," which includes "Racist Special Interests groups, 'cheap labor' corporations and the globalist power-mongers." Respondents suggested that Bush's seditious behavior is almost more troubling than Davis's actions. Bush's stances on immigration and amnesty further evidence that the invading forces now have control over *both* parties.

The concept of racial realism is essential to understanding the restrictionist response to the aftermath of Proposition 187. The concern over political invasion centers on the idea that Hispanics or Mexicans have interests that are attributable to their membership in a racial group. Those interests inherently conflict with, and therefore are in a constant state of war with, the interests of other racial groups. The gendered, racialized schemas about the hyperfertile immigrant central to the passage of the measure were transformed in its aftermath. In the face of the increased politicization of the Latino population and the failure of the measure to be implemented, the focus shifted to the electoral arena as the important site of struggle. The events and changes of the political landscape after the passage of Proposition 187 were read through the defensive bridging strategy that highlighted political invasion. While the other two bridges collapsed, the racialized image of the Mexican migrant embedded in those two strategies was used to supplement and strengthen the idea of a political invasion and race consciousness. This led to a shift in understanding the central dilemma with the hyperreproductive female Mexican immigrant. Environmental concerns were lost as concerns about electoral takeover came to the fore.

The War on Terror has served as simply another weapon in the arsenal of restrictionist groups working for the same agenda with the same racial terrain. However, radical shifts in the racial terrain as a result of the Bush administration's War on Terror are probable and will cause a substantial change in the restrictionist agenda. The focus on electoral politics may wane as new characterizations of dangerous immigrants come to the fore. The dangerous immigrant will be reraced and regendered by restrictionist groups. In this case, however, the restrictionist groups will follow the lead of the American public and the elected officials, noting that these new schemas may enable them to achieve their agendas: tougher border enforcement, firmer and more meaningful lines between noncitizens and citizens, and stricter limits on access to American institutions and services. Schemas that came to the fore in the aftermath of Proposition 187 are easily transposed in post-9/11 America. The schema of defense against a racializing other and notions of invasion can easily be used on the new political terrain.

Conclusion

During the 2004 California gubernatorial recall campaign, reporters asked Arnold Schwarzenegger about his voting record on Proposition 187. People and groups of all different political stripes made claims about his fitness or unfitness for office based on his reply that he had voted in favor of the measure. In 2006, Schwarzenegger made headlines again when he came out with the statement that he had decided his vote for the measure was wrong. This nearly decade-old measure, which was never implemented, still serves as a critical marker for understanding contemporary immigration and race politics. The struggle that occurred over the measure in 1993 and 1994 radically altered the racial terrain.

Proposition 187 emerged from a renewed nativist movement that began in the late 1980s and peaked in the mid-1990s. The struggle over the measure occurred at the height of this nativist movement and altered its meaning and trajectory, as well as the racial politics of our country. The movement represented a powerful coalition of ideas and groups. Color-blind conservatism and racial realism worked together to create a broad-based coalition. This coalition, however, fell apart in the aftermath of Proposition 187. By the end of the 1990s, the movement focused on invasion, consisted of a smaller set of groups, and had lost much of its power (Freeman and Birrell 2001). The events of September 11 gave the restrictionist movement possibilities for forming a different coalition of conservative forces focused on invasion and national security. Certain bridging strategies that survived the campaign of Proposition 187 were easily transposed in the aftermath of the terrorist attacks on America. Additionally, when bridges did break down, racial realism came to the fore after 9/11. Proposition 187 generated lasting schemas that criminalized Mexican migration and highlighted Mexican cultural and political threat to democracy. These served to tie concerns over Mexican invasion to the newly salient threat from other "others," Muslims and individuals of Arab descent.

The breakup of the coalition of restrictionist forces and the primacy of the language of invasion over fairness are evident in the most recent debates over immigration. The Republican Party, a firm supporter of immigration restriction in the mid-1990s (as evidenced by the party platform), is splintered on the issue to the highest levels of party leadership. Since entering office in 2000, President George W. Bush has supported a guest worker program and a way to regularize the undocumented. This is far from the crackdown that restrictionists would like to see, and immigration restrictionist groups have labeled President Bush a traitor for his approach. Bush made immigration his top domestic agenda in the latter part of 2005, and in response to his renewed campaign for immigration reform, House Republicans passed a bill to crack down on illegal immigration through increased enforcement and tougher penalties. They did not offer any avenue for regularization or any form of a guest worker program. This rebuff of the president's long-held goals on immigration revealed the deep splinters in the Republican Party on the issue of immigration.

In March and April 2006, cities around the country witnessed some of the largest protests they had seen in decades. These protests were a response to the renewed debate about illegal immigration on Capitol Hill. That debate has reverberated around the country through citizens, organizations, and city and state governments. In the six months following the protests, over thirty municipalities considered proposals to make English the official language, to fine landlords who rent to the undocumented, and punish employers who hire the undocumented. Seventeen of these were located in Pennsylvania, some in towns with a population under one thousand with not a single person of Latino descent living there. Such towns claimed consideration of these ordinances as "preventative measures." These local debates reflect the intensified discussion focusing on invasion and the connections between the discussions over security and the discussions over immigration.

New racism cannot explain the lasting impact of Proposition 187, the new definitions of citizenship that emerge, or the rise and fall of restrictionist coalitions. Because new racism lacks a dynamic notion of race, campaigns such as the one for Proposition 187 are read as tapping into existing racial views. Agency appears only in the hands of elites who use race to attract voters. According to new racism, commitments to equality expressed by the restrictionist movement in the early and mid-1990s were necessary covers. Coded racial messages were the powerful mobilizing force. Commitments to equality and fairness and other American ideals are used to hide racism, since overt racism is understood as unacceptable after the civil rights movements in the 1960s. This, however, does not help us to understand why some of the color-blind conservative arguments were jettisoned in the aftermath of Proposition 187 or lost their salience. If, as new racism might suggest, fairness is a necessary cloak for unacceptable racism, subsequent state action did not change that political imperative. Therefore successive campaigns should have been pursued with a similar set of tactics, and the racial terrain should not have been radically altered.

Omi and Winant's racial formation theory suggests mobilization around a racial project does not just use the notions of race found in the racial terrain but transforms racial meanings. They point to social movement theories to understand this phase of racial formation. Current social movement theories, however, cannot serve as a framework for understanding how racial projects are transformed because of an undertheorized notion of agency.

Rational-choice accounts of social movements assume static goals that individuals and organizations strive to achieve. This includes both resource mobilization accounts, which focus on the activities of organizations, and micromobilization accounts, which use a rational actor at the base. Neither provides insight into how those goals are established. Because rational-choice accounts stress structural and material factors, such theories have difficulty addressing the lasting impact of a measure that was never implemented. The measure can therefore only be understood as symbolic, but the very real effects that resulted from its passage challenge such a notion. Without greater power given to cultural forces and a stronger account of agency, these theories cannot explain the legacy of Proposition 187.

Identity-oriented theories about social movements use culture as an important tool for understanding protest. They focus on the ways that grievances and goals are constructed and understood and make room for expressive goals. From this perspective, agency matters in explaining why social movements arise and how they unfold. However, identity-oriented approaches also draw a strict line between culture and structure, leaving agents detached from their historical context and the material world around them. Agents appear unbounded, and in turn their impact on structures is hard to explain. The ways that the racial terrain channels action and is affected by agents are lost in a focus on culture at the expense of the material.

Theorizing the connections between material and culture is important to understanding change. A theory of schemas, tools of thought that rely on and create resources, is a critical starting point. Schemas highlight how resources are in fact a combination of interpretation and material conditions. A resource does not exist as solely a material or a cultural phenomenon. Additionally, we cannot remove culture or interpretation from the resources on which it is based. Such a view allows us to understand human agency as contextualized creativity. In transposing schemas from one structure or one field to another, people change the meaning of resources, the way they are distributed, and in turn the schemas themselves. Using a notion of creative human action and schemas, which incorporates culture and structure, provides insight into the racial formation process and the legacy of Proposition 187.

If we use these tools, proponents' accounts of participation in the campaign are illuminating. Individuals creatively bridged central schemas about race to re-create new notions of citizenship and new meanings behind race. Bridging commitments between seemingly competing understandings of race generated new racial meanings and a new set of schemas through which to view state action.

Proponents were mobilized to act on Proposition 187 as they connected color-blind conservatism and racial realism. Respondents demonstrated that on each central issue in the campaign there was a color-blind conservative schema and a racial realist mirror schema. Concerns about fairness and invasion worked together through three central bridging strategies: racialization, association, and defense. Each of these strategies provided a way to connect the metaschemas of color-blind conservatism and racial realism and schemas about immigration and the law, the economy, culture, and population. Within each theme, the basic bridging strategies were used to connect those mirror schemas. The bridges became the frames through which respondents viewed the court injunction and state response to the measure. Some bridges were reinforced by the state response; some were challenged. Through an investigation of the particular outcomes for each bridge, we can see how the racial terrain was transformed; respondents generated lasting narratives of a criminalized, dependent Mexican immigrant where concerns of cultural and political invasion were at the fore.

Such insights do two things. First, an awareness of the transformative bridges gives us leverage to understand immigration politics after the measure. Second, such understandings provide possibilities for escaping the polarized debate generated around Proposition 187. Alternatives for addressing the measure and immigration politics can be found.

Beyond Proposition 187

Understanding the specific logics of each bridge and how respondents understood them in the wake of the court injunction provides insight into subsequent immigration politics. I provide examples from each chapter, exploring the impact of the bridging strategies after Proposition 187.

Supporters during the campaign constructed a notion of criminal Mexican migration. State action on the measure did not alter the bridges responsible for this construction. If anything, the state action ensured that the bridges would remain, as respondents viewed the court injunction as evidence of lawlessness precisely at the locus of the rule of law. The bridges that connected rule of law and criminality therefore became a new reference through which other political events were viewed. Reading the events of September 11 through these bridges, restrictionists understood the terrorist attacks as a reason to tighten the border with Mexico because criminal undocumented Mexican migrants might help terrorists just as easily as they helped drug dealers. Criminality is linked with schemas on national security, and border control becomes central for protecting the United States.

The power of these schemas can also be seen in the debate over granting driver's licenses to the undocumented.[1] Governor Davis had committed to granting licenses to the undocumented. The bill, however, appeared on his desk in the wake of September 11. Davis requested that the legislative sponsor remove the bill. The sponsor obliged Davis, citing security concerns. In 2002 the bill reappeared on Davis's desk; the governor vetoed the bill, again citing national security concerns. Davis requested the law be modified to include, among other things, criminal background checks. Finally, in 2003, facing a recall campaign, Davis signed the bill. Arnold Schwarzenegger attacked Davis for flip-flopping on the issue, for a crass attempt at courting Latino voters, and for increasing danger to the country by granting licenses to the undocumented. The first legislative move Schwarzenegger promoted upon entering office resulted in the repeal of the law.

The bridges that constructed the criminal Mexican migrant with notions of the rule of law remain powerful and are a central framework for viewing the debate over driver's licenses. These bridges were reinforced and reconstructed by the events of September 11. Rule of law was connected with notions of danger to the individual and the nation-state. This has been reframed as a national security issue. This becomes clear as Schwarzenegger moves to reconsider how to provide driver's licenses to the undocumented. He suggests that proper criminal background checks are essential to providing licenses to the undocumented. The bridge between criminal Mexicans and race-neutral law enforcement allows for a focus on Mexican undocumented immigrants as a security threat, but also for the possibility of using greater scrutiny on a racialized criminal element to reinstitute rule. These dynamics would not be evident if the politics surrounding the issue were just about racial realism or just about color-blind conservatism.

While the bridges constructed around criminality and illegality survived the rise and fall of the restrictionist movement in the 1990s, the bridges that constructed a notion of a dependent Mexican migrant proved immediately powerful but less salient in the long run. The schemas were useless to interpret the state response and had no leverage in addressing the terrorist attacks in 2001. As we saw in chapter 4, reconstructions of economic citizenship in the campaign for Proposition 187 relied, in part, on a regendering of the problem immigrant. The female problem immigrant in the mid-1990s was not easily transferable to a terrorist threat, which was understood as having a masculine nature.

Bridges between work ethic and dependency informed politics in the immediate years after the campaign but lost power over time. Proposition 187 is credited with making immigrants one centerpiece of the 1996 Personal Responsibility and Work Opportunity Reconciliation Act. This act restricted services to legal immigrants, an indication of the power of the bridges that conflated the documented and the undocumented. A year later, however, some services were returned at the federal level, and most states have decided to fill in the gap for legal immigrants. Important events following the passage of the measure did not resubstantiate the schemas, and this theme as a whole moved to the background in the restrictionist movement in the late 1990s. This is evidenced by a spate of copycat initiatives in other states, none of which got very far, which appeared only in the immediate years after the measure.

A copycat initiative in Arizona is the exception. Proposition 200 appeared on the 2004 Arizona ballot—much later than the other copycat initiatives, which arose in the years right after Proposition 187, and was passed by 56 percent of the voters. The Arizona initiative contained many of the same provisions as Proposition 187 but had one additional component that is telling of the shift in immigration politics. The first two sections of the measure required that individuals show proof of citizenship before registering to vote and before voting. Political citizenship was prior to concerns over economic citizenship.[2] This is representative of what happened as a result of Proposition 187; as we will see, notions of political invasion came to the fore.

Concerns over cultural invasion also emerged from the struggle over Proposition 187, but in a limited form. Bridges connecting color-blind conservative ideas of assimilation and concerns over an invading uncivilized race generated during the campaign remained intact in the wake of the immediate state response. The racialization bridge was used in other campaigns immediately following the passage of Proposition 187. Shortly after Proposition 187, the California electorate passed Proposition 227, formally ending bilingual education. However, as most proponents noted, bilingual education continues in many forms; the policy as envisioned by supporters has not been implemented. This does not seem a particularly salient issue today. The connections between assimilation and civilization are heightened through the association bridge, focusing on loyalty. As evidenced in the restrictionist movement, after the measure, concerns about assimilation are important to the extent that they represent patriotism. Cultural assimilation is a shortcut for identifying those who support America and can be counted on to defend the country's well-being. We saw this with CCIR's connections between Mexicans and communism, the ultimate enemy of American culture and existence. September 11 strengthened this bridge between loyalty, assimilation, and race and expanded the targeted racial groups. Now, Mexicans are understood as additionally disloyal, as proponents view them as a potential conduit for Middle Eastern terrorist groups.

In his book *Who Are We?* (2004), Samuel Huntington exemplifies a contemporary incarnation of this bridging between culture and loyalty. Huntington argues that recent immigration challenges American national culture and identity: "Cultural America is under siege." For Huntington, patriotism and American culture are linked, and recent immigration, which he understands as uniquely opposed to assimilation, is one of our gravest threats. He connects this problem to the dangers of terrorism both in his book and in numerous articles since. Huntington's work uses, and reifies, the frame of assimilation and loyalty that powerfully emerged from the decline of the restrictionist movement in the 1990s.

During the campaign for Proposition 187, America was also threatened with political takeover. Concerns about population were important to the measure, as evidenced by environmental arguments and the groups that supported it. Population was understood by supporters as threatening quality of life and environment and also the electoral system. The three bridges central to this set of twin schemas were hyperfertility, control, and power. The first bridge, hyperfertility, revolved around a regendering of the immigrant as female and inclined toward higher rates of reproduction. The second bridge, control, noted that the border was evidence of out-of-control population growth. The third revolved around the power of a growing Latino population owing to the race consciousness of others, politicians and minorities. Growth becomes problematic both in its race-neutral incarnation and in its race-specific form.

Given the court injunction, the power of Latinos and race-conscious forces appeared to be so great as to overturn the will of the people. The electorate had expressed its desire at the voting booth, and the court case was seen as a subversion of the democratic system. It was evidence of political takeover. Though Latinos were not yet a dominant force at the ballot box, politicians were looking into the near future and responding to the growing power and strength of the Latino population. The state response thus brings invasion to the fore, and issues of growth and quality of life fall into the background. In the wake of the court injunction, environmental concerns with population become separated from concerns about political invasion. This is seen both in individual respondents and in coalitions. The focus on invasion is also apparent in the Arizona copycat initiative, which included concerns about noncitizens voting. The restrictionist movement began to focus on invasion, and people supporting immigration restriction were unable to persuade mainstream environmental groups, like the Sierra Club and Population Connection, to come out on the side of immigration restriction.[3]

With a focus on political and cultural invasion, the restrictionist movement in the immediate moment isolated itself from potential allies. While the Republican Party at the state level heartily endorsed the measure in 1994 and a Democratic president passed a more extreme version of Proposition 187 at the federal level with the 1996 welfare reform, by the late 1990s the restrictionist movement could not turn to either party for support. In 1996 the national Republican Party platform included a plank denouncing birthright citizenship, but by 2000 the platform did not mention the issue revolving around the Fourteenth Amendment at all. During the gubernatorial recall campaign, Voices of Citizens Together and CCIR did not endorse either Arnold Schwarzenegger or Gray Davis; both were depicted as traitors. Similarly, President George W. Bush is seen as an enemy, leaving the restrictionist movement with few political options of whom to endorse. The focus on invasion left the movement in a less powerful position, with fewer allies.

Nonetheless, the changing international political terrain after 2000 got the restrictionist agenda back on the table. Restricting student visas and tightening border control have long been agenda items for the restrictionist movement. The War on Terror and conflict in the Middle East have provided a window of opportunity for the movement to make gains and create new allies.

The new possibilities for immigration restriction are highlighted by the headline grabbers that emerged during the latest round of discussions of immigration: the Minuteman Project, a citizen group formed in 2004 that engages in its own border patrol activity. The Minutemen certainly do not represent the mainstream or only incarnation of the restrictionist movement in the decade's middle years. Their acceptance by, and influence on, citizens, politicians, other restrictionist organizations, and the media, however, are telling of the transformations in the political and racial terrain since the mid-1990s.

The Minutemen, while adamantly denying the role of race ("MMP has no affiliation with, nor will we accept any assistance by or interference from, separatists, racists, or supremacy groups"), focus on the schemas of invasion. In August 2006, their Web site featured articles on the Reconquista movement, "Hezbollah Invading U.S. from Mexico," undocumented immigrants' claims about political takeover, and a recent MMP demonstration at Ground Zero. Demonstrating at the site of the World Trade Center attacks is a graphic example of the powerful pull of the invasion schema.

The Minuteman Project in the 1990s would have been a fringe group from which the mainstream restrictionist forces would have attempted to distance themselves. In 2006 the line between mainstream and extreme restrictionist forces is not so clear. CCIR, a central organization supporting Proposition 187, hosted Jim Gilchrist, cofounder of the Minuteman Project, and highlights MMP's work. Other immigration reform groups, such as Arizonans for Immigration Reform, support MMP. The Minutemen also have the support of California state politicians such as Dick Mountjoy, who was coauthor of Proposition 187, and Arnold Schwarzenegger, as well as aspiring California state politicians who hope that demonstrating support for the Minuteman Project will help their campaigns.[4] Support from national political figures includes Senator Wayne Allard and Representative John Culberson of Houston. The Minuteman Project also has access to supportive media from Fox News to CNN's Lou Dobbs. Gilchrist, running as an independent for Congress, received 24 percent of the vote in Orange County.

Given the tenor of the immigration debate today, it is even more important to understand how Proposition 187 shaped the current racial terrain. Understanding the role of agency and the schemas essential to mobilization behind Proposition 187 gives us leverage to address and criticize restrictionist projects. Viewing the situation through a lens provided by new racism led to accusations of racism being leveled at supporters. This is what new racism proscribes. Because overt racism is not a legitimate public platform, by identifying the underlying racism, by calling the racist a racist, scholars of new racism hope to diminish the power of racial code words and issues. In the end, however, this tactic generated an extremely polarized political struggle. Opponents called proponents racists. Proponents denied such accusations and in turn leveled accusations of reverse racism. Each side vilified the other.

Recognition of the mobilizing bridging strategies opens up possibilities for finding common ground or alternative politics. Opponents misread proponents by either addressing their color-blind conservative arguments directly or simply denouncing their racial realist concerns as racism. Neither properly targeted the mobilization.

Opponents' failure to recognize this campaign as a struggle over defining citizenship was one of the reasons they were unable to defeat the measure, even with over three times as much money as supporters. For example, by accepting the cost-benefit calculation and addressing the measure as a policy designed to save money, they failed to challenge proponents. Ono and Sloop (2002) point to this in their discussion of the dominant discourse surrounding the measure and the central theme of a cost-benefit analysis. They state that a cost-benefit analysis was the most-used argument in the national media about the measure and in relation to Wilson's campaign as well as by opponents of the measure (29). But by using a cost-benefit calcu-

lation, both sides agree on "economic enterprise as a social good and undocumented migrant laborers as expendable; they simply differ on which
position, for or against, leads to the greatest economic advantage for the
state" (31). Ono and Sloop suggest that opponents were therefore already
doomed from the start by engaging in cost-benefit calculations. They
observe that given the nature of the argument used by the *Los Angeles
Times,* which bought into the framework of proponents, it is not surprising
that the measure passed despite this major paper's opposition (110). The
opposition's use of dominant discourse, and specifically cost-benefit calculations, granted the constructions of immigrants as economic units and
citizens as those who contribute capital (120). Because they accepted the
centrality of contribution, opponents did not present a compelling counter-
narrative of migrants' economic citizenship. Additionally, opponents mis-
understood how proponents were defining economic citizenship. Opponents
addressed only the color-blind conservative argument about contribution,
not the racial realist schema to which it was tied about independence, ambition, and individualism. Opponents granted the categories of citizen,
foreigner, and American and left unaddressed the racialized construction
of those categories that was occurring from below.

In doing so, opponents missed an opportunity to engage in a democratic dialogue on the connections between labor and services. Opponents
addressed a cost-benefit calculation, missing the importance of a work ethic
to proponents. The racialization bridge, which depicted Mexicans as hardworking but pliant and dependent, suggested alternative possibilities for
reconstructing American economic citizenship. Recognition of this bridging strategy could have provided opponents of the measure with a doorway
to talk about alternatives to Proposition 187 that would have addressed a
similar concern. A schema that expanded and included Latinos in an American work ethic through an accentuated relationship between old and new
immigrants would have been more powerful than a cost-benefit calculation
and addressed the role of citizenship. Opponents could have attempted to
take power away from the ascriptive strands of American political culture
by tapping into others, such as the still-powerful Horatio Alger myths, and
drawing on the schemas of Mexicans and hard work.

Recognizing the bridging strategies could have created a better democratic debate by allowing the two sides to address the same set of issues and
concerns. Opponents could have addressed concerns about expanding cultural and political citizenship, which undergird mobilization. By explicitly

discussing reconceptualizations of citizenship, the sides could have engaged in a debate, instead of name-calling. Opponents may have been able to offer a new version of citizenship that also appealed to supporters' concerns; opponents could have suggested a new set of schemas to transpose onto the battle. Through a recognition of creative action central to the reconstruction of the racial terrain, we can begin to consciously chart our course. Understanding the legacy of Proposition 187 is one step in that direction.

APPENDIX

Research Methods

Interviewee Selection

Respondents were solicited from two pools of names. The first set came from a survey of letters to the editors of the *Los Angeles Times* and the *San Francisco Chronicle* between September 1993 and the election in November 1994. I identified individuals who expressly or implicitly supported Proposition 187 or Proposition 187–type policies. There were ninety-five such individuals. Using the Internet, I found the addresses of twenty individuals who matched the name and the city from the original letter to the editor. Of these twenty, twelve indicated they wanted to participate, seven declined, and one letter was returned. Of the twelve who wanted to participate, I was able to arrange for six in-person interviews and two telephone interviews; the remaining four could not find a time to interview during a field trip and eventually changed their minds about participation.

The second set came from Campaign Disclosure Statements of the "Yes on 187 — Save Our State" committee, the largest committee working toward passage of the measure. I sent a letter to 293 individuals who donated money during September and October 1994. Fifty-nine of these letters were returned. (The individuals had either moved or died since 1994.) Fifty-eight individuals replied, and there was no response from the rest. Of those who responded, twenty-five wanted to participate, twelve did not, and the rest indicated they might be interested.

In five cases, individuals who had agreed to be interviewed brought additional supporters of the measure. Two interviews were conducted with married couples, two interviews were conducted with a pair of friends, and one interview was conducted with six individuals. This group interview came about as a result of needing to gain access to female respondents. A female member of a central organization got five midlevel activists, four of whom were women, to agree to speak with me as a group.

I interviewed thirty-one individuals. (See Table A.1 for descriptions of each interviewee.) Twenty-nine respondents were white and twenty-one were male. Twenty-two of the respondents were in southern California, eight were in northern California, and one was out of state but had lived in both areas of California. In the initial planning for the project, I had wanted to keep an even gender distribution, and an eye toward geographical distribution within California. This proved problematic. In the end, my interview sample was mostly made up of white men from southern California. Although this was not planned, it mirrors the largest population voting in favor of the measure (Alvarez and Butterfield 2000).

Gender

Obtaining an even distribution between men and women was extremely difficult. More women than men voted in the 1994 California election; however, women seemed to be less engaged in other forms of political activity surrounding this issue. This seems to mirror what is found in American politics in general (Verba et al. 1993; Schlozman et al. 1995; McGlen and O'Connor 1995).

Of the individuals who expressed support for Proposition 187–type policies through letters to the editor in the year leading up to the election, based on gender-specific names, 75.8 percent appeared to be men, 16.8 percent appeared to be women, and the remainder had non-gender-specific names. Of the twenty whom I was able to locate, seventeen were male, two were female, and the gender of one was unknown.

Of the original 293 individuals who donated money, there were 197 men, or 67.2 percent, and 95 women, or 32.4 percent. While the use of titles "Mr./Ms./Mrs." on the Federal Elections Commission reports makes it easier to tell a female contributor from a male, there is the potential, as I found out in one case, for the female to have been contributing in name only. When soliciting a "Mrs." donor, I received a reply from her husband indicating that it was in fact he who was concerned about the issue and that his wife did not know anything about it. Of the twelve donors who declined to participate, eight were female. Of the twenty-five who indicated a desire to participate, only three, or 12 percent, were female. Women not only were less represented in the initial pool but had a much higher decline rate as well. The reasons why women would not participate were the most telling. Of the eight female contributors who declined to participate, three were sick, two were taking care of sick family members, one suggested she didn't "air" her opinions, another feared recrimination, and the last felt that while she supports such policies, it is futile work.

While previous work has suggested there is not a gender gap on the issue of immigration (Alvarez and Butterfield 2000; Burns and Gimpel 2000), I was unable to test that claim in this study.

North–South Divide

Additionally, I wanted to consider the impact of the divide between northern and southern California. Eight of the thirty-one respondents were from northern California. This was because southern Californians were disproportionately represented in my initial pool of possible interviewees. While forty-three of the ninety-five letters to the editor appeared in the *San Francisco Chronicle*, only four of the twenty respondents for whom I could locate mailing addresses lived in northern California. Of those four, only two replied that they would be interested in being interviewed. Only 30 of the 294 people who donated money were from northern California, and 6 of those 30 agreed to be interviewed. However, I was still able to get some sense of the ways that local racial terrains played a role. See the discussions of proximity to the border in chapter 3 and of racial triangulation in chapter 2.

Political Activities of Respondents

Some respondents supporting Proposition 187 engaged in more than one form of political activity during the campaign. Nine of the interviewees wrote letters to the editors of California newspapers. Twelve donated money. Ten circulated petitions to get the measure on the ballot. Ten also worked with organizations supporting Proposition 187 in some other capacity (e.g., stuffing envelopes, making phone calls, etc.). Seven attended a demonstration. One engaged in a public debate during the campaign, and another organized a local meeting on the issue.

Interview Process

The interviews were conducted between June 2001 and June 2002, seven to eight years after the passage of the measure. The interviews lasted between one and three hours at a location selected by the respondent. During the

Table A.1. Respondents' characteristics and political participation

	Age at the time of interview	Northern or southern California	Occupation	Race	Family heritage
Ed	64	S	professor	W	German/Irish
Bob	56	S	electronics (self-employed—used to be in aerospace)	W	*
Maria	53	S	retired aerospace administration	H	Guatamelan
Jason	52	S	accountant	A	Japanese
Kyle	35	S	TV journalist	W	Armenian
John	49	S	electronics engineer	W	English
Steve	56	N and S	education	W	*
Philip	54	N	conservation scientist	W (Jewish)	Polish
Donald	36	N	public education administration	W	Italian/British
Sue	45	N	farmer	W	German
David	50	S	education	W	Irish/Scottish
Jack	76	N	furniture maker (currently unemployed)	W	*
Chris	48	N	salesman	W	5th generation Californian
Milton	76	N	marketing	W (Jewish)	Polish
Robert	45	N	not employed (trust fund)	W	*
Richard	66	N	retired teacher	W	English
Scott	77	S	human resources	W	German

Highest level of education attained	Activities in Proposition 187 campaign	Political affiliations	Military service
graduate degree	wrote letter to the editor; participated in community events	Republican	Y
BA	wrote letter to the editor; volunteered with an organization	Reform Party	
*	vocal supporter		
BA	wrote letter to the editor	Republican	Y
postgraduate	wrote letter to the editor	Republican	Y
postgraduate	wrote letter to the editor	Republican Party; Zero Population Growth	
postgraduate	wrote letter to the editor	Republican	
postgraduate	wrote letter to the editor; donated money	Democrat	
postgraduate	wrote letter to the editor; donated money	Libertarian	
college	vocal supporter	Republican	
postgraduate	vocal supporter	Republican	Y
high school	donated money; circulated petition		Y
college graduate	donated money; volunteered with an organization	Republican	Y
*	donated money; circulated petition		
some college	donated money		
college graduate	donated money; attended pro-187 demonstration	Republican Party; National Immigration Organization	
*	donated money	Republican	Y

Table A.1. Respondents' characteristics and political participation *(continued)*

	Age at the time of interview	Northern or southern California	Occupation	Race	Family heritage
Vivian	74	S	preschool teacher	W	German
Jill	42	S	housewife	W	*
Denise	39	S	housewife	W	*
Bernie	69	S	retired	W	*
Kathy	47	S	housewife	W	*
Fran	66	S	political sctivist	W	*
Tony	50	S	sales	W	*
Dean	55	S	marketing	W	*
Charles	68	S	engineer	W	American Revolutionary War
Maurice	72	S	retired	W	*
Sharon	48	S	secretary	W	*
Vicky	46	S	secretary	W	*
Sam	63	S	retired, computers	W	*
Jim	45	S	unemployed truck driver	W	*

Highest level of education attained	Activities in Proposition 187 campaign	Political affiliations	Military service
some college	donated money	Republican	
*	volunteered with an organization	Republican	
*	volunteered with an organization		
*	volunteered with an organization		
*	volunteered with an organization		Y
*	volunteered with an organization		
*	volunteered with an organization		
college graduate	donated money	Republican	
college graduate	donated money; attended pro-187 demonstra-tion; volunteered with an organization		
*	vocal supporter		
*	volunteered with an organization		
*	volunteered with an organization		
college graduate	wrote letter to the editor; volunteered with an organization	Reform Party	
high school	donated money	Republican; Judicial Watch; FAIR	Y

interviews, I tried to generate a natural conversational style. I ensured that each interview covered a list of topics to facilitate comparability (Figure A.1).

Data Analysis

I used letters to the editors of major newspapers, propaganda put out by elites and groups supporting the measure, and newspaper accounts of events in the early 1990s to contextualize the interview data. I conducted a survey of articles in the *Los Angeles Times* addressing immigration from 1990 to 1994. Additionally, I looked at Pete Wilson's speeches during his first term as governor (1990–94), highlighting the central themes that emerged and his discussion of immigration and immigrants.

Every interview, except one, was audiotaped and then transcribed. The interview transcripts were entered into Nu*dist, a qualitative data software program. This software permitted many iterations of coding, flexibility in exploring the interrelationships between coded categories, and quick text and string searches, and made my mistakes much less costly. Because of the decreased investment in creating coded categories, I was able to code all categories suggested by the data. In the end, I was left with well over one hundred categories that proved to be dead ends. This, however, allowed the relevant coded categories to emerge from the data rather than being created a priori. Additionally, with a click of the button I could nest (and unnest) coded groups or create lateral and hierarchical relationships. This was especially important in understanding the various components of the schemas and the relationships between schemas. Easy text and string searches helped ensure once I was nearing the end of the analysis process that the relevant coded categories were complete. By maintaining an open-ended data-collection process and allowing the categories of analysis to be grounded in the data, I hoped to allow the voices of the respondents as much room as possible to create their own individual stories about mobilization and, in turn, their collective story about the legacy of their activity.

Figure A.1. Interview guide

I. Background information
  A. Basic information
    1. Family composition
    2. Employment
    3. Length of residency in California
  B. Childhood history
    1. Places raised
    2. Family structure
    3. Religion
    4. Economics
      a) Jobs of immediate caretakers
    5. Neighborhood
      a) Class
      b) Racial composition of neighborhood
    6. Education
      a) Of immediate caretakers
      b) Primary and secondary school experience
        (1) Location
        (2) Racial composition of classmates
          (a) Effect on social experience
          (b) Effect on educational experience
        (3) Degree of achievement
        (4) Degree of involvement
      c) College education
        (1) Location
        (2) Degree
        (3) Racial composition
        (4) Comparisons with previous experiences
    7. Politics
      a) Affiliation and activity of immediate caretakers
      b) Affiliation and activity of other influential family members
  C. Political activity
    1. Political affiliation
    2. Sources of news
    3. Individuals or groups with whom politics are discussed
    4. Memberships
    5. Perceived level of political intensity and involvement
    6. Editorials
    7. Activism

Figure A.1. Interview guide *(continued)*

II. Citizenship
  A. Definition(s)
     1. Importance
     2. Spheres to which the concept applies
  B. Responsibility
     1. Political participation
     2. Economic contribution
     3. Military service
     4. Other service
  C. Privileges
     1. Freedoms
     2. Community
  D. Allegiance
     1. Dual citizenship
     2. Military service

III. Immigration—part I
  A. Connections
     1. Personal connections
     2. Familial connections
     3. Friends' connections
  B. Demographics
     1. Immigrants
        a) Country
        b) Class
        c) Education
        d) Reason(s) for immigration
     2. Illegal immigrants
        a) Country
        b) Class
        c) Education
        d) Reason(s) for immigration
  3. Change in immigration patterns over time

IV. Proposition 187
  A. 1994
     1. Job held
     2. Household composition
     3. Economy
     4. Significant personal events

Figure A.1. Interview guide *(continued)*

---

      5. Political events
          a) National politics
          b) Local politics
              (1) Most important issue(s)
              (2) Issues or events relating to immigration
   B. Content
      1. Explicit goals
      2. Stated impacts
      3. Perceived impacts
   C. Appearance of the initiative
      1. Surprising or expected
      2. Precedents to this campaign
      3. Events that gave rise to measure or sentiments
   D. Level of involvement
      1. Formal
      2. Informal (e.g., personal discussions)
   E. Personal decision to support the measure
      1. When
          a) Time
          b) Events surrounding
      2. Why
          a) General reaction
          b) Most compelling reason
          c) Agreement with other reasons proposed by those supporting the measure
   F. Friends and family views
      1. Description
      2. Impact
   G. Role of elites
      1. Political races
          a) Gubernatorial race
               (1) Influence on decision to vote for proposition
              (2) Influence of views on proposition to vote for candidate
              (3) Influence of commercials
          b) Senatorial race
               (1) Influence of candidates on decision about proposition
              (2) Influence of views on proposition on decision of candidates
          c) Local races
          d) Other political elite influences
               (1) Party stances
               (2) National figures

Figure A.1. Interview guide *(continued)*

    H. Reaction to counterarguments during the campaign
- 1. Children
  - a) Not guilty for parents' actions
  - b) Education benefits country
  - c) Will be on streets
  - d) Will be refused medical attention
- 2. Health care—will increase infectious diseases
- 3. Economic contributions
  - a) Illegal immigrants perform needed jobs
  - b) Illegal immigrants contribute to economy
- 4. Special relationship with Mexico due to history
- 5. "No Human Being Is Illegal"
- 6. Displays of opposition to the measure
- 7. Personal discussions with opponents

    I. Court Challenge
- 1. Initial injunction
- 2. Appeals
- 3. Removal from appellate process

    J. Changes in views on initiative

  V. Immigration—part II

    A. America's reception of immigrants
- 1. Historical view
  - a) Acceptance
  - b) Assimilation
- 2. Today
  - a) Acceptance
  - b) Assimilation
- 3. Change over time

    B. Impact
- 1. Immigration
  - a) Historically
  - b) Today
  - c) Change over time
- 2. Illegal immigration
  - a) Historically
  - b) Today
  - c) Change over time

    C. Problems
- 1. Of immigration
- 2. Of illegal immigration

Figure A.1. Interview guide *(continued)*

    D. Views on a good U.S. immigration policy
        1. Numbers
        2. Types
            a) Country
            b) Education
            c) Reason for immigration
        3. Priority status
    E. Current elite activity around immigration
        1. National
        2. California
    F. Current mood in California on immigration and illegal immigration

VI. Other political issues
    A. Political activity since 1994
    B. Government assistance
    C. Affirmative action
        1. Education
        2. Employment
    D. English as official language

Notes

Introduction

1. The initiative's proposed increases in penalties for document forgery, however, were implemented.

2. Arnold Schwarzenegger and his competitors in the governor's race in 2003 were asked about their stance on Proposition 187. George W. Bush was asked about his stance during his 2000 presidential campaign.

3. Nativism refers to the targeting of a minority group because of a perceived "foreignness."

4. The role of undocumented immigrants in American society was being talked about nationally, in part, because an appointee for U.S. attorney general had hired a person to take care of her children who was not legally allowed to work in this country. Zoe Baird, President Clinton's appointee, did not make it through the nomination process because of this, and even after she was no longer in contention for the office, the nation continued to talk about what entices immigrants without legal papers to enter the United States, in what ways illegal immigrants contribute to our society, and whom do we punish.

5. Among the resolutions introduced to the state assembly in 1993 and 1994, one asked the federal government for $1.5 billion to reimburse the state for money spent on illegal immigrants (Ferguson 1993). Another asked the federal government to deny emergency relief to illegal immigrants in the wake of the January 1994 earthquake (Nolan 1994). Yet another urged Congress to abolish the first sentence of the Fourteenth Amendment and to grant citizenship at birth only to those born to American citizens or to legal residents (Mountjoy 1993b). Some bills were introduced with the intent of getting a better count of the undocumented using state services: one required schools to count the number of undocumented students; another required social services to do the same. Other bills were designed to use state power to make it more difficult for illegal immigrants to remain in the country. In the 1993–94 legislative session, a bill was introduced and passed that required the Department of Motor Vehicles to obtain proof of citizenship or legal residence before issuing a driver's license or identification card

(Allen 1993a). Another bill attempted to ensure illegal immigrants did not receive employment and public benefits "including but not limited to, unemployment compensation insurance, welfare, medical, public assistance, and job training" (Allen 1993b). Two other bills dealt with public education, one attempting to make it a felony for an undocumented person to attend a postsecondary public institution; the other would "prohibit the expenditure of any state funds . . . for the education of undocumented aliens" (Conroy 1994; Mountjoy 1993).

6. Before 1993, Wilson had advocated prenatal care for all indigent women as a way to save California money in the long run. During election year, Wilson altered this stance and advocated banning illegal immigrants from receiving prenatal care, despite the fact that it might cost California more over time. Wilson, as senator, had not asked previous federal administrations to pay for state services to illegal immigrants; in fact, he had voted for a number of bills that made it easier for immigrants to come to the United States. Wilson had championed a number of causes as governor, including crime and the economy, but immigration came to the fore as polls began to indicate the issue was one that people cared about.

7. Not only did many organizations, including the Christian Coalition, refuse to take a stance on Proposition 187, but Jack Kemp, who at the time was a leading candidate for the 1996 Republican presidential nomination, came out, along with other national figures, against the measure (Martinez 1994).

8. By 1980, four out of five immigrants entering the United States came from Asia or Latin America (Gibbs and Bankhead 2001, 77).

9. As with any rule, there are exceptions. And some wonderful ones, too. Desmond King (2000), for example, recognizes how recent development in immigration "coupled with multiculturalism, demonstrates how the United States is a political system whose members self-consciously construct and contest the content of its core identity and values" (283).

10. The commonality of claims of un-Americanness or foreignness points to connections between nativism and racism. Early studies may have downplayed this connection because of an emphasis on color; however, Matthew Jacobson (1998) urges us to "admit of a system of 'difference' by which one might be both with *and* racially distinct from other whites" (6). Thanks to the revealing work of scholars on the European immigrant experience, we can challenge another distinction—the one that differentiates studies of race relations among native-born populations from studies that focus on race relations between the foreign born and native born. Both, in fact, are the same struggle, the struggle over citizenship, formal and substantive: the struggle fought to determine who counts as "us," who gets to define the contours of the political body along racial lines.

11. For excellent histories of nativism in the United States, see Higham's classic *Strangers in the Land* (1988), Roger Daniels's *Guarding the Golden Door* (2004), and David Reimers' *Unwelcome Strangers* (1998), which focuses on the nativist impulse in the latter part of the twentieth century.

12. Voters supported the measure two to one. Looking at voters' declared intentions in October, which seem to closely match the outcome at the polls in November, we see 60 percent of whites supporting the initiative, but only 15 percent of blacks. Sixty-one percent of Asians indicated they would vote no on the measure, as did 53 percent of Mexican Americans (Wolfinger and Greenstein 1968, 757–59).

1. Bridging Race

1. We don't need to dig very deep to find evidence of the continuing import of race. Public opinion polls on everything from direct democracy to our response to 9/11 display significant differences according to race. Voting patterns differ by race. Whites disproportionately hold elected offices. In the 109th Congress, African Americans held forty seats as representatives in the House and one seat in the Senate. Hispanics held twenty-six seats in the House and two in the Senate. Five representatives are Asian American or Native Hawaiian–Pacific Islander. Minorities are disproportionately represented in state prisons and jails (64 percent in prisons in 2001). There are persistent disparities across a range of health and economic indicators. In 1998, infant mortality rates among African Americans were twice that of white Americans of non-Hispanic origin and were 93 percent higher than the national average. Native Americans had an approximately 30 percent higher infant mortality rate than the average and over a 50 percent higher rate than white Americans (Keppel, Pearcy, and Wagener 2002). The unemployment rate for whites over the age of twenty-five in 2001 was 3.25 percent; 6.2 percent of African Americans were unemployed in the same year (U.S. Department of Labor 2002). We cannot wish race away.

2. Numerous scholars have shown that Proposition 187 was far from race neutral (e.g., Ono and Sloop 2002; Santa Ana 2002; Hasian and Delgado 1998; Lennon 1998; Perea 1997). Building on the valuable work that proves race was salient, the present study defines the role race played.

3. "Race resentment," as introduced by Kinder and Sanders (1996), was a reformulation of symbolic racism that they argue was an "unfortunate choice" of words (293). But their renaming also includes a reformulation. They are careful to say that they cannot determine if race resentment is a form of prejudice, since they cannot judge how inflexible their respondents' views would be to counterevidence, despite the fact that racial resentment exhibits many of the same characteristics one normally expects to find in prejudice (e.g., coherence, stability, relation to stereotypes, etc.) (109).

4. A key question revolving around the claim of subtlety is the implied stance of the person evaluating the claim of racism. If racism is expressed and constructed through action, then only those in the dominant group have the luxury of trying to discern the subtlety of racism. This highlights yet another privilege of whiteness. Color judgments may allow whites to discuss the explicit or covert nature of racism. Whites might not see or feel the daily impact of color judgments even if they recognize their existence, and therefore can label them as "subtle." But to a black man who cannot catch a cab, to the Mexican American citizen who is intensely questioned by the border patrol, or to the Asian American who is asked repeatedly where he or she comes from, color coding, contemporary racism, is anything but subtle.

5. For field discussions on the material-culture divide, as well as some examples of attempts at integration, see Morris and Mueller 1992; and Meyer, Whittier, and Robnett 2002.

6. Here I am relying on the work of William Sewell Jr., who reformulates the concept of structure using Bourdieu's notion of the habitus and Anthony Giddens's work to eliminate the culture-structure divide.

7. Capital, then, is the thing over which one struggles in any given arena (or, in Bourdieu's words, field) and is what gives the field meaning. For example, Bourdieu

explores the field of art in France and shows how cultural capital drives the field of art; people strive for "cultural nobility" (Bourdieu 1984, 2). Legitimacy in the realm of art is achieved by distinction from others. Capital is important in a relative sense and is used to create hierarchies and domination. Resources are like capital for Bourdieu except that in any given field, one may bring multiple resources to bear in the struggle for capital. Again, here we see the breakdown of the material-culture divide.

8. Sewell gives a few examples of how what may appear as the most concrete resources depend on schemas for their power. The factory (and all its components, the gate, the time clock, the assembly line) relies on schemas found in the capitalist structure, and communion wafers require interpretation through religious schemas. "Resources, we might say, are *read* like texts, to recover the cultural schemas they instantiate" (13).

9. See the appendix for more detailed information on who the respondents were and what sorts of activities they engaged in during the campaign.

10. Consider the following examples: "The recurrent themes in their early lives... created a general attitude that life was difficult. The women carried a legacy of hard work and the need for perseverance into their adult years" (Zavella 1987, 84); "Most of these workers had lived through the Mexican revolution of 1910–1920, and they utilized both the experience and the legacy within the new context of a strike-torn California" (Weber 1989, 53); "Through the daily struggle to survive in an oftentimes hostile environment, these newcomers [Mexican immigrants] constructed a world for themselves, shaped both by their memories of their past lives and by the reality of their present situation" (Sanchez 1993, 11).

11. This allowed me much more room to talk about race without suspicion than if I had brought it up myself. This tactic was designed to avoid some of the most extreme problems of social desirability bias when talking about race.

12. For classical realism, see Morgenthau 1978; for neorealism, or structural realism, see Waltz 1979.

2. Color-Blind Conservatism and Racial Realism

1. By using the term "realism," I am in no way suggesting this schema is a more realistic assessment of the world. I use the idea of realism, borrowing from international relations, to highlight the key roles of self-interest and power and the constant state of conflict embedded in this worldview. Racial realism encompasses Winant's other two restrictionary responses to the contemporary racial terrain. In addition to neoconservatism, he identifies a Far Right project, which sees race as a natural division that indicates genuine inequality among people, and a New Right project, in which "racial mobilization [is] a threat to 'traditional values.'" The New Right sees racial conflict as focusing on the state; the Far Right sees whites needing to form their own organizations to pressure the state for white rights. Neither really captures the notion of racial realism, but both contain some elements of what I am attempting to describe here.

2. In interviews, I never introduced the issue of race. It is therefore more suggestive that race was frequently raised by respondents in a defensive context first.

3. The contact thesis, introduced by Gordon Allport in 1954, argues that contact between individuals of different groups can reduce prejudice.

4. For example, interviews in the Glendale area also included discussions of Armenian populations, while in interviews in a rural area outside Sacramento, Ukrainians took a central role in discussions of welfare abuse. Around Temple City there was a discussion of the impact from Russian immigrants, and in Cupertino the Chinese population took on increasing importance. However, while these groups are equated with immigrants, there is generally a moment of distinction between illegal and legal that focuses on the country of origin; when talking about a statewide initiative, respondents were engaged in a collective dialogue with others in the state. They are responding predominantly to a state racial terrain rather than a local one.

5. See Lucy Salyer's excellent work *Laws as Harsh as Tigers* (1995) for a discussion of the construction of Asians as the quintessential illegal immigrant during the first couple of decades in the twentieth century.

6. However, arguments associated with color-blind conservatism are still used, as evidenced by the California Coalition for Immigration Reform's continued alliance and support of Ward Connerly, author of the initiative to dismantle affirmative action in California.

3. Criminalizing Mexican Migration

1. At the same time that Wilson was terribly concerned about people breaking immigration laws, he was arguing for a reform of red tape that prevented business and small entrepreneurs from succeeding. While the immigration law was immutable and good by virtue of being law, laws regarding business conduct were regulations to be done away with, and businesspeople who circumvented the laws were sympathized with, not demonized.

2. It is interesting to note that it did not arise in all interviews. That is, while the propaganda focuses on illegality as central, some supporters would not raise the issue once during the course of a two-hour interview. This suggests that formal legal citizenship and official documentation status was not the prime or central motivating issue for all supporters, but was one of many. This highlights that to understand mobilization we need to consider multiple versions of citizenship under contestation, and multiple schemas and how they worked together.

3. Surprisingly, drugs were not as central a notion when compared with gangs and corruption. Three respondents mentioned drugs as being associated with the undocumented or with Mexican immigration in general. I call this surprising because of the contemporary associations between Mexico and the war on drugs as well as a historic connection between drug smuggling and border crossers. Ngai (2004) points out that "Prohibition supplied an important cache of criminal tropes, the language of smuggling directly yoking illegal immigration to liquor running," and those tropes depicted illegal aliens as "vicious and criminal" (62). In the 1920s, the general public, vigilante groups including the Klan, and public officials focused attention on stopping drug and liquor smuggling from Mexico (Rosales 1999, 71–74). This attention to smuggling and the border connected Mexicans with drugs in U.S. film and news and in the American popular imagination.

4. For example, the *Los Angeles Times* featured a story on an undocumented Hispanic man who broke into a house and raped an elderly woman. The woman died of

a heart attack after the attack, and the prosecutor attempted to charge the man with murder.

5. The poll question was "Do you think any of these groups in Orange County— whites, Asians, Blacks or Latinos—is more inclined to be violent than the others?" Twenty-five percent answered that blacks were more prone to violence, and 26 percent suggested that was true of Asians. Only 5 percent suggested that was true of whites.

6. See Ngai 2004 for an incredible analysis of the Immigration Act of 1924. She demonstrates the new racial map that the act and its enforcement drew, which was not through Europe but around it. She illustrates how the illegal Mexican immigrant was created by this legislative act, which on its surface did not change the entry requirements for Mexicans.

7. This bridge has historical precedence. In the 1950s, INS officials argued that once a person enters illegally, he or she becomes more prone to criminal activity. For example, in 1953 an INS official explained because the " 'wetback' starts out by violating a law . . . 'It is easier and sometimes appears even more necessary for him to break other laws since he considers himself to be an outcast, even an outlaw'" (Ngai 2004, 149). However, the bridge revealed by respondents in this study is somewhat different; the act of illegally crossing the border serves as evidence of a criminal nature, as opposed to creating a slippery slope of criminal activity.

8. For clarity, I have eliminated writers from out of the area. From a total of eighty-three letters arguing for restriction or pro–Proposition 187 stances in the *Los Angeles Times*, I excluded only one that was written by an individual in the central valley. Out of fifty-one possible letters to the *San Francisco Chronicle* in that time that displayed either pro–Proposition 187 stances or anti–illegal immigrant sentiments, I excluded three, all from out-of-state authors. If those letters were not removed, the percentages were within 2 points.

9. Proximity to the border and its importance in serving as an easy conduit for schemas of threat and for a greater intensity around the issue may also explain the disproportionate response rates from the north and the south, with southern Californians being more willing to be interviewed. See the appendix.

4. Economic Citizenship

1. Alvarez and Butterfield (2000) also fail to explain why voting Hispanics would not perceive illegal immigrants as an economic threat. They state that "because the debate over Proposition 187 was focused on Mexico, we would expect the Hispanic population to vote against it" (170). This statement is not self-evident and needs further exploration. If what is really at stake in Proposition 187 are economic issues, then one could hypothesize that Hispanic voters, similar to blacks, may find themselves in direct competition with illegal immigrants for jobs.

2. In March 1994, a poll of California adults found that people were feeling the best about the economy than they had since December 1991, and 65 percent of those polled felt their financial situations were "secure." Sixty-two percent of those polled also supported the Save Our State measure (Decker 1994). This trend continued. In June, exit polls showed that people were becoming more concerned with illegal immigration and less concerned with the economy (Stall 1994).

3. Not only did opponents point to the millions of dollars that California would have needed to spend to set up the bureaucratic systems and hire the personnel needed to implement the proposition, but they also noted the billions that California would have lost in federal funds had Proposition 187 ever made it past the courts (Davis 1994; Feldman 1994a). The summary of the legislative analyst's estimate of costs in the 1994 California Voter Information Sheet published by the attorney general noted that while the proposition would save "roughly $200 million," the annual administrative costs would be in the tens of millions (possibly more than $100 million) and would place billions of dollars of federal funds at risk "due to conflicts between the measure's provisions and federal requirements."

4. The notion of dependence is central to this strategy as well. Mexicans who do not work and those who do are both characterized by dependency. This allows supporters to hold two competing versions of Mexican immigrants simultaneously: Mexicans as takers and Mexicans as hard workers.

5. This reconstruction of the immigrant as family is associated with the regendering of the Mexican immigrant in the contemporary moment, which is explored in chapter 6.

6. In fact, the decline in California was so significant that it creates the appearance of a national decline in immigration rates after the implementation of the Personal Responsibility and Work Opportunity Reconciliation Act: "The data clearly indicate that the welfare participation rate of immigrants declined relative to that of natives *at the national level*. It turns out, however, that this national trend is *entirely* attributable to the trends in welfare participation in California" (Borjas 2002).

5. Assimilation and Civilization

1. For an interpretation of the epigraphs by Perea and Kesler, see King 2000, 284–86.

2. Ed, a college professor in southern California, was concerned about the economic problems associated with a multilingual society. He did feel very strongly about cultural ties binding Americans. Language was not the critical juncture for John; he spoke many languages and had traveled all over the world. This travel, he suggested, reinforced his views that Americans did in fact share a similar culture, even if they did not recognize it when at home. Don shared in this mixed assessment of cultural concerns. While he supported the recognition of English as an official language, he seemed resigned to the continuing spread of a Spanish-speaking infrastructure. He turned the tables on the question of English as the official language and asked what was wrong with doing just that. This move highlights the reinscription of English as the natural official language, and asserting it through law therefore does not alter reality. So while it will not affect anything, according to Don, he sees no problem with reifying in law English as the official language. Here we see a respondent turn the tables on the opponents by portraying them as challengers to the status quo when they express opposition to a new law. This move is replicated throughout the campaign. Proposition 187 is merely enforcing laws, according to proponents, and therefore opponents are the ones challenging the current structures, not those actually working toward the passage of a *new* law.

6. Population and Hyperreproductivity

1. Evidence of this is seen in Governor Wilson's approach to the issue of growth. When Governor Wilson wanted to talk about attracting businesses with more people and more jobs during his first term in office, he stressed the idea of "smart growth." This theme was one of the most frequently recurring ideas in speeches between 1990 and 1994. Smart growth meant identifying ways to grow the economy without contributing to the problems associated with high-density populations; it meant bringing the right sorts of people into the state, those who could provide jobs and invest in California. Wilson needed to create commissions, lay out plans, and clarify what he meant by smart growth, as the idea of growth troubled many Californians.

2. "No to racism, Yes to environmentalism: We support U.S. population stabilization purely for ecological reasons. This requires we reduce both birth rates and migration to the U.S. to sustainable levels. Unending population growth and increasing levels of consumption together are the root causes of the vast majority of our environmental problems, as is the case in many other countries. As environmentalists, we in SUSPS are fully aware of the value of biodiversity. An ecosystem is healthier when it has a wide variety of animal and plant species. Similarly, we see value in ethnic and cultural diversity. A nation with human diversity is better able to survive crises, and it benefits from the creativity that diversity inspires. We are shocked and repulsed by the actions and statements of Neo-Nazis, xenophobes and racists of any kind. We repudiate any support from people who have racial motives for reducing immigration. Racists and their offensive ideas and actions have no place in modern civilized society" (SUSPS).

3. I spoke with Dean in the third round of interviews in June 2001, right after a major California energy crisis.

4. Maria is the only interviewee who continually stresses the importance of drawing a distinction between "Mexican" and "Latin American" populations. Even her husband continually retreats to the use of the word "Mexican," despite her pestering. The importance for Maria to use the term "Latin American" could be twofold. First, from personal experience, she understands that Latin American immigrants come from many different countries, not just Mexico. Second, she repeatedly uses stories about other immigrants to draw a contrast between "good immigrants," those who work hard, wave American flags, and join American society, and "bad immigrants," those who use the system, keep strong political ties with their countries of origin, and "bring their tamales and tortillas." She creates this distinction and then repeatedly places herself and her family and friends on the side of the independent Americanized immigrants.

5. The debate focused on men despite the fact that in 1920 the Bureau of Labor estimated that 50 percent of all Mexican immigrants were women and children (Foley 1997, 43).

6. For example, during the years 1953 and 1954, Congress held six hearings regarding Mexican–U.S. migration. The hearings, which debated needs of growers and the complaints of unions, focused on male migrant laborers.

7. This shift drew on an earlier transition in the welfare debate. In the 1960s, America witnessed the birth of the image of the "welfare queen." The picture of the black, hyperreproductive woman that was inserted into the American imagination was transposed to the immigration debate and reraced as Mexican.

8. Comments like this were also made in my first nine interviews despite the fact that I was eight months pregnant at the time. Respondents either broached the subject of my pregnancy after the interview or used me, a white woman of eastern European descent, as a contrast to prove their racialized depiction of the dependent pregnant Mexican woman. Maria, when beginning a story to illustrate that women use their reproductive powers to take advantage of the system, says: "And the young girls, now that's not your case, but the young girls like in your age," and Maria proceeds to tell the story of a nanny who came, got pregnant, and expected her employer to take care of her.

9. This moment arrived in 1998. There is currently no majority in California. Whites make up approximately 47 percent of the state's population, and Hispanics make up at least 32 percent (State of California 2003).

10. In fact, however, citizen children cannot file a petition for residency or citizenship for their parents until they turn eighteen. Even after they file, residency can take many years to obtain.

11. These individual respondents mirror Tanton's narrative about his reasons for founding FAIR.

12. This distrust of the federal government emerged during the campaign for Proposition 187. Throughout, the measure was depicted as California finally acting because of the federal failure to do so. Wilson depicted this as a struggle between the federal government and the states early on as he attempted to sue the federal government for reimbursement for services provided at first to immigrants and later to "illegal immigrants." Letters to the editors suggested that those in other states simply could not understand the problems Californians were facing. The idea that the federal government benefited from undocumented migration through extra social security taxes while the states paid all the costs emerged in Wilson's speeches, in interviews with mid- and low-level activists, and in letters to the editor.

13. Davis did sign such a bill before his recall in 2003; see conclusion.

14. Spencer still occasionally used the name VCT, but it appears to be the same organization with the same Web site, the same funding sources, and the same membership base.

15. I determined that it was still a centerpiece because of conversations with CCIR leaders and because it is included in their press packet and is highlighted in numerous places on CCIR's Web site. A shortened series of excerpts from the tape and the accompanying booklet was highlighted in their December 2001 newsletter.

Conclusion

1. This debate was ongoing even before Proposition 187. With a powerful restrictionist movement throughout the mid-1990s and Wilson still in office, no progress was made on getting licenses into the hands of the undocumented. New political space, however, opened up for the possibility as the immigration restrictionist movement began to lose power.

2. The state attorney general, in the wake of the vote, declared that the measure applied only to a handful of small welfare programs. The judicial challenges surrounding Proposition 200 that continue today focus on the voting rules rather than on provision of social services.

3. A 1998 Sierra Club ballot proposal to take a stance connecting immigration to environmental degradation was defeated. A group of Sierrans have run a slate of candidates in each Sierra Club election in an attempt to elect club officials friendly to immigration restriction. Thus far this group has failed to make inroads.

4. Brenda Salas, a member of CCIR who was running for the 65th District in California, stood watch with the Minuteman Project in April 2006.

References

Allen. 1993a. AB 983, *Drivers' Licenses: Identification Cards; Citizenship or Legal Residence.* California Assembly.

———. 1993b. ACR 16, *Relative to Illegal Immigration.* California Assembly.

Allport, Gordon W. 1954. *The Nature of Prejudice.* Boston: Addison Wesley.

Almaguer, T. 1994. *Racial Faultlines: The Historical Origins of White Supremacy in California.* Berkeley: University of California Press.

Alvarez, R. M., and T. L. Butterfield. 2000. "The Resurgence of Nativism in California? The Case of Proposition 187 and Illegal Immigration." *Social Science Quarterly* 81 (1): 167–79.

Andreas, Peter. 2000. *Border Games: Policing the U.S.–Mexico Divide.* Ithaca, N.Y.: Cornell University Press.

Ayres, J. M. 1997. "From Competitive Theorizing towards a Synthesis in the Global Study of Political Movements: Revisiting the Political Process Model." *International Sociology* 12 (1): 47–60.

Berkman, Leslie. 1994. "Some Attach Strings to the Spirit of Giving." *Los Angeles Times,* Orange County Edition. November 24.

Bobo, Lawrence D. 2000. "Reclaiming a Du Boisian Perspective on Racial Attitudes." *Annals of the American Academy of Political and Social Science* 568 (March): 186–202.

Bonilla-Silva, Eduardo. 2000. "The New Racism: Racial Structure in the United States, 1960s–1990s." In *Race, Ethnicity, and Nationality in the United States: Toward the Twenty-first Century,* ed. Paul Wong, 55–101. Boulder, Colo.: Westview Press.

Borjas, G. J. 1999. *Heaven's Door: Immigration Policy and the American Economy.* Princeton, N.J.: Princeton University Press.

———. 2002. "The Impact of Welfare Reform on Immigrant Welfare Use." Center for Immigration Studies, Center Report (March). http://www.cis.org/articles/2002/borjas2.htm (accessed January 31, 2004).

Bourdieu, Pierre. 1984. *Distinction: A Social Critique of the Judgement of Taste.* Cambridge, Mass.: Harvard University Press.

Brimelow, P. 1995. *Alien Nation: Common Sense about America's Immigration Disaster.* New York: Random House.

Burns, P., and J. P. Gimpel. 2000. "Economic Insecurity, Prejudicial Stereotypes, and Public Opinion on Immigration Policy." *Political Science Quarterly* 115 (2): 201–26.

Calavita, Kitty. 1996. "The New Politics of Immigration: 'Balanced-Budget Conservatism' and the Symbolism of Proposition 187." *Social Problems* 43 (3): 284–305.

California Voter Information. 1994. Attorney General, California Secretary of State's Office.

Camarota, Steven A. 2002. "Study Examines Effects of Welfare Reform on Immigrants: Findings Indicate Decline in Use Relative to Natives, but Only in California." Center for Immigration Studies, December 20. http://www.cis.org/articles/2002/borjaspr.html (accessed January 31, 2004).

Citrin, Jack, Donald P. Green, Christopher Moste, and Cara Wong. 1997. "Public Opinions towards Immigration Reform: The Role of Economic Motivations." *Journal of Politics* 59 (3): 858–81.

Chang, G. 2000. *Disposable Domestics: Immigrant Women Workers in the Global Economy.* Cambridge: South End Press.

Conroy, Mickey. 1994. ABX1 70, *Illegal Aliens: Postsecondary School Attendance.* California Assembly.

Crawford, J. 1992. *Hold Your Tongue: Bilingualism and the Politics of English Only.* New York: Addison-Wesley.

Crossley, N. 2002. *Making Sense of Social Movements.* Philadelphia: Open University Press.

Daniels, Roger. 2004. *Guarding the Golden Door: American Immigration Policy and Immigrants since 1882.* New York: Hill and Wang.

Davis, M. 1994. "$50 Million in School Funds Are Threatened by Prop. 187." *Los Angeles Times.* October 10.

"Debate over Immigration." 1994. *Los Angeles Times.* January 3.

"The Debate over the Rights and Wrongs That Is Proposition 187." 1994. *Los Angeles Times.* October 30.

Decker, C. 1994. "Wilson Trails Despite Brighter Economic View." *Los Angeles Times.* March 31.

Delgado, R., and J. Stefancic. 1992. "Images of the Outsider in American Law and Culture." *Cornell Law Review* 77 (1258): 170–77.

De Genova, Nicholas. 2002. "Migrant 'Illegality' and Deportability in Everyday Life." *Annual Review of Anthropology* 31: 419–47.

Di Rado, Alicia. 1993. "The Times Poll: Fear of Crime Is the Unifying Factor in O.C." *Los Angeles Times.* October 25.

Elbel, Fred. 2001. "Social Issues." SUSPS Frequently Asked Questions, Sierra Club U.S., Population Stabilization. http://www.susps.org/info/faq.html#social (accessed June 4, 2003).

Feldman, P. 1994a. "Proposition 187: Opponents of the Measure Vow to Sue If It Passes." *Los Angeles Times.* October 11.

———. 1994b. "The Times Poll: Anti–Illegal Immigration Prop. 187 Keeps 2–1 Edge." *Los Angeles Times.* October 15.

———. 1994c. "Dispute Erupts over Planned Radio Spots for Prop. 187." *Los Angeles Times.* October 26.

Ferguson. 1993. AJR 8, *Relative to Immigrants.* California Assembly.

Fields, B. J. 1982. "Ideology and Race in American History." In *Region, Race, and Reconstruction,* ed. J. M. Kousser and J. McPherson, 143–77. London: Oxford University Press.

Foley, N. 1997. *The White Scourge: Mexicans, Blacks, and Poor Whites in Texas Cotton Culture.* Berkeley: University of California Press.

Foner, Eric. 1970/1995. *Free Soil, Free Labor, Free Men: The Ideology of the Republican Party before the Civil War.* New York: Oxford University Press.

Freeman, G. P., and B. Birell. 2001. "Divergent Paths of Immigration Politics in the United States and Australia." *Population and Development Review* 27 (3): 525–51.

Frey, W. H. 1996. "Immigration, Domestic Migration, and Demographic Balkanization in America: New Evidence for the 1990s." *Population and Development Review* 22 (4): 741–63.

Gibbs, J. T., and T. Bankhead. 2001. *Preserving Privilege: California Politics, Propositions, and People of Color.* Westport, Conn.: Praeger.

Habermas, J. 1984. *The Theory of Communicative Action.* Boston: Beacon Press.

Hale, G. E. 1998. *Making Whiteness: The Culture of Segregation in the South, 1890–1940.* New York: Pantheon Books.

Hasian, Marouf, Jr., and Fernando Delgado. 1998. "The Trials and Tribulations of Racialized Critical Rhetorical Theory: Understanding the Rhetorical Ambiguities of Proposition 187." *Communication Theory* 8 (3): 245–70.

Higham, J. 1988. *Strangers in the Land: Patterns of American Nativism, 1860–1925.* New Brunswick, N.J.: Rutgers University Press.

Hochschild, J. L. 1981. *What's Fair? American Beliefs about Distributive Justice.* Cambridge: Harvard University Press.

Huntington, S. P. 2004. *Who Are We? The Challenges to American National Identity.* New York: Simon and Schuster.

Irving, Katrina. 2000. *Immigrant Mothers: Narratives of Race and Maternity, 1890–1925.* Chicago: University of Illinois Press.

Jacobson, Matthew Frye. 1998. *Whiteness of a Different Color: European Immigrants and the Alchemy of Race.* Cambridge: Harvard University Press.

Keppel, K. G., J. N. Pearcy, and D. K. Wagener. 2002. "Trends in Racial and Ethnic-Specific Rates for the Health Status Indicators: United States, 1990–98." *Statistical Notes,* Center for Disease Control, no. 23: 1–66.

Kesler, C. R. 1998. "The Promise of American Citizenship." In *Immigration and Citizenship in the Twenty-first Century,* ed. N. Pickus. New York: Rowman and Littlefield.

Kinder, Donald R. 1998. "Still Divided by Color." *Journal of Applied Behavioral Science* 34, no. 4 (December): 420–25.

Kinder, Donald R., and Lynn M. Sanders. 1996. *Divided by Color: Racial Politics and Democratic Ideals.* Chicago: University of Chicago Press.

King, D. S. 2000. *Making Americans: Immigration, Race, and the Origins of the Diverse Democracy.* Cambridge: Harvard University Press.

Klandermans, B. 1992. "The Social Construction of Protest and Multiorganizational Fields." In *Frontiers in Social Movement Theory,* ed. A. D. Morris and C. M. Mueller, 77–103. New Haven, Conn.: Yale University Press.

Landrith, J. A. 2001. "Statement on the Racial Privacy Initiative." The Multiracial Activist (www.multiracial.com). http://www.multiracial.com/abolitionist/word/landrith3.html.

Lennon, Tara M. 1998. "Proposition 187: A Case Study of Race, Nationalism, and Democratic Ideals." *Policy Studies Review* 15 (2–3): 80–100.

Libertarian Party. 1997. "Abolish the Government's 'Official' Racial Classifications, Libertarians Say." The Multiracial Activist (www.multiracial.com), January 28. http://www.multiracial.com/news/announcements.html (accessed February 2003).

Lipsitz, G. 1998. *The Possessive Investment in Whiteness: How White People Profit from Identity Politics.* Philadelphia: Temple University Press.

Lopez, I. F. H. 1996. *White by Law: The Legal Construction of Race.* New York: New York University Press.

Mahar, Cheleen, Richard Harker, and Chris Wilkes, eds. 1990. *An Introduction to the Work of Pierre Bourdieu: The Practice of Theory.* New York: St. Martin's Press.

Martinez, Gebe. 1994. "Kemp Defends Criticism before Hostile Audience." *Los Angeles Times.* October 20.

McAdam, D. 1982. *Political Process and the Development of the Black Insurgency.* Chicago: University of Chicago Press.

McCarthy, J. D., and M. Zald. 1977. "Resource Mobilization and Social Movements." *American Journal of Sociology* 82 (6): 1212–41.

McConahay, John B. 1986. "Modern Racism, Ambivalence, and the Modern Racism Scale." In *Prejudice, Discrimination, and Racism: Theory and Research,* ed. John F. Dovidio and Samuel L. Gaertner. New York: Academic Press.

McDonnell, Patrick J. 1994. "Prop. 187 Turns Up Heat in U.S. Immigration Debate Election." *Los Angeles Times.* August 10.

McDonnell, Patrick J., and Robert J. Lopez. 1994. "L.A. March against Prop. 187 Draws 70,000 Immigrants." *Los Angeles Times.* October 17.

McGirr, Lisa. 2001. *Suburban Warriors: The Origins of the New American Right.* Princeton, N.J.: Princeton University Press.

McGlen, N. E., and K. O'Connor. 1995. *Women, Politics, and American Society.* Englewood Cliffs, N.J.: Prentice Hall.

Meertens, Roel W., and Thomas F. Pettigrew. 1997. "Is Subtle Prejudice Really Prejudice?" *Public Opinion Quarterly* 61: 54–71.

Melucci, A. 1988. "Getting Involved: Identity and Mobilization in Social Movements." *International Social Movement Research* 1: 392–48.

Mendelberg, T. 2001. *The Race Card: Campaign Strategy, Implicit Messages, and the Norm of Equality.* Princeton, N.J.: Princeton University Press.

Meyer, D., N. Whittier, and B. Robnett. 2002. *Social Movements: Identity, Culture, and the State.* New York: Oxford University Press.

Moran, Juan, Otto Santa Ana, and Cynthia Sanchez. 1998. "Awash under a Brown Tide: Immigration Metaphors in California Public and Print Media Discourse." *Aztlan: A Journal of Chicano Studies* 23 (2): 137–40.

Morgenthau, Hans. 1978. *Politics among Nations: The Struggle for Power and Peace.* 5th ed. New York: Alfred A. Knopf.

Morris, A. D., and C. M. Mueller. 1992. *Frontiers in Social Movement Theory.* New Haven, Conn.: Yale University Press.

Mountjoy, Richard. 1993a. AB 149, *Educational Funding: Undocumented Aliens.* California Assembly.

———. 1993b. AJR 49, *Relative to Aliens and Citizenship.* California Assembly.

Negative Population Growth. 2003. "Is Opposition to High Immigration Rooted in Racism?" NPG Frequently Asked Questions. http://www.npg.org/faq.html#anchor23 (accessed June 4, 2003).

Nesbet, B., and S. K. Sellgren. 1995. "California's Proposition 187: A Painful History Repeats Itself." *UC Davis Journal of International Law and Policy* 153 (Winter).

Ngai, M. 2004. *Impossible Subjects: Illegal Aliens and the Making of Modern America.* Princeton, N.J.: Princeton University Press.

Nolan, Patrick. 1994. AJR 59, *Relative to Earthquake Relief for Citizens and Legal Residents of the United States*. California Assembly.

Novkov, J. 2002. "Deconstructing Whiteness? Miscegenation and the Institutionalization of Race." Paper presented at Law and Society Association.

Omi, Michael, and Howard Winant. 1986/1989. *Racial Formation in the United States: From the 1960s to the 1980s*. New York: Routledge.

Ono, Kent A., and John M. Sloop. 2002. *Shifting Borders: Rhetoric, Immigration, and California's Proposition 187*. Philadelphia: Temple University Press.

Pascoe, Peggy. 1999. "Miscegenation Law, Court Cases, and Ideologies of 'Race' in Twentieth-Century America." In *Sex, Love, Race: Crossing Boundaries in North American History*, ed. Martha Hodes. New York: New York University Press.

Patterson, Orlando. 1997. *The Ordeal of Integration: Progress and Resentment in America's Racial Crisis*. Washington, D.C.: Civitas.

Perea, J. F., ed. 1997. *Immigrants Out! The New Nativism and the Anti-immigrant Impulse in the United States*. New York: New York University Press.

———. 1998. "'Am I an American or Not?' Reflections on Citizenship, Americanization, and Race." In *Immigration and Citizenship in the Twenty-first Century*, ed. N. Pickus. New York: Rowman and Littlefield.

Pettigrew, T. F., and R. W. Meertens. 1995. "Subtle and Blatant Prejudice in Western Europe." *European Journal of Social Psychology* 25: 57–75.

"The Politics of Population." 2003. Living on Earth. World Media Foundation, May 23. http://www.loe.org/ETS/organizations.php3?orgid=33&action=printNewest ContentItem&typeID=17&templateID=48&User_Session=686c58c915ea2acd01571a85 38b11eda#feature5 (accessed May 28, 2003).

Racetraitor.org. 2003. "What We Believe." http://racetraitor.org/welcome.html (accessed June 2003).

Ramos, George. 1994. "Prop. 187 Debate: No Tolerance but Abundant Anger." *Los Angeles Times*. October 10.

Reimers, D. M. 1998. *Unwelcome Strangers: American Identity and the Turn against Immigration*. New York: Columbia University Press.

Roediger, David R. 1991. *The Wages of Whiteness: Race and the Making of the American Working Class*. New York: Verso.

Rogin, Michael. 1996. *Blackface, White Noise: Jewish Immigrants in the Hollywood Melting Pot*. Berkeley: University of California Press.

Rohrabacher, Dana. 1994. "Illegal Immigration." *Los Angeles Times*. October 14.

Romo, R. 1983. *East Los Angeles: A History of a Barrio*. Austin: University of Texas Press.

Rosales, F. A. 1999. *Pobre Raza! Violence, Justice, and Mobilization among Mexico Lindo Immigrants, 1900–1936*. Austin: University of Texas Press.

Salyer, Lucy E. 1995. *Laws as Harsh as Tigers: Chinese Immigrants and the Shaping of Modern Immigration Law*. Chapel Hill: University of North Carolina Press.

Sanchez, G. J. 1993. *Becoming Mexican American: Ethnicity, Culture, and Identity in Chicano Los Angeles, 1900–1945*. New York: Oxford University Press.

Santa Ana, Otto. 2002. *Brown Tide Rising: Metaphors of Latinos in Contemporary American Public Discourse*. Austin: University of Texas Press.

Schlozman, Kay Lehman, Nancy Burns, Sidney Verba, and Jesse Donahue. 1995. "Gender and Citizen Participation: Is There a Different Voice?" *American Journal of Political Science* 39 (2): 267–93.

Schmidt, R., R. Hero, A. Aoki, and Y. Alex-Assensoh. 2002. "Political Science, the New Immigration, and Racial Politics in the United States: What Do We Know? What Do We Need to Know?" Paper presented at the 2002 American Political Science Association Conference, Boston, Mass.

Schuman, H., C. Steeh, and Lawrence Bobo. 1985. *Racial Attitudes in America: Trends and Interpretations.* Cambridge, Mass.: Harvard University Press.

Sears, David O., and Donald R. Kinder. 1971. "Racial Tensions and Voting in Los Angeles." In *Los Angeles: Viability and Prospects for Metropolitan Leadership,* ed. Werner Z. Hirsch. New York: Praeger.

Sears, David O., Colette Van Laar, Mary Carrillo, and Rick Kosterman. 1997. "Is It Really Racism? The Origins of White Americans' Opposition to Race-Targeted Policies." *Public Opinion Quarterly* 61: 16–53.

Sewell, William H., Jr. 1992. "A Theory of Structure: Duality, Agency, and Transformation." *American Journal of Sociology* 98 (1): 1–29.

Sheridan, C. 2002. "Contested Citizenship: National Identity and the Mexican Immigration Debates of the 1920s." *Journal of American Ethnic History* 21 (3): 3–36.

Shklar, Judith. 1991/1998. *American Citizenship: The Quest for Inclusion.* Cambridge, Mass.: Harvard University Press.

Skerry, Peter. 2000. "Do We Really Want Immigrants to Assimilate?" *Society* 37 (3): 57–62.

Smith, R. M. 1997. *Civic Ideals: Conflicting Visions of Citizenship in U.S. History.* New Haven, Conn.: Yale University Press.

Sniderman, Paul M., and Michael G. Hagen. 1985. *Race Inequality: A Study in American Values.* Chatham, N.J.: Chatham House.

Sniderman, Paul M., and Thomas Piazza. 1993. *The Scar of Race.* Cambridge, Mass.: Harvard University Press.

Snow, D. A., and R. D. Benford. 1992. "Master Frames and Cycles of Protest." In *Frontiers in Social Movement Theory,* ed. A. Morris and C. M. Mueller. New Haven, Conn.: Yale University Press.

Stall, B. 1994. "News Analysis: Governor's Race to Be Run in Middle of Political Road." *Los Angeles Times.* June 9.

State of California, Department of Finance. 2003. *Race/Ethnic Population Estimates: Components of Change for California Counties, April 1990 to April 2000.* Sacramento.

Stefancic, Jean. 1997. "Funding the Nativist Agenda." In *Immigrants Out! The New Nativism and the Anti-immigrant Impulse in the United States,* ed. Juan F. Perea. New York: New York University Press.

SUSPS. 2004. "SUSPS." August 14. http://www.susps.org/index.html.

Tilly, C. 1978. *From Mobilization to Revolution.* Reading, Mass.: Addison-Wesley.

Tolbert, C. J., and R. E. Hero. 1996. "Race/Ethnicity and Direct Democracy: An Analysis of California's Illegal Immigration Initiative." *Journal of Politics* 58 (3): 806–18.

Touraine, A. 1985. "An Introduction to the Study of Social Movements." *Social Research* 52 (4): 749–87.

U.S. Department of Labor. 2002. "Unemployed Persons by Marital Status, Race, Age, and Sex." Bureau of Labor Statistics Labor Force Statistics from the Current Population Survey. http://www.bls.gov/cps/home.htm#charunem (accessed March 2003).

Verba, Sidney, Kay Lehman Schlozman, Henry Brady, and Norman H. Nie. 1993. "Citizen Activity: Who Participates? What Do They Say?" *American Political Science Review* 87 (2): 303–18.

Waltz, Kenneth. 1979. *Theory of International Politics.* New York: McGraw Hill.

Weber, D. A. 1989. "*Raiz Fuerte:* Oral History and Mexicana Farmworkers." *Oral History Review* 17 (2): 47–62.

Wilson, P. 1993a. "Closing the Door on Illegal Immigration." Speech at Ronald Reagan State Building, Los Angeles. August 9.

———. 1993b. Press statement. "I-5, South of San Clemente." 10:15 a.m., August 9.

———. 1993c. Speech at the California School Boards Association. Final Draft. 10:00 a.m., May 3.

———. 1994a. Budget Press Conference. June.

———. 1994b. Report to the Heritage Foundation.

Winant, Howard. 1994. *Racial Conditions: Politics, Theory, Comparisons.* Minneapolis: University of Minnesota Press.

———. 2000. "Racism Today: Continuity and Change in the Post–Civil Rights Era." In *Race, Ethnicity, and Nationality in the United States: Towards the Twenty-first Century,* ed. Paul Wong, 14–24. Boulder, Colo.: Westview Press.

Wolfinger, Raymond E., and Fred I. Greenstein. 1968. "The Repeal of Fair Housing in California: An Analysis of Referendum Voting." *American Political Science Review* 62 (3): 753–69.

Wong, Paul, ed. 2000. *Race, Ethnicity, and Nationality in the United States: Towards the Twenty-first Century.* Boulder, Colo.: Westview Press.

Zavella, P. 1987. *Women's Work and Chicano Families.* Ithaca, N.Y.: Cornell University Press.

Index

academic performance, 99–100

acquisitiveness: of Mexicans, 68, 73–76

activists/activism: environmental, 111–12, 115, 142, 170n3; grassroots, 72, 99; post–Proposition 187, 127–28, 131–34, 169nn14–15; respondents' characteristics, 147–53. *See also* conservative activism

aerospace industry, xvi, xx

affirmative action: debate about, 2, 27–28; initiatives to end, xiv, xxiv, 132, 165n6

African Americans: crime associated with, 62–63, 166n5; early exclusion, xxiv; support of Proposition 187, xix, 69, 162n12; work ethic, 74, 77, 85

agency theory, xxv, 2, 17; in social action theory, 13–15, 24; in social movement theory, 9–12, 67, 137–38

alcohol smuggling, 54, 56, 165n3

Allard, Wayne, 144

allegiance. *See* loyalty

Alliance for Stabilizing America (ASA), 114

American Border Patrol, 113, 132

American flag, 97

American Reform Party, xviii

amnesty, 129–30, 133

anchor babies, 78, 122–25, 131, 169n10

Anderson, Terry, 44

"Anti-Okie" law, 70

Arab terrorists, 65, 136

Arizona: copycat initiatives, 132, 140–42, 144

Armenian immigrants, 165n4

arrest rate: of Mexicans, 54

Asian immigrants: assimilation, 92–93, 99–100, 165n4; crime associated with, 62–63, 166n5; early politics, xxi–xxii, xxiv, 39, 70, 165n5; political power, 35, 120; support of Proposition 187, xix, 25–26; work ethic, 74, 77, 85

assimilation, cultural, 89–108; allegiance concerns, 91, 97–98, 101–3; civilization aspects, 94–98; coerced, 100–101, 105; of immigrants, xxii, xxvi, 26, 31, 89–91, 93, 141–42; language acquisition as, 92, 96–99, 104–6; after Proposition 187, 106–8; race-neutral notion of, 91–94, 97, 103, 116

association bridge, 19, 21; criminality and, 48, 58–62, 166n7; culture and, 90–91; economics and, 68, 84–86; fairness/invasion focus, 36–40, 138, 141

Aztlan, 33–34, 113, 118

Baird, Zoe, 161n4

balanced-budget conservatism, 70–71, 73

bilingual education, xiv, xxiv, 100, 104–5, 132; Proposition 227 ending, 141, 167n2

Robin Dale Jacobson is assistant professor of political science at Bucknell University. She has written and spoken about issues of immigration, race, and social movements.